LONG TRAIL GUIDE

p. 8
11
12

LONG TRAIL GUIDE

Vermont Hiking Trails Series

The Green Mountain Club
Waterbury Center, Vermont 05677

Editions

First Edition 1917	Thirteenth Edition 1947
Second Edition 1920	Fourteenth Edition 1951
Third Edition 1921	Fifteenth Edition 1956
Fourth Edition 1922	Sixteenth Edition 1960
Fifth Edition 1924	Seventeenth Edition 1963
Sixth Edition 1924	Eighteenth Edition 1966
Seventh Edition 1928	Nineteenth Edition 1968
Eighth Edition 1930	Twentieth Edition 1971
Ninth Edition 1932	Twenty-first Edition 1977
Tenth Edition 1935	Twenty-second Edition 1983
Eleventh Edition 1937	Twenty-third Edition 1985
Twelfth Edition 1940	Twenty-fourth Edition 1996

The Green Mountain Club, Inc.
4711 Waterbury-Stowe Road
Waterbury Center, Vermont 05677
(802) 244-7037

The information in this guide is the result of the best effort of the
publisher, using information available at the time of printing.
Changes resulting from maintenance and relocations are constantly
occurring, and, therefore, no published route can be regarded as
precisely accurate at the time you read this notice.

Cover and book design by The Laughing Bear Associates,
Montpelier, Vermont
Illustrations by Ed Epstein
Format by Electric Dragon Productions, Montpelier, Vermont
Copyedited by Susan Bartlett Weber

Printed by The Leahy Press, Inc., Montpelier, Vermont,
on recycled paper.
Twenty-fourth Edition
(fourth printing with revisions)

ISBN 1-888021-01-2

*To those who have
worked to protect
the Long Trail,
Vermont's "footpath in
the wilderness" and
the oldest long-distance
hiking trail in
America.*

Managing Editor
Sylvia Plumb

Volunteer Editors
John Dunn
Dave Hardy
Don Hill

It is impossible to list every person who assisted in the production of this edition of the guidebook, but many deserve special recognition. Thank you for your creativity, patience, and enthusiasm for the *Long Trail Guide*.

Contributors

Rolf Anderson	Reidun Nuquist
Dick Andrews	Herb G. Ogden, Jr.
Lars Botzojorns	Kevin Peterson
Brenda Clarkson	Dot Pirkanen
Ben Davis	George Plumb
Kate Donaghue	Louise Lloyd Prescott
Russ Eastwood	Fred Putnam
Smith Edwards	Gary Salmon
Brian T. Fitzgerald	Gary Sawyer
Don Groll	Polly Schoning
GMC Sections	Dennis Shaffer
Don Harvey	Susan Shea
Kathleen Hayes	Kimball Simpson
Lisa Hughes	Mason Singer
Charles Johnson	Brian Stone
Sue Johnston	Tim Tierney
David Lacy	Doris Washburn
Ed Leary	Susan Bartlett Weber
Paul Neubauer	

Many thanks to Don Hill who painstakingly updated the division maps and the state of Vermont map. These maps were originally drafted in 1977 by University of Vermont students Stewart D. Arnold, Martin L. DeWitt, and Douglas Paulsen under the direction of Dr. H. Gardiner Barnum. Northern Cartographic, Inc., assisted with map updates on previous editions and produced the original Appalachian Trail maps. Jane Dosdall created the Camel's Hump and Mount Mansfield maps.

Contents

Contributors vi

A New Look for the Guide x

Using This Guide xii

Welcome to the Long Trail 1

Guidelines for Use of the Long Trail 2

    Overnight Sites 3

    Leave No Trace 4

    Water 6

    Camping and Fires 7

    Group Use 8

    Spring and Fall Mud Seasons 9

    Special Natural Areas and Wildlife 10

    Trip Planning and Safety 11

    Climate and Weather 14

    Hypothermia 14

    Winter Use 18

    Parking 21

The Green Mountain Club and the Long Trail . . . 22

    Membership 23

    Headquarters 24

    GMC and Long Trail History 25

Management of the Long Trail 30

Protecting Vermont's Mountain Lands 34

The Green Mountains 36

Division 1
Massachusetts-Vermont State Line to Vt. 9
Trail Description 48
Summary and Map. 190–191

Division 2
Vt. 9 to Arlington–West Wardsboro Road
Trail Description 56
Summary and Map. 192–193

Division 3
Arlington–West Wardsboro Road to Mad Tom Notch
Trail Description 64
Summary and Map. 194–195

Division 4
Mad Tom Notch to Vt. 140
Trail Description 74
Summary and Map. 196–197

Division 5
Vt. 140 to U.S. 4
Trail Description 86
Summary and Map. 198–199

Division 6
U.S. 4 to Vt. 73 (Brandon Gap)
Trail Description 96
Summary and Map. 200–201

Division 7
Vt. 73 (Brandon Gap) to Cooley Glen Shelter
Trail Description 102
Summary and Map. 202–203

Division 8
Cooley Glen Shelter to Birch Glen Camp
Trail Description 110
Summary and Map. 204–205

Division 9
Birch Glen Camp to Bolton Mountain
    Trail Description 118
    Summary and Map 206–207
Division 10
Bolton Mountain to Vt. 15 (Lamoille River Bridge)
    Trail Description 134
    Summary and Map 208–210
Division 11
Vt. 15 (Lamoille River Bridge) to Tillotson Camp
    Trail Description 162
    Summary and Map 212–215
Division 12
Tillotson Camp to the Canadian Border
    Trail Description 170
    Summary and Map 216–217
Appalachian Trail 1
Long Trail (Maine Junction) to Vt. 12
    Trail Description 178
    Summary and Map 218–219
Appalachian Trail 2
Vt. 12 to the Connecticut River
    Trail Description 184
    Summary and Map 220–221

Public Campgrounds Near the Long Trail 222

Post Offices and Stores 225

Useful Addresses 226

GMC Publications 228

Additional Reading 230

Index 232

A New Look for the Guide

The editors of the 23rd edition of the *Guide Book of the Long Trail* could not have foreseen that eleven years would pass before their work would see a revision. Thus the contributors to the 24th edition of the guide faced a formidable task: to cover not only a decade of relocations, shelter construction, and other changes to the Long Trail System, but also to answer the calls for more information from the ever-growing number of hikers.

An Easier Guide to Use

As the majority of LT users are not "End-to-Enders" making the trip in one trek, but rather day hikers and short-distance backpackers, the guidebook committee hoped to make the guide easier to use for this group of hikers. Side trails are identified in greater detail and described from the trailhead to the Long Trail, rather than the Trail to the trailhead, as had been previously done. Rather than including the side trails in the LT description, they are now grouped at the end of each division. There are improved directions and parking information for all Long Trail System trailheads, as well as a paragraph on suggested day trips and winter use at the start of each division. Also new are: an expanded section on natural history, a reading list, the locations of campgrounds near the Trail, and an expanded index.

Perhaps the most noticeable change is the location of the division summaries and maps, which are now grouped at the end of the book rather than mixed with the trail description. Hikers should find this arrangement useful in moving from one division to another, and viewing sections of trail at a glance.

A New Size and Format

To accommodate this expanding body of information, the committee changed the dimensions of the book from the shirt-pocket size, in use since 1920, to a slightly larger format. The new size and design make the book easier to use and information easier to find. One other slight change is the renaming of the book to *Long Trail Guide*, a title more to the point than *Guidebook of the Long Trail*. Doubtless some will decry these changes as heresy, while others will say "It's about time." Only the future will tell us which voice is louder.

A guidebook, like a trail, is not a static creation. Your contributions are vital to this process. Please send your comments on this book to the GMC along with any corrections to trail or shelter descriptions. Thank you in advance and enjoy the Trail.

Paul Hannan
President, GMC

Using This Guide

For guidebook purposes, the Long Trail has been divided into twelve divisions, numbered from south to north. Also included in this guide is trail information for the Appalachian Trail in Vermont. Division boundaries are indicated on the pocket map in the back of the book. Each trail division has three components: (1) trail description, (2) summary, and (3) map. Trail descriptions for all trails are found on pages 48 to 188. The summaries and maps are grouped from page 190 to 221.

(1) Trail Description

The Long Trail (LT) and Appalachian Trail (AT) descriptions read from south to north. Distances are cumulative within the division. Distances between shelters are given in both miles (mi.) and kilometers (km) and include northbound hiking times. Southbound time (SB) is in parentheses. Cumulative distances from Massachusetts and Canada are given at the top of the first page of each division. Shelters, summits, side trails, and road crossings are set in boldface type. Most features are listed in the summary charts.

Side trails are described after the LT descriptions; however, they are mentioned in the Trail description at the point they intersect the LT. Hiking times are given in the direction the side trail is described as well as the reverse (Rev.).

(2) Summary

A summary of mileage and elevation is found opposite each map. These charts correspond to the adjacent maps, with the northernmost features at the top, so that the northbound hiker reads from the bottom up. The charts are useful in quickly determining the distance and net elevation gain or loss between one point on the Trail and the next. The listed features correspond with those features in boldface in the trail description. Mileages are cumulative. With a nod to the future, the LT elevations are given in both feet and meters.

(3) Map

The scale of the maps is about three miles to the inch. The contour interval is two hundred feet. The Long Trail is shown as a dotted line with grey shading. Dashed lines distinguish roads that may not be driveable from those roads that probably are driveable.

Abbreviations

AT. . . . . Appalachian Trail
ATC. . . . Appalachian Trail Conference
CCC . . . Civilian Conservation Corps
DOC . . . Dartmouth Outing Club
GMC . . . Green Mountain Club
GMNF . . Green Mountain National Forest
h . . . . . hour(s)
km . . . . kilometer(s)
LT. . . . . Long Trail
mi. . . . . mile(s)
Rev. . . . . Reverse time for side trails
SB . . . . . southbound
USFS . . . U.S. Forest Service

Welcome to the Long Trail

Vermont's Long Trail, with its 270-mile footpath, 175 miles of side trails, and nearly 70 primitive shelters, offers endless hiking opportunities for the day hiker, weekend overnighter, and extended backpacker. The Long Trail (LT) follows the main ridge of the Green Mountains from the Massachusetts-Vermont state line to the Canadian border. Its 445 miles cross Vermont's highest peaks.

Although the Long Trail is known as Vermont's "footpath in the wilderness," its character may more accurately be described as backcountry. As it wends its way to Canada, the Trail climbs rugged peaks and passes pristine ponds, alpine bogs, hardwood forests, and swift streams. The Long Trail is steep in some places, muddy in others, and rugged in most. Novice and expert alike will enjoy the varied terrain of the Trail as it passes through the heart of Vermont's backwoods.

Built by the Green Mountain Club (GMC) between 1910 and 1930, the Long Trail is the oldest long-distance hiking trail in the country. It was the inspiration for the Appalachian Trail, which coincides with the Long Trail for one hundred miles. As the protector, manager, and maintainer of the Long Trail, the Green Mountain Club works to ensure that the Trail—one of Vermont's most significant natural and recreational features—will be protected and maintained for the enjoyment of future generations.

The *Long Trail Guide* is the official guide to the Long Trail and its network of side trails. This guidebook and the

Club's companion publication *Day Hiker's Guide to Vermont,* which includes trails outside the Long Trail System, together cover the majority of hiking trails in Vermont.

Guidelines for Use of the Long Trail

With proper care, a hiker of almost any ability and experience can enjoy an excursion on the Long Trail. Hikers are encouraged to plan their hikes with both their ability and weather conditions in mind. For the latest information on trail and shelter conditions, contact the GMC.

Please treat all trail lands with respect. Portions of the Long Trail in northern Vermont cross private land. Just one inconsiderate hiker could cause a landowner to close the Trail. Park so as not to block access to roads or driveways. Leave no trace. Carry out all trash. Landowners may be farming, grazing, maple sugaring, or logging on lands adjacent to the Trail, activities that are an integral part of Vermont's economy and way of life. Because the Long Trail passes over state, federal, GMC-owned, and private land, camping and fire restrictions vary from one portion of the Trail to the next. See camping information on page 7.

Trail Marking

The Long Trail is marked by two-by-six-inch white blazes. Along the Trail, intersections are usually marked with signs. Double blazes may mark important turns. In open areas or on rocky summits, blazes are often painted on rocks, or cairns and scree walls may mark the Trail. Property lines, snowmobile routes, and cross-country ski trails marked in various colors are often encountered, but the well-worn footpath and standard white blazes distinguish the Long Trail from these. Side trails are blazed in blue and signed. Hikers should always pay special attention at trail intersections as signs could be missing and blazes could be worn.

Overnight Sites

There are nearly seventy GMC overnight sites, spaced no more than a moderate day's hike apart, along the Long Trail System. These range from fully enclosed lodges to three-sided lean-tos and tent sites. All sites, although primitive, have a water source (purity and reliability cannot be guaranteed) and privy. Visitors must carry food, a backpacking stove, and overnight gear.

The overnight structures along the Trail are designated as shelters, camps, and lodges. Shelters usually have open fronts in the Adirondack style. Some camps are enclosed and have doors and glazed windows. The larger enclosed structures are lodges. Any exceptions to these classifications are noted. In the trail description the word "shelter" is also used in referring to trail structures in general.

These facilities are first-come, first-served. Please fit fellow hikers in. Use of any overnight facility is limited to three consecutive nights.

Groups should follow group hiking guidelines and restrictions on page 8. Anticipated shelter changes are noted in each division. A moderate fee is charged at overnight sites with caretakers. See below and on page 4.

To improve outhouse efficiency and reduce odors, whenever possible urinate in the woods well away from water sources. As part of its waste management efforts, the GMC composts sewage at some overnight sites. Please follow any special instructions posted on the outhouse door.

Site and Summit Caretakers

Throughout the hiking season, from early May to early November, hikers may find GMC caretakers at several sensitive, high-use overnight sites along the Trail (identified in the trail description). Through informal conversation and example, these caretakers educate hikers about leave-no-trace practices and perform trail and shelter maintenance. At many of the sites, caretakers manage sewage through composting.

GMC caretakers are experienced hikers. They are happy to provide backpacking suggestions and tips, as well as basic information about the Trail and the Club.

To help support this important program, a modest overnight use fee is charged at caretaker sites: $4 for non-members; GMCers with membership cards pay a $3 fee except at shelters on National Forest land where the discount is not allowed. (These fees were for the 1996 season and are subject to change.) This is a use fee and applies to tent as well as shelter users.

As part of an effort to protect Vermont's alpine areas and fragile summits, the GMC fields summit caretakers on Mount Mansfield, Camel's Hump, Mount Abraham, Stratton Mountain, and the Coolidge Range (Killington and Pico Peaks). These caretakers talk with hikers about the fragile summit ecosystems, enforce camping and fire regulations, and provide first aid and assistance.

Leave No Trace

You can help preserve Vermont's "footpath in the wilderness" as you enjoy it by leaving no trace of your visit. While you hike, please follow a few guidelines to ensure that the trail and the backcountry experience will be there for others to enjoy. Please leave no trace of your passing.

Travel Only on Foot. Motorized vehicles, pack animals (including horses and llamas), and bikes are not permitted on the Long Trail System.

Stay on the Footpath. Short cuts can cause erosion and make more work for the volunteers who take care of the trail for you.

If You Packed It In, Pack It Out! Help by picking up trash others have left behind.

Use a Backpacking Stove. Wood fires are strongly discouraged and are prohibited at high elevations. Fires severely impact surrounding areas by depleting vegetation, causing soil compaction and erosion. Fires should be built only in fireplaces provided. Keep fires small. Burn only dead and downed wood. Never cut live branches or trees for firewood.

Travel and Camp in Small Groups. Four to six hikers to a party is ideal; ten is maximum for overnight and twenty-five for day use. Be considerate of other hikers and make space for them in shelters.

Camp at Established Overnight Sites. Use the existing shelters and tenting areas whenever possible to avoid wide-spread impact.

If Camping Off Trail, Camp at Least Two Hundred Feet (Seventy-five Paces) from any Trail, Stream, or Pond. Never camp where someone has clearly camped before (unless a designated site). Mountain summits are especially susceptible to damage and should not be used as campsites. Camp below 2,500 feet in elevation.

Wash and Rinse Dishes Away from Open Water. Use the designated wash pit or, if primitive camping, wash dishes and "self" at least two hundred feet (seventy-five paces) from any water source. Avoid soap: it is difficult to rinse and is more often the source of gastrointestinal distress than water contamination. If you use soap, use it sparingly; a few drops go a long way.

Use the Privy If the Site Has One. Otherwise, dispose of human and pet waste in a "cat hole" between four and six inches deep and at least two hundred feet (seventy-five paces) away from water sources. Bury toilet paper. Treat your dog's waste in the same way as your own—bury it. And, above timberline, carry it out.

Carry Out All Tampons and Sanitary Napkins. Carry a personal trash bag for this purpose. Please do not dispose of these products in outhouses.

Don't Carve Your Name or Anything Else into Trees or Shelters. Although it may be fun to leave your mark, please refrain. It alters the experience of fellow hikers and is an insult to the careful work that went into these creations.

Take Only Pictures. Be Sure to Leave Only the Lightest of Footprints.

Respect Other Hikers and the Wildlife. Travel and Camp Quietly.

Pets Are Best Left at Home. If you bring a dog along, make sure it is well trained and keep it away from water sources. Leash it above treeline and at shelters when you cannot give your dog your full attention. Be thoughtful of shelter mates. Pet waste should be buried just like human waste. Pets are likely to encounter their own trail problems, especially painful battles with porcupines.

Leave No Trace. Leave no signs of your presence anywhere along the trail.

Water

Although the Green Mountain Club makes every effort to locate shelters and campsites near water sources, the quality and quantity of water cannot be guaranteed. Water may be polluted and, during dry weather, water sources may fail. Areas that are particularly prone to water shortages are noted in the trail description.

WATER PURITY. Contamination of water supplies is a problem, even in remote areas. Water may look and taste clean but still be contaminated. Giardiasis, caused by the intestinal parasite *Giardia lamblia*, is just one of many illnesses caused by drinking contaminated water. Other bacteria and viruses may be present in water sources. If giardiasis symptoms such as severe cramping and diarrhea occur, consult your physician.

PREVENTION. Hikers and dogs are probably the main carriers of *Giardia*. Often, they carry the parasite and unknowingly contaminate water supplies through the careless disposal of waste. People often pass it on to others by failing to wash their hands after making a pit stop. Follow leave-no-trace guidelines on pages 4 to 6.

TREATMENT. Treat all drinking water. To kill *Giardia*, water must be boiled for three minutes, filtered with a water purifier guaranteed to remove the *Giardia* parasite (filters may not remove all contaminants, such as viruses), or treated with an iodine-based chemical purifier (follow the directions on the bottle). To kill all viruses and bacteria, water must be chemically treated or boiled for ten minutes.

Camping and Fires

Because the Long Trail System passes through private, state, and federal lands, regulations may vary from one part of the Trail to the next. Guidelines for each type of land ownership are described below. Unless you know you are on federal or state land and in areas where primitive camping is permitted, camp only at designated sites. The guidebook gives simplified information about where dispersed camping is allowed in each division. For more information, contact the appropriate state or federal agencies.

PRIVATE LANDS. Camping on private lands is limited to designated sites. Fires are permitted only in the permanent fireplace at each site. Use of these areas is permitted through the generosity of the landowners. Abuse of this long-standing arrangement could result in closure of the Long Trail on private lands. If you are unsure whether or not you are on private land, camp only at designated sites.

STATE LANDS. With the exception of state lands north of Mount Mansfield State Forest, and some areas on Camel's Hump and Mount Mansfield, primitive camping is permitted below 2,500 feet if leave-no-trace practices are followed. Any other exceptions are noted in each division. Fires are permitted but discouraged below 2,500 feet unless otherwise noted in the divisions. Camping is limited to no more than three consecutive nights in the same area. Groups larger than ten require a state primitive camping permit. For more information, contact the state regional offices of the Department of Forests, Parks, and Recreation listed on pages 226 and 227.

FEDERAL LANDS. Camping between shelters is permitted along much of the Trail in the Green Mountain National Forest between the Massachusetts border and Vt. 140 and between Sherburne Pass and Mount Ellen if leave-no-trace practices are followed. Exceptions are noted in each division. Small wood fires are allowed unless noted in the division. See page 9 for information regarding Outfitter-Guide Special Use permits.

Group Use

Use of the Long Trail by organized groups is popular. Experienced leadership, a good leader-to-participant ratio (one to four), and a manageable size are essential for a successful trip. The GMC group use policy limits group size to twenty for day hikes and ten for overnights (including leaders). An overnight group of four to six is far better and leaders should consider limiting day hikes to ten participants.

All members of groups should be properly equipped. At high-use sites such as Camel's Hump, Mount Mansfield, Stratton Pond, Griffith Lake, and Little Rock Pond, groups are encouraged to use designated tenting areas rather than shelters. Elsewhere groups should be prepared to tent as shelters may be full. Groups should be especially accommodating to new arrivals and make space for them. Leaders should be sure that their group is considerate of other hikers. Break large groups into smaller groups and leave at half-hour intervals. Use different trails to get to the summit or hike in opposite directions on the same trail and trade car keys at the middle point. Better yet, break groups up and hike in different areas.

The GMC asks organized groups planning a hike on the Long Trail to contact its office. Staff can guide leaders toward areas suitable for group use, help them plan a safe and enjoyable hike, and offer suggestions to keep impact on the resource and other hikers to a minimum. While the GMC likes to see school groups, camps, scouts, and others hike the Long Trail, proper use, consideration, and trail ethics are as much a part of the experience as "getting into the woods." A free brochure, "A Group Hiking Guide for Vermont's Long Trail and Appalachian Trail," is available from the GMC.

PERMITS. Groups hiking the LT System south of the northern boundary of the Green Mountain National Forest on Mount Ellen should contact the Green Mountain National Forest to determine if an Outfitter-Guide Special Use permit is needed. Groups of eleven or more people hiking the LT System on state land (generally the Killington-Pico area, and most of the land north of Appalachian Gap) should contact the Department of Forests, Parks, and Recreation to obtain a primitive camping permit. (See pages 226 and 227 for phone and address information.)

Spring and Fall Mud Seasons

The Green Mountain Club strongly encourages hikers to avoid higher-elevation trails during the spring "mud season" (usually late March through the end of May). Snow melt creates extremely muddy trails and makes them vulnerable to damage from foot traffic, which is often compounded when hikers walk beside the trail to avoid the mud.

GUIDELINES

- If a trail is so muddy that you need to walk on the vegetation beside it, turn back, and seek another area to hike.
- Plan hikes in the hardwood forest at lower elevations.
- Avoid the spruce-fir (conifer) forests at higher elevations.
- The State of Vermont closes trails in the Camel's Hump and Mount Mansfield areas from mid-April until Memorial Day weekend. Please do not hike here. Also avoid Stratton Mountain, the Coolidge Range (Killington to Pico Peaks), Lincoln Ridge (Lincoln Gap to Appalachian Gap), and Jay Peak during this time of year.

Late fall presents similar muddy conditions and hikers are asked to follow the same guidelines. From late October until snowpack, early snows leave large amounts of moisture but don't cover the ground enough to protect it from damage. The freeze and thaw cycle during this period can wreak havoc on overused trails. Severe winter thaws create similar conditions. During these times hikers should find other recreational activities and let the mountain trails freeze up or dry out to protect them from further damage.

Special Natural Areas and Wildlife

ALPINE AREAS. Vermont is fortunate to be home to three arctic-alpine areas. These fragile ecosystems, found on the summits of Mount Mansfield, Camel's Hump, and Mount Abraham, contain plants normally found 1,500 miles to the north in Canada. Although these plants are hardy enough to survive the harsh climate of mountain summits, they are vulnerable to trampling. Please help protect these special natural areas by staying on the marked trail, walking only on the bare rock, and leashing your dog to ensure that it does not wander. Camping is not permitted above timber line.

WILDERNESS AREAS. In parts of the Green Mountain National Forest, the Long Trail crosses federally designated wilderness. These generally remote areas were established by the United States Congress as places where the impact of man is minimal. Appropriate recreation and scientific research are encouraged. Hunting and fishing are allowed, but logging, roads, and mechanical equipment (including mountain bikes) are not. In time, the forest will regenerate from past clearing, and the wilderness will approximate the primeval lands early European explorers found. The Long Trail crosses four wildernesses: Lye Brook (Division 3), Big Branch and Peru Peak (Division 4), and Breadloaf (Divisions 7 and 8).

Restricting day and overnight group sizes to fewer than ten people is particularly important in wilderness areas. Campers should leave no trace. Trail blazing and brushing are limited. Signs are less frequent and they often omit mileage figures. There may be more downed trees across the trail, reflecting a reduced emphasis on trail maintenance. Bridges are often more primitive and there are occasional stream fords.

PEREGRINE FALCONS. After almost a thirty-year absence, peregrine falcons have returned to nest in Vermont. But they are still rare with only eleven nesting sites reported in 1994. Peregrines prefer high cliffs and outcrops, with many of these locations on or near the Long Trail such as Smugglers' Notch and Mount Horrid. They are easily disturbed, especially by hikers above their cliffside nests.

During the nesting season, from mid-March to mid-August, hikers may encounter portions of the Long Trail or side trails that have been closed or relocated. Please help by staying away from the area until the young have fledged. For information call the Green Mountain Club or the Vermont Department of Fish and Wildlife at 103 South Main Street, Waterbury, Vermont 05671-0501; (802) 241-3700.

Trip Planning and Safety

Planning a hike is almost as much fun as doing it. It is also just as important. A mix of good planning, common sense, proper gear and clothing, food, and water is needed for a safe and enjoyable trip in the Green Mountains. Proper precautions may prevent a small problem from becoming a large one. Remember, there is safety in numbers. It is always wise to hike with other people.

When planning your hike take into consideration the experience and conditioning of all members of your group, the terrain you plan to cover, the season, the weather, and the hours of daylight. Leave a copy of your itinerary with a reliable person.

Try out your equipment, new or old. Know how to deal with emergencies. Become familiar with the area you are visiting. (This is particularly important for winter trips.) Determine where roads and towns are located in relation to the trail. Learn basic first aid. Most importantly, know how to prevent problems in the first place. During periods of high water, streams may be impassable. Hikers may need to wait, backtrack, or detour.

For long hikes, plan conservatively, allowing at least one day's leeway in case of unforeseen weather conditions. Start your hike slowly to get accustomed to your pack and strengthen your legs.

Volumes of books have been written about hiking, backpacking, equipment, clothing and trail food. Pages 230 and 231 list a number of excellent references.

Going light is critical to a pleasant backpacking trip. Beginning hikers tend to forget that they must carry everything they pack and almost invariably take along more than they need. Few hikers can comfortably carry more than onefourth of their own weight. Below are some basic items that are needed to make a hike safe and comfortable.

DAY HIKES

- guidebook or map
- lunch, snacks, and water
- sturdy boots
- wind jacket/rain gear/breathable shell (remember it's colder on the summits than in the valleys)
- warm layer (wool or synthetic fleece) or overshirt (summer)
- hats and mittens (spring, fall, or winter)
- flashlight/headlamp (extra bulb and batteries)
- compass
- first-aid kit
- waterproof matches
- insect repellent and sunscreen
- toilet paper and trowel
- whistle

OVERNIGHT HIKES

Add the following items to those carried on a day hike:

- backpacking stove and fuel
- cook kit and eating utensils
- sleeping bag and pad (in a waterproof sack)
- tent
- extra clothes and socks (in a waterproof sack)
- litter bags

Reduce pack weight on long-distance hikes by forwarding parcels marked "General delivery—hold for Long Trail hiker—arriving about (date)" to post offices near the trail (see list of post offices on page 225), or by caching supplies in a metal container near road crossings. People making an extended backpacking trip on the Long Trail may want to purchase the GMC's *Long Trail End-to-Ender's Guide.*

Mileages and Hiking Times

Mileages used in the summaries and trail descriptions are actual hiking distances, including twists and turns. The hiking times given in the book are based on the formula commonly used: one-half hour for each mile plus one-half hour for each one thousand feet of ascent. These figures are for actual hiking time. Allowances should be made for lunch breaks, viewing and resting, ruggedness of terrain, hiking experience, and also for trips to summits and other viewpoints reached by side trails.

These guidelines are not necessarily times you will or should take. After comparing a few of your times with those given, you can determine a personal ratio, which can be applied to the guidebook figures. As you gain ability and experience, your hiking times may change.

Hiking times for the Long Trail and side trails are given for both directions. Two abbreviations are used. Southbound is abbreviated as SB and reverse is indicated as Rev.

Staying Found

Should the next blaze ahead not be found within a reasonable distance, stop, look, and backtrack if necessary. It is better to lose a moment looking for the correct route than to forge ahead on the wrong route. If, by chance, you do lose the trail, a compass and map will help you get back on the trail or to the nearest road. The guidebook maps serve only for reference and should not be considered suitable for map and compass work. In Vermont, the compass points about fifteen degrees west of true north.

Climate and Weather

Although summers in the Green Mountains are often cool and pleasant, hot, humid days are quite frequent. Never underestimate the variability of Vermont weather. Conditions along the crest of the Green Mountains are not the same as in the lowlands; temperatures will often vary dramatically, sometimes as much as 5°F per 1,000 feet. There is also a marked increase in the amount of precipitation at higher elevations. The annual average precipitation in Vermont is thirty-eight inches. Other conditions such as rain, fog, and sudden drops in temperature can occur at any time, even in the summer. Always carry a warm layer and wind protection when hiking to higher elevations. On the higher peaks the rain exceeds one hundred inches. Summer nights are usually cool and hikers should always be prepared for rain.

Hypothermia

The threat of hypothermia, a dangerous and deadly condition, exists year-round. Hypothermia is the cooling of the body core temperature caused by heat loss and the body's inability to keep the internal temperature constant. This condition is not limited to winter. In fact, what is often referred to as "hypothermia weather" is not –20°F, but those rainy, windy 40° to 50° or even 60°F days that occur in Vermont's mountains at any time of the year.

Hypothermia symptoms include poor judgement, forgetfulness, and confusion. Motor control may suffer, leading to problems with coordination (such as being unable to fasten one's clothing), an unsteady gait, or even slurred speech. Other warning signs include being unable to keep one's fingers and toes warm, uncontrollable shivering, or extreme unexpected fatigue. In the most severe cases this can lead to lethargy, coma, and death.

Prevention is the key to avoiding hypothermia. Body heat can be lost by heat radiating from uncovered surfaces (e.g., a bare head), from direct contact, such as sitting on frozen ground, from wind blowing away the warm air in clothing, and evaporation from breathing or sweating.

Proper food, water, clothing and pacing are critical. Always be sure to eat and drink plenty while hiking, and bring along extra food in case of emergency. A hard day of winter hiking can burn four thousand to five thousand calories. Dress in layers including, as needed, wicking underwear, an insulating layer, and a wind and waterproof shell. Wear wool or synthetics like polypropylene or pile or, if it's warm, keep some of these in your pack just in case.

Remember: mountain weather can change suddenly and unexpectedly. Keep your pace steady. When it's cold try not to sweat and dampen your clothes, and keep rest stops brief so as not to cool off too much. Carry some emergency gear such as a foam pad to sit on, a tarp or a tent fly to make an emergency shelter, waterproof matches, and possibly a stove, and consider packing at least one sleeping bag per group on a day hike.

If hypothermia is spotted early, it's easy to treat. If the victim is still walking and talking, get him or her out of the wind and into dry and warm clothing as quickly as possible. Don't forget a hat, as a large percentage of body heat is lost through the head. Then give him something to eat and drink, take a brief rest, and get moving again. This is usually all it takes to warm up. If this doesn't work, then you must try to rewarm him. Prewarm a sleeping bag with a healthy companion and then put the two in together, or place either chemical hot packs or bottles filled with warm water heated on a stove around the person's neck, armpits and groin. Build a fire, if you can. If the person becomes unconscious (fortunately an extremely rare occurrence), then he must be handled extremely gently and evacuated as quickly as possible.

Lightning

Injury from lightning, although fortunately rare, is a serious risk for the hiker, and the relatively low altitudes of the Green Mountains of Vermont are by no means a guarantee of protection.

Avoidance of lightning is critical. Whenever you feel there's a threat: (1) Avoid summits and ridges where strikes are most apt to occur. This includes areas such as the open summits of Mount Mansfield, Camel's Hump, and Mount Abraham, as well as many lower bald summits and prominent ridges. If you are stuck on a ridge and can't get off quickly, go for the middle rather than a shoulder on either end. (2) Avoid open fields. (3) If in the forest, seek an area amid shorter trees. (4) Avoid moist areas such as wet gullies and crevices, and stay out of small depressions where ground currents may travel. (5) Also stay out of small caves (large, dry ones are usually good, however). (6) Sit or crouch on insulating objects such as a dry sleeping bag or mattress, making yourself as small as possible. (7) Set aside exposed metal objects (things inside a pack are usually all right).

About 70% of people hit by lightning survive, probably because much of the current often "flashes over" and not through one's body. If the person is conscious and breathing, the chance of survival is excellent. Even if the person is not breathing or is pulseless, prompt and effective CPR may be lifesaving. Continue CPR as long as possible, as there is a much greater chance of survival in this situation than in most other causes of cardiac arrest.

Hunting

Most of the Long Trail crosses land that is open to hunting. Hikers should be aware that various hunting seasons are underway from September 1 through mid-December. The hunting that might be of most danger to hikers occurs from mid-to-late November, the regular deer season. Wild turkey season is usually the month of May.

Late fall offers some of the best hiking of the year, with no bugs, and leafless trees affording greater long-range visibility, but it is necessary to take precautions. Wear bright visible colors, preferably fluorescent orange. During hunting season, avoid wearing brown, tan, black or patches of white that might be mistaken for the white tail of a deer. For information on hunting seasons, write or call the Department of Fish and Wildlife, 103 South Main Street, Waterbury, Vermont, 05671-0501; (802) 241-3700.

Local Residents

Deer mice, raccoons, and squirrels are particularly adept at gnawing through packs in search of food. Be sure to take food, trash, and items resembling food (toothpaste, peppermint soap) out of your packs and hang them in separate bags. Mice will chew through pockets for anything that smells like food. Hang packs and unzip the pockets so mice can freely run in and out without chewing through the fabric.

Porcupines enjoy gnawing on shelters and outhouses. Be sure to close and latch outhouse doors to keep them from chomping on the seat platform (you may be sorry later if you don't). They love salt; never leave your boots where porcupines may reach them. Hang boots to keep porcupines away and also to help them dry out.

Although black bears exist in Vermont, they are generally not a problem, being shy and seldom seen. Please follow leave-no-trace practices so bear do not become a problem.

Although minuscule, blackflies and mosquitoes can make hiking in the Green Mountains very uncomfortable and at times unbearable. Blackflies breed in running water so are most abundant in early summer. They usually disappear by mid-July. Mosquitoes are around most of the summer and like low, wet areas. Wearing headnets is helpful. Be sure your tent has no-see-um-proof netting. Almost nothing works against blackflies, except long-sleeve shirts and pants. Although insect repellent containing D.E.E.T is most effective, there is some concern about its safety. If you do choose to use it, apply it to clothing rather than directly to the skin and avoid using it on children. Alternative repellents are available.

Rabies

Like other areas in the Northeast, rabies has arrived in Vermont. Although at present human cases are rare, and your danger of contacting the disease remains greater at home than on the trail, it is best to take precautions. Hang your food, keep your campsite clean so as not to attract animals, carry out food wastes and trash, refrain from feeding animals, and stay away from any wild animal that is acting strangely, such as too tame or unafraid, or too aggressive. Leave any dead animal alone.

If you are bitten by a wild animal, wash the wound thoroughly with soap and water and get to a doctor as soon as possible. Rabies today is generally successfully prevented—as long as medical treatment is received soon after contact, otherwise it is virtually 100% fatal.

Winter Use

Snowshoeing and cross-country skiing are popular on much of the Long Trail System. The winter hiking experience can be rewarding, filled with solitude, challenge, clear skies, and breathtaking views, but it can also be dangerous. A winter trip *must* be planned and conducted with caution. The margin for error on a winter hike is small.

Unlike many trails in neighboring states, the Long Trail and its shelters are not designed for winter use. The white blazes that mark the Long Trail are usually made four to five feet from the ground, a height that could be at knee-level or even completely buried under snow during winter. Overhanging branches, well out of reach for summer hiking, may obstruct the hiker's way.

Vermont winters are severe and prolonged, with abrupt temperature changes. Unpredictable and changing weather conditions, deep snow, short daylight, and the need to carry extra warm clothing and safety gear can make the going slow. Breaking trail is strenuous and exhausting. Conditions at higher elevations will be much more severe, and wind may make winter travel impossible. On open ridges and summits hikers may encounter icy, windswept conditions. Crampons may be needed. Hypothermia, always a threat, is especially dangerous in winter. (See more about hypothermia on page 14.) Be prepared to get lost—but try not to. Carry a map and compass and know how to use them. Be prepared to spend a night in the woods, if necessary.

Only a few Long Trail shelters have wood stoves. Those that do are not insulated and the tiny stoves do not heat the shelter all that well. Long Trail hikers should be prepared to spend a night in a shelter without a stove for warmth. The presence of a stove at a shelter on a summer trip is no guarantee of a stove on a winter trip. Shelters may be covered or filled with snow. An open-faced lean-to provides little protection against the elements. A winter tent and below-zero sleeping bag are far better.

Winter conditions occur from November to May in the Green Mountains, with snow lasting until early June at higher elevations just below treeline. At 3,800 feet snow lingers for eight to twelve weeks longer than at 1,800 feet. Maximum snow depth usually occurs in March.

If you are new to winter outings, gain some experience before you set out. Go on outings with friends who have experience, take a class, or join a guided hike. Many GMC sections offer winter trips as do outing goods stores. There are a number of good books available on the subject of winter hiking and camping (see pages 230 and 231).

Each trail division includes a note about winter use. Some divisions are better suited for snowshoeing and require more technical equipment, while the rolling terrain of other sections makes them ideal for cross-country skiing. Always give yourself extra time; the estimated hiking times in the guidebook do not apply during the winter months.

The GMC sells cross-country skiing guidebooks and maps at the Gameroff Hiker Center.

USE SKIS OR SNOWSHOES. Please think of your fellow hikers and those who come after you. Avoid post-holing through the snow. These knee-deep holes can make it unpleasant, unenjoyable and even dangerous for the person who comes next. Wear snowshoes or skis on all winter treks.

WINTER SANITATION. Carry a shovel and dig out the outhouse whenever possible. The fastest way to discourage a volunteer maintainer is the annual spring chore of burying the toilet paper found when the snow melts. Be aware of where streams are and avoid making a pit stop near them.

CATAMOUNT TRAIL. The Catamount Trail provides the full range of skiing opportunities. Fashioned after the Long Trail, it traverses the length of Vermont from Massachusetts to Canada, linking cross-country areas with long stretches of backcountry trail. For more information about the Catamount Trail, contact Catamount Trail Association, P.O. Box 1235, Burlington, Vermont 05402; (802) 864-5794.

Trail Access

The Long Trail is easily reached from many major roads. This guide gives directions to all LT road crossings at the beginning of each division. Directions to side trails are included in the side trail descriptions. The pocket map in the back of the book is intended primarily to show the overall route of the Long Trail. For a road map, hikers may request the Official Highway Map of Vermont from the Vermont Department of Travel and Tourism, P.O. Box 1471, 134 State Street, Montpelier, Vermont, 05601-1471; (802) 828-3236 or (800) VERMONT.

Access to the Trail is also shown in many road atlases. Northern Cartographic, South Burlington, Vermont, publishes *The Vermont Road Atlas and Guide,* and DeLorme Mapping publishes *Vermont Atlas and Gazeteer.* Both atlases can be useful for locating routes to the Long Trail as well as side trails.

Transportation

BUS. Public transportation in the vicinity of the Long Trail is provided primarily by Vermont Transit Lines, a component of the Greyhound bus system. Vermont Transit busses pass over parts of the following highways, crossing or closely paralleling the Long Trail: U.S. 7, Vt. 9, Vt. 103, U.S. 4, U.S. 2, I–89, Vt. 15, and Vt. 100. Timetables are available from Vermont Transit Company, 135 St. Paul Street, Burlington, Vermont 05401. (802) 862–9671.

AIR. The Burlington International Airport is served by several major carriers, while smaller companies provide air service to the Rutland, Springfield, Barre-Montpelier, and Stowe-Morrisville airports.

RAILROAD. Amtrak provides passenger rail service to Vermont from Washington, D.C. and New York and many other cities. Although Amtrak crosses the Trail at Jonesville, it does not stop closer than Waterbury or Essex Junction.

Parking

There are many small, and some larger, parking areas at trailheads on both the Long Trail and its side trails. Parking information is included with road directions to trailheads. When parking vehicles at trailheads and road junctions, hikers should take special care to avoid obstructing traffic or blocking access to homes, farms, or woodlots.

Vandalism is a problem at some trailheads. Overnight trailhead parking is always risky. If possible, leave your vehicle in town. It is sometimes wiser to leave a car away from the trail near major public transportation routes. Police and service stations will usually provide a place to park (in the case of the latter for a small fee), and the Long Trail may then be reached by walking, taxi, or other public transportation.

Leave valuables at home, or at the very least keep them locked in the trunk or otherwise hidden. Remove your stereo if possible. Don't leave a note on the car advising of your plans. Leave the glove compartment open and empty and park in the open and parallel to the highway if possible. If you have a problem at a trailhead, call the local or state police and the GMC.

Public Campgrounds Near the Trail

State and U.S. Forest Service campgrounds make ideal base camps for hikers. They are inexpensive and nearby to many trailheads. Many are situated near lakes or ponds with excellent swimming. For a listing of campgrounds and the closest trailheads, turn to pages 222 to 224.

The Green Mountain Club
and the Long Trail

In 1910 the Green Mountain Club, declaring a mission "to make the mountains of Vermont play a larger part in the life of the people," began building the Long Trail. Although the GMC's mission philosophically remains the same as when the Club was founded in 1910, what that entails as the Club heads towards the year 2000 is much different than it was in 1910. With the modern-day pressures of encroaching development and damage to natural resources from overuse, providing hiking opportunities now involves much more than building and maintaining trails. Today, the Green Mountain Club and its 8,000 members are involved in all aspects of protecting and managing the trails and facilities of the Long Trail System.

Membership

Membership in the GMC is an important way to support hiking opportunities in Vermont. It is open to anyone with an interest in hiking and the preservation of Vermont's backcountry. Annual membership dues support trail maintenance, education, publications, and trail protection.

Those wishing to participate in outings and organized trail maintenance activities may choose to join a GMC section. Sections provide a four-season schedule of outings, including hiking, biking, cross-country skiing, and canoeing. They also maintain portions of the Long Trail and its shelters.

The Club offers an at-large membership for those who wish to support the work of the GMC but are not interested in affiliating with a local section. Both section and at-large members enjoy the same benefits including a subscription to the Club's quarterly newsletter, *The Long Trail News*, which provides up-to-date information on trail and shelter conditions, hiking, statewide trails, Club history, and a Club activities calendar. Members receive discounts on Club publications and items carried in the GMC bookstore, reduced fees at some overnight sites served by GMC caretakers, opportunities to participate in a wide range of Club activities, and discounts on admission to most GMC events. Section members also receive a section activities schedule and newsletter.

There are twelve GMC sections. Ten are based in Vermont: Bennington, Brattleboro, Bread Loaf (Middlebury), Burlington, Killington (Rutland), Laraway (Northwestern Vermont), Manchester, Montpelier, Ottauquechee (Woodstock), and Sterling (Stowe-Morrisville). Two sections are based out of state: Connecticut and Worcester (eastern Massachusetts). Turn to pages 31 and 32 for a description of section maintenance responsibilities.

TO JOIN THE GMC. Send payment for dues ($27 Individual, $35 Family) to the Green Mountain Club, 4711 Waterbury-Stowe Road, Waterbury Center, Vermont 05677 or call the GMC with your VISA or MasterCard number at (802) 244-7037. GMC dues are subject to change.

Publications

The GMC publishes a number of books, maps, and brochures. Those wishing to complete their collection of guides to the hiking trails of Vermont may wish to purchase the GMC's *Day Hiker's Guide to Vermont*. Other GMC publications and brochures are listed on pages 228 to 229.

Headquarters

Information and Education Services

The Green Mountain Club headquarters are located in the heart of Vermont's hiking country, on Route 100 in Waterbury Center, Vermont, midway between Waterbury and Stowe. To reach the GMC from I-89 in Waterbury (Exit 10) take Vt. 100 north four miles. The headquarters are in the red barn and office building on the west (left) side of Vt. 100. From the intersection of Vt. 108 and 100 in Stowe, the GMC is six miles south on Vt. 100.

The Marvin B. Gameroff Hiker Center houses the Club's information services, educational displays, bookstore, and field programs. At the Hiker Center, the Club provides information about backcountry recreational opportunities throughout Vermont.

The GMC is happy to answer questions about the Long Trail and other trails in Vermont. Hikers are encouraged to stop by the center for trail information. The GMC will also gladly respond to written or telephone inquiries. During the winter months the Club hosts the James P. Taylor Winter Series—a slide show and lecture series celebrating outdoor recreation.

The Hiker Center is open seven days a week (9:00 AM to 5:00 PM) from Memorial Day to Columbus Day. During the remainder of the year, information services are located in the GMC administrative offices in the Ted and Anne Herrick Office Building across the driveway from the Gameroff Hiker Center. Business hours are Monday through Friday from 9:00 AM to 5:00 PM year-round.

End-to-End

Hiking the Long Trail end-to-end is very popular. Although many people hike the Trail in one continuous trip, the majority complete it in sections, one person having taken as long as fifty-two years to finish. Each year about seventy people add their names to the roster of those who have made this journey from Massachusetts to Canada. Such notables as the Three Musketeers (the first women to hike the entire Trail), GMC Long Trail Patrol founder Roy Buchanan, and the U.S. Ski Team are among the over two thousand certified End-to-Enders. Many have hiked the Trail more than once.

Any hiker who has completed the Long Trail—in one season or many—is entitled to an End-to-End certificate. Guidelines for a written summary, necessary for certification, are available from the GMC office. Club members who have completed the Long Trail may purchase an End-to-End emblem for sleeve or pack.

GMC and Long Trail History

The Early Years: 1910–1920

The history of the Green Mountain Club *is* the history of the Long Trail. The LT is the oldest long-distance hiking trail in the United States. Conceived by James P. Taylor (1872–1949) as he waited for the mist to clear from Stratton Mountain, the LT took its first step from dream to reality at a gathering of twenty-three people on March 11, 1910, in Burlington when the Green Mountain Club was formed.

Taylor, associate principal of Vermont Academy in Saxtons River, had been frustrated by the lack of suitable hiking trails in the state. Unlike the mountains in neighboring states, the Green Mountains remained largely unappreciated and unused for recreation until Taylor promised that the new organization would "make the Vermont mountains play a larger part in the life of the people."

Work began almost immediately in the Camel's Hump and Mount Mansfield areas; by the end of 1912 Burlington members had cleared a path from Sterling Pond to Camel's Hump. Early the following season a Forestry Department crew cut a route from Killington Peak to Brandon Gap, and from Camel's Hump south to Lincoln Gap. Later that summer trail builders were busy between Lincoln and Brandon Gaps. Concurrently, the Trail expanded in the north from Johnson to Sterling Pond.

In 1914 the slogan was "Killington to Massachusetts," and by 1917 that goal had been reached. Also that year the first *Guide Book of the Long Trail* was published. It listed fourteen overnight accommodations, including private camps, the Mount Mansfield Hotel, abandoned lumber camps, and five new GMC shelters. Nine farmhouses off the Trail were available for lodging and meals.

The second edition of the guidebook (1920) showed the Trail running from Johnson to the Massachusetts line, with another nine GMC shelters and twelve more farms or other lodgings along the way. Thus, in the first decade members built 209 miles of trail and provided forty-four overnight facilities, fourteen of which were raised by the GMC.

Completion of the Long Trail

The next decade saw the extension of the Long Trail north from Johnson, culminating at Jay Peak in 1927. Many Club members felt Jay was "almost" to Canada and far enough, but Bruce Buchanan of Brattleboro vowed, "We better get rid of the 'almost'." Two years later Roy O. Buchanan, professor of electrical engineering at the University of Vermont, and his brother Bruce marked the remaining ten-odd miles to the Canadian border. In 1930 Charles G. Doll and Phillips D. Carleton cut the final link to Canada.

On its twenty-first birthday the GMC could celebrate the completion of Taylor's footpath from Massachusetts to Canada. The occasion was marked by a large gathering at the Club's headquarters, the Long Trail Lodge at Sherburne Pass, a gift from the Proctor family, early and dedicated supporters of the Long Trail. The highlight of the celebration was the lighting of flares from mountaintop to mountaintop along the spine of the Green Mountains.

Besides regularly updating the *Guide Book of the Long Trail*, the GMC began publishing a bimonthly newsletter, *The Green Mountain News*, in 1922. It was later retitled *The Long Trail News*. Today, this membership quarterly continues to inform members and hikers about Long Trail and Club issues.

Many GMCers belong to local sections whose members maintain designated parts of the Trail and overnight shelters. The oldest is Burlington, first known as the Mount Mansfield Section when it was formed in 1910. Other sections have also existed for many years, while some have come and gone as local interest waxed and waned.

Long Trail Patrol and End-to-End

With the Trail completed, the Club continued to expand its network of shelters. A prime mover in this effort was Roy Buchanan. In 1931 the Club's board of trustees authorized formation of a salaried Long Trail Patrol with Buchanan as the first crew leader. Each summer he assembled groups of students and worked with them on trail maintenance, construction of new shelters, and repairs to existing ones. During the next ten years, the Long Trail Patrol, sections, and other groups built or rebuilt twenty-nine shelters and lodges.

Not surprisingly, the war years saw reductions in trail use and trail work. One GMC program, however, began during this period. In 1942 Club trustees authorized formal recognition of GMCers who had tramped the full length of the Trail and awarded thirty-two special certificates that began the long roster of End-to-Enders.

Back to the Woods

Shelter construction and reconstruction resumed at a modest rate through the 1950s, then accelerated in the next decade. The reason for renewed activity was a significant increase in the number of hikers, especially young people, who sought recreation in the backcountry as part of a new back-to-the-land movement. Between 1966 and 1975, responding to heavy trail traffic, the Club launched a variety of initiatives, including removal of dumps at shelters and promotion of a "carry-in, carry-out" policy, dissemination of information on responsible trail and camping practices, stationing of caretakers at the most popular shelters and ranger-naturalists (now called summit caretakers) on the summits of Mount Mansfield and Camel's Hump, where they taught hikers to respect the rare, fragile alpine ecosystems. The caretaker program was the revival of an informal program of the late 1930s when caretakers were stationed at Taft Lodge to care for the site.

During most of its history the GMC has chosen not to become involved in national conservation causes, concentrating its energy on preserving the wilderness character of the Long Trail. In the mid-1930s, however, when a scenic highway, called the Green Mountain Parkway, was proposed for the length of the Green Mountain Range, the Club mounted energetic opposition. (Vermonters ultimately rejected the idea in a statewide referendum.) Again, in 1958 when the U.S. Air Force dropped its plan to erect a missile communications facility on the Chin of Mount Mansfield, it was in part due to GMC objection.

Perhaps the largest endeavor for the Green Mountain Club in recent years was the initiation of the Long Trail Protection Campaign in 1986. See page 34 for complete information on this critical GMC program.

A Place of Our Own

When the GMC adopted its first vision statement in 1990, it could not foresee that one goal, owning its own headquarters, would become reality within two years. In 1992 the Club bought the former 1836 May Farm on Route 100, a popular tourist avenue into the Green Mountains, in Waterbury Center. After renting office space for many years, first in Rutland, then in downtown Montpelier, the GMC was at last its own landlord.

With the Club's relocation into the heart of hiking country, wide support for the Long Trail Protection Campaign, and continued public interest in healthy outdoor activity, including hiking, membership in the Club has climbed steadily. In 1999 it stood at 8,000.

"Founder, sponsor, defender, protector"

On the GMC's fiftieth anniversary in 1960 the Vermont General Assembly adopted a resolution "expressing its gratitude and recognition to the Green Mountain Club" for its role in establishing and maintaining the Long Trail. In 1971 the legislature passed yet another resolution, recognizing the Club as "the founder, sponsor, defender, and protector" of the Long Trail System and delegating to it responsibility for developing policies and programs for "the preservation, maintenance, and proper use of hiking trails for the benefit of the people of Vermont."

Although the General Assembly's continued recognition has meant very different challenges to different generations of GMCers—from pioneer trail blazing to environmental concerns and land acquisition—the Club's main responsibility remains the same: to maintain and protect the Long Trail for all Vermonters, now and in the future.

Management of the Long Trail

A Private-Public Partnership

Managing the 445-mile Long Trail System is a complex task, involving Club volunteers and staff, federal and state agencies, organizations, and businesses. Over the years, as use of the Long Trail has risen and outside pressures such as development have increased, management of the Trail has evolved from merely trail building and maintenance into a program also focused on protecting natural resources from overuse, upholding landowner rights, protecting the Trail from development, safeguarding special natural areas, educating hikers, and publishing guidebooks and maps.

The Long Trail is maintained by the Green Mountain Club in cooperation with the Vermont Department of Forests, Parks and Recreation, U.S. Forest Service, National Park Service, Appalachian Trail Conference, and private landowners. The cooperation and assistance of these agencies, organizations, and individuals are indispensable. In the Green Mountain National Forest, the U.S. Forest Service actively manages the Long Trail and its side trails with the GMC, providing funding for trail crews, managerial expertise, and staff support. On state lands, the Vermont Department of Forests, Parks, and Recreation works in a similar way on matters pertaining to the Long Trail System. The department also provides grants from the Vermont Recreational Trails Fund. The GMC is also a maintaining club of the Appalachian Trail Conference (ATC) and, together with the ATC, U.S. Forest Service, and National Park Service, is working to secure a protected route for the Long/Appalachian Trail in Vermont (the southern one hundred miles of the Long Trail).

The GMC also works with private landowners to ensure access to the Trail on their land and with Vermont ski areas who in some instances provide financial and logistical support for Long Trail projects.

Volunteer Activity

Volunteers are the backbone of the Green Mountain Club and the Long Trail. Without them the Long Trail would never have been built nor would it be managed as it is today. They serve on committees and blaze and maintain not only the Trail itself but the Club's spirit as well.

The GMC welcomes volunteers. There are many opportunities for all GMC members to be involved with the Club. Newcomers are always welcome. To volunteer or learn about Club skills workshops, contact the GMC.

SECTIONS AND ADOPTERS. GMC sections maintain a portion of Trail, side trails, and shelters. They host work parties throughout the year. Anyone interested in joining a section in its maintenance activities may contact the GMC.

In recent years section maintenance efforts have been supplemented by the Club's Trail and Shelter Adopter Program. Adopters agree to care for a shelter or portion of the Trail and work independently to do inspections, basic maintenance, and cleanup. Cooperation among sections and adopters is encouraged. Volunteers also assist GMC field staff throughout the hiking season as site and summit caretakers and trail maintainers. Portions of the Long Trail maintained by GMC sections are listed below.

- *Bennington:* Harmon Hill to Glastenbury Mountain
- *Brattleboro:* Winhall River to Vt. 11 and 30
- *Bread Loaf:* Sucker Brook Shelter to Emily Proctor Shelter
- *Burlington:* Jonesville to Smugglers' Notch
- *Connecticut:* Glastenbury Mountain to Arlington–West Wardsboro Road
- *Killington:* Vt. 140 to U.S. 4
- *Laraway:* Vt. 15 to Vt. 118
- *Manchester:* Vt. 11 and 30 to Mad Tom Notch
- *Montpelier:* Gorham Lodge to Jonesville and Smugglers' Notch to Chilcoot Pass

- *Ottauquechee:* U.S. 4 to Maine Junction and Appalachian Trail: Maine Junction to Vt. 12
- *Sterling:* Chilcoot Pass to Vt. 15
- *Worcester:* Arlington–West Wardsboro Road to Winhall River

Caretaker Program

The Green Mountain Club manages and minimizes hiker impact through a combination of education, maintenance, and trail design. Since the late 1960s the GMC has hosted site and summit caretakers at a number of high-use sites and vulnerable natural areas along the LT.

These caretakers educate hikers about leave-no-trace practices, maintain trails and shelters, compost sewage, and assist hikers. To help support this important program, a modest overnight use fee is charged at caretaker overnight sites.

At the core of the GMC caretaker program is the belief that education will provide for generations of hikers who know how to travel in the backcountry without harming the Trail, the natural resource, or the backwoods experience of fellow and future hikers. For more about the caretaker program, turn to pages 3 and 4.

Long Trail Patrol

The Long Trail Patrol (LTP) is the Green Mountain Club's official trail crew. Directed by University of Vermont professor Roy O. Buchanan from its inception in 1931 until the mid-1960s, the LTP is the oldest of the GMC's nonvolunteer programs. Patrol crews concentrate on trail relocation and reconstruction projects such as installing rock waterbars and steps. Each crew lives under primitive conditions for five days per week near the work site.

The Long Trail also benefits from a recent cooperative effort of the GMC, ATC, and the U.S. Forest Service. From midsummer to early fall, the Volunteer Long Trail Patrol spends an intensive five days per week doing trail maintenance and construction. This successful program draws volunteers from far and wide as well as local GMCers.

Appalachian National Scenic Trail

Vermont and the Long Trail hold a prominent place in the history of the Appalachian Trail (AT), for it was on the summit of Stratton Mountain, after construction of the Long Trail was begun, that the idea of an extended footpath linking the scenic ridges of the East crystallized in the mind of AT visionary Benton MacKaye.

First proposed in 1921 by MacKaye, a forester, author, and philosopher, the Appalachian Trail was completed in 1937. It extends for 2,150 miles from Katahdin in Maine to northern Georgia's Springer Mountain. The Appalachian Trail Conference, founded in 1925, works with its member clubs and federal and state agencies to preserve and maintain the Appalachian Trail.

In Vermont, the AT coincides with the Long Trail from the Massachusetts border to Maine Junction at Sherburne Pass (U.S. 4), and then swings easterly to cross the Connecticut River near Hanover, New Hampshire, a distance of 146 miles. The GMC maintains the AT from the Massachusetts border to Vt. 12. From there to Norwich, the AT in Vermont is maintained by the Dartmouth Outing Club. For more information about the Appalachian Trail, contact the Appalachian Trail Conference, P.O. Box 807, Harpers Ferry, WV 25425; (304) 535-6331.

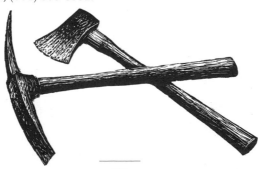

Protecting Vermont's Mountain Lands

In 1986, the GMC launched the Long Trail Protection Campaign in an ambitious effort to acquire land or easements where the Trail crossed private land. By 2000 the GMC had protected sixty-four miles of the Long Trail System. Over 18,500 acres of backcountry land with important wildlife habitat and recreational value had been safeguarded. This effort has been made possible in large part through state legislative appropriations for Long Trail acquisitions totalling $3.725 million.

The Long Trail protection effort began when the Green Mountain Club learned that land crossed by almost thirty miles of the Long Trail in northern Vermont was up for sale, threatening the future of the Trail. An additional thirty miles was in private ownership and potentially at risk due to rapidly changing ownership patterns, development, clear-cutting and log-skidding on the Trail, and posting by some private landowners. A protracted economic slump in the timber industry made it unprofitable for forest owners to hold on to their land and several large landholdings came on the market at an alarming rate.

For the first time in the history of the Long Trail, a simple handshake wasn't enough to ensure passage for hikers or protection of the trail corridor. Between Mount Ellen and the Canadian border, in areas outside the Camel's Hump, Mount Mansfield, and Jay State Forests, over sixty miles of the Long Trail and twenty-two miles of side trail were unprotected. Much of the southernmost two hundred miles of the Trail had been protected through acquisition for the Green Mountain National Forest and the Appalachian Trail.

Much of the acquired land has gone into state ownership. During the early years of the campaign, the Vermont Field Office of the Nature Conservancy assisted the GMC with closing services and interim capital when needed.

Hundreds of GMC members, friends, schools, businesses, organizations, foundations and the Vermont Housing and Conservation Board have generously given to the cause to protect the country's oldest long-distance hiking trail.

About ten miles of Long Trail and six miles of side trail along the length of the Trail remain in private ownership and are still in need of permanent protection.

The GMC thanks the landowners who have generously allowed the Long Trail to cross their land since Club volunteers cut the first section of Trail in 1910, and the thirty landowners who continue to allow it to do so.

265-Mile Club

The success of the Green Mountain Club's 265-Mile Club, named for the length of the Long Trail, illustrates the depth of passion that people have for the Trail. Over 475 people, foundations, businesses, civic groups, and GMC sections are members of the 265-Mile Club, having pledged or given $1,000 to the Long Trail Protection Campaign. In 1992 two plaques were unveiled at the Club headquarters in Waterbury Center with the names of the 265-Mile Club members. Additional plaques are planned as 265-Mile Club membership continues to grow.

Anyone wishing to support the Club's protection effort should contact the GMC headquarters in Waterbury Center. Donating to the Long Trail Protection Fund is a special way to commemorate a hike on the Long Trail.

The Green Mountains

by Charles Johnson

History of the Land

The Ancient Foundation

It is said that Vermont was given its present name in 1609 by the French explorer Samuel de Champlain, the first white man reputed to see it. *"Voila, les verds monts"* (Behold, the green mountains), he was supposed to have remarked as he looked at the mountains that dominate Vermont's landscape.

Geographically, physically, and spiritually the Green Mountains are the backbone of the state. People can see them from almost every region. They take up a sizable portion of the land base, running the entire 160-mile length of the state (extending, under different names, into Massachusetts and Québec) and ranging from twenty to thirty-six miles wide throughout. They contain the highest peaks in the state, some over four thousand feet. In times before quick transportation and paved roads, their height, terrain, and climate were formidable barriers to east-west movement and communication.

The Greens are a segment of the Appalachian Mountain chain extending from Alabama through the Gaspé Peninsula in Canada. They include remnants of the most ancient rock formations in New England, dating back over a billion years; the cores of previous ranges long since worn down from heights estimated between ten thousand and twenty thousand feet (Killington and Pico Peaks are examples of these nubs). The eroded materials—rocks, gravels, sands, silts, and clays—carried by water, ice, and gravity itself, worked their way downslope over the eons and came to rest in the coastal waters of an earlier (proto) Atlantic Ocean.

For over 200 million years, from 445 to 200 million years ago, slowly but inexorably the shifting continental plates converged, with Europe, Africa, and North America colliding and the proto-Atlantic sea floor buckling into volcanoes and earthquakes. Ultimately, under tremendous pressure and heat, the sediments transformed into metamorphic ("remade") rocks—the most common is the wavy and convoluted *schist*, often green due to a constituent mineral, chlorite. They were crumpled and pushed up into new mountain ranges, today's Green and Taconic Mountains.

The Long Trail runs over the main Green Mountain Range. To the east of the main range lie three shorter parallel ranges from south to north: the Northfield, Worcester and Lowell Mountains. To the west of the Green Mountains, south of Brandon, are the Taconics. These prominent ranges are easily viewed from the Long Trail.

The Green Mountains are broken by two west-flowing rivers, the Winooski and the Lamoille, which rise on the uplands to the east. These rivers have cut impressive water gaps.

After crossing the summit of Camel's Hump (4,083 feet), one of Vermont's highest mountains, the Long Trail descends 3,758 feet to the Winooski River at Bolton, the lowest point on the Long Trail.

Since the development of the Green Mountain ranges, the continents have been inching away from each other, to where now they are over three thousand miles apart and the Atlantic Ocean has filled the chasm between.

The Ice Age

Four, perhaps more, times within the past two to three million years massively thick and widespread ice sheets, visible demonstrations of significant climate change, have descended upon and retreated from North America. In the process and by their weight and movement, they reshaped the land in substantial ways. The latest episode in this Pleistocene epoch, the Wisconsin glaciation, lasted in our region about ten thousand years (from twenty thousand to ten thousand years ago). At its maximum, the Laurentian Ice Sheet, as it is called, blanketed a huge region from the Arctic south to what is now New York City and west to the Rockies. In Vermont it was a sea of ice a mile or more deep, which covered the entire land surface, including the highest peaks.

As the ice worked its way south and overrode the mountains, it smoothed them on the north-facing slopes and summits, then as it descended the southern flanks plucked rocks from the leeward slopes, often making them steeper and more jagged (e.g., the cliffs of Camel's Hump).

Everywhere the glaciers have left their legacy: roughly smoothed peaks and broad U-shaped valleys whose bedrock shows deep scratches from dragged boulders. Bowl-shaped gulfs lie against mountains, made by their own personal glaciers after the main ice sheet left. Rock-infested soil, the debris of melting glaciers—and the bane of farmers—was scattered everywhere. Sinuous sand and gravel terraces follow next to rivers. The resulting impeded drainages have given rise to lakes, ponds, bogs, and other wetlands by the thousands.

People on the Land

Into the terrestrial and aquatic places left vacant by the disappearance of the glacier came plants and animals, most of which had been displaced by the ice. Some, however, were new. Among them were humans, the native peoples.

Here during the earlier postglacier environment were peoples who had migrated from the south and west. The Paleo-Indians, as archaeologists have called them, were hunter-gatherers whose way of life revolved largely around big game such as caribou, elk, even the extinct mammoth (whose bones were discovered in western Vermont in 1848) and who moved with the herds.

As the climate warmed and forests supplanted tundra over a six thousand-year period, the Native American culture changed in response. The Archaic Indians lived in more defined, though still large, territories and focused on local game (fish, deer, bear) and vegetation that could be eaten in season or stored for winter use. Their culture seemed designed around settlements, albeit settlements that shifted with the seasons: spring and summer in the valleys near rivers and lakes for fish and plant foraging, fall and winter in the forests for game and protection of trees.

With still further warming, to a maximum temperature perhaps five thousand to four thousand years ago (the so-called hypsithermal interval), Vermont's climate took on the character of modern-day Pennsylvania or New Jersey. Since then and up to the present, the climate has cooled again, with corresponding displacements of forest types.

From three thousand years before present to just three or four hundred years ago, the native peoples were more and more influenced by social changes associated with the rise of agriculture to the south and west, particularly a shift away from territorial hunting-gathering and towards settlements. This Woodland Period shows evidence of well-established sites, especially near major waterways.

It is clear that the earliest Vermonters and their descendants, known to us historically as the Western Abenaki people, have always had a special relationship with the Green Mountains. It is virtually certain that some, and perhaps many, stretches of the Long Trail run atop routes once favored by the Abenaki. Edible and medicinal plants were found and gathered in the mountains, and high quality raw materials for making stone tools were quarried here as well. Mountain regions, particularly summits, have been used for religious purposes from time immemorial. During periods of conflict, especially later in history, native people used the mountains as places of refuge, which may have led to the establishment of larger, longer-term mountain settlements.

During the latter stages of this long prehistory, the native peoples apparently became more distinctly divided into five regional language groups, those in New England belonging to the Eastern Algonquian group. Of this group, several bands lived in Vermont—various Abenakis over most of the state and Mahicans in the southwestern corner. These were the native peoples white European explorers and trappers first encountered here in the early seventeenth century.

For the new arrivals, this surely was a land rich and beautiful in its natural splendor yet undoubtedly daunting in its wildness, deep forests, and trackless mountains. Except for the five percent or less of the landscape in treeless mountaintops, lakes, ponds, rivers, wetlands, and the relatively small areas disturbed by Native Americans for agriculture or game production, this region was all forested. But it was soon to change. The coming and settlement of white people, mostly from southern New England in the eighteenth century, and the supplanting of Native American ways by western attitudes towards the land and its resources transformed the landscape with a blink of the historic eye.

Except for the forests in the Northeast Kingdom of Vermont, the trees fell in waves before the early farmers who cleared the land for crops, pastures, firewood, homes, and tools. Big pines were cut indiscriminately for ship masts and large areas of woodland were burned off to produce potash, an essential ingredient in the manufacture of soap and for a time Vermont's most valuable export. Still later, large areas of woodland were cleared to produce timber and provide space for Vermont's booming sheep farms. Many prominent mountains, heavily forested from base to summit, were cleared far up their slopes to provide sheep pasturage. Within 150 years of settlement, from 1700 to 1850, the state had gone from virtually 100% forested to almost completely deforested. With the forests went the associated plants and animals, such as mountain lion, wolves, moose, deer, beaver, passenger pigeons, wild turkeys, and many others.

From about 1850 to the turn of the century, however, many events and forces halted, then reversed, this trend. Newly constructed railroads provided relatively easy access to homestead range and croplands in the Midwest and attracted farmers to a more forgiving terrain and climate. The Civil War drew men from the fields into battle, and later, the cities south and west, hubs of the Industrial Revolution, attracted many in search of easier and better paying jobs.

As a result, mountain farms were abandoned by the score and the fallow fields and meadows soon became new forests, most notably white pine that throve in full exposure to the sun. All that remains of most of these hill farms today are the stone walls and cellar holes found throughout the Vermont woods—some along the Long Trail itself. Over the next quarter-century, the white pines grew to a size merchantable by the emerging logging industry. As these trees were taken, the young seedlings and saplings beneath them were given room to grow and became the forests within which today we live and work and recreate. With the forests' reclamation of former territory returned many of the animals and plants once displaced by land clearing.

The Green Mountains today see a variety of uses. Vermont's farms continue to decline, struggling to compete in a world economy. Those farms managing to survive are located largely in fertile valleys and flatlands, but even they are gravely threatened by high property taxes, low milk prices, and development. The forests cloak the higher slopes, where logging, maple sugaring, and recreation are the main activities. Recreation is increasing: hundreds of thousands of people enjoy hiking, hunting and fishing, ski touring, snow-mobiling, and mountain biking. Downhill ski areas and resorts are prominent on many high peaks of the Green Mountains. Minimizing confrontations and conflicts among these many uses has become an integral part of land and recreation management in Vermont.

Plants and Animals

The Northern Hardwoods

Progressing upslope from the lowlands to about 2,500 to 2,800 feet (depending on geographical location or site), one passes through the northern hardwood forests that so characterize much of the Vermont landscape. This forest type accounts for up to 70% of the 4.5 million acres of forests in the state. Vermont is presently 75% forested.

These established hardwood forests are predominantly sugar maple, red maple, beech, yellow birch, and eastern hemlock (actually a softwood or conifer) mixed with other species. For example, on rich, moist sites white ash is common; on places newly exposed by logging or windthrow, quaking and bigtooth aspens may come in quickly; on burned sites paper and gray birches are the pioneers; and in abandoned fields white pine often grows in profusion. In the southern half of the state, oaks and hickories are often significant contributors to tree species diversity.

This hardwood forest is the one of magical spring wildflowers that, bathed in the strengthening sun, bloom so beautifully before the trees are fully leaved. There are lavenders, pinks, and purples of hepaticas and spring beauties, the whites, yellows, and deep blues of violets, the white sprays of foamflower, the burgundy of red trillium, and many more. It is also the forest of indescribable autumns, of colors of massed leaves matched by few other places on earth. Mountainsides are here ablaze with reds and yellows of maples, there muted with browns and coppers of beech and oak.

With more available food within reach, the wildlife of the northern hardwoods is more diverse and plentiful than in the spartan boreal forest above it. Small mammals are many, including several species of shrews, mice, voles, and bats; red, gray, and flying squirrels—all or one—are likely present.

Many of the larger mammals, predators and herbivores alike, are here for the "second time around," so to speak. Such forest-identified species as white-tailed deer, moose, black bear, fisher, beaver, bobcat, and others dwindled with the dwindling forest of the 1700s and 1800s. They became virtually extinct in the state during that time and have returned or been restored only over the past hundred years or so of forest regrowth. Some, like deer and fisher, had our help in recolonizing old ground; they were caught elsewhere, transported here, and released. Some say (and others hope) the mountain lion—or catamount—has returned to the Green Mountains as well.

Like mammals, birds of this forest are plentiful and varied also. In the exuberant rush of spring come species by the score: wood warblers; thrushes (hermit, wood, and the veery); flycatchers; woodpeckers such as sapsuckers and flickers; broadwinged hawks; and many others. Some stay through the summer to nest and raise young, others move on. By fall, these visitors leave and the quieter woods are left to the resident seed-, nut-, and bud-eaters (e.g., ruffed grouse or partridge, wild turkey, the ever-present black-capped chickadees and white-breasted nuthatches), and vigilant predators (e.g., great horned and barred owls and sharp-shinned hawks).

Alpine (Montane) Boreal Forest

The higher in the mountains, the tougher life becomes: winters are longer, temperatures colder, soils thinner. A phenomenon called fog precipitation occurs at these upper elevations. Moisture from low-lying clouds is removed by the branches and needles of the conifers. Tiny cloud droplets collect and then coalesce, becoming a major source of water above 2,500 feet. For animals, food is scarcer. Between roughly 2,800 and 3,000 feet, the northern hardwood forest yields—sometimes gradually, sometimes more abruptly—to Vermont's high-elevation boreal (subarctic) forest, a realm of balsam fir, red spruce, and moisture- and shade-loving understory mosses, lichens, and a few wildflowers such as goldthread, Canada mayflower, and bunchberry. Towards timberline (3,800 to 4,000 feet) the trees become ever more stunted, tangled, and virtually impenetrable. Where trees have been distorted and sheared by winds and ice, the low, craggy forest is known as krummholz, a German word meaning crooked wood.

Year-round bird or mammal residents are few in this demanding environment. In winter, birds most likely to be seen are the black-capped chickadee (and more rarely its cousin the boreal—formerly brown-capped—chickadee) and red-breasted nuthatches, as they work tree bark and branches for seeds, grubs, and hibernating insects. Besides the smaller voles and shrews, the most common mammals are red squirrels and snowshoe hares (also called varying hares, for their change of color from summer brown to winter white). More dramatic species do pass through this zone: moose moving up from the lower forests to browse in winter and predators such as goshawks, bobcats, and fisher (a large, sleek, weasel-like creature) in search of prey.

Spring brings not only the pesky, stream-born blackflies but a host of birds who stay to nest or pass on through to Canada. As many as fourteen species of wood warblers are spring visitors; a few stay for the breeding season, such as blackpoll and Nashville warblers. Ground-nesting Bicknell's gray-cheeked thrushes and, more commonly, Swainson's thrushes are the highest elevation thrushes here, their distinctive flutelike songs evocative of their cousins of the lower, deciduous forests.

Tundra

Above timberline, only the summits of three of Vermont's highest mountains, Mount Mansfield (the highest, 4,393 feet), Camel's Hump (tied for third, 4,083 feet), and Mount Abraham (4,006 feet) support small and precarious vestiges of the post–Ice Age, alpine tundra. These barrenland zones above timberline—250 acres on Mount Mansfield, ten on Camel's Hump, and a very small area on Mount Abraham—have, in miniature, much the appearance, ecology, and natural history of the true Arctic, with some significant differences.

The frost-free growing season is short, often less than ninety days. The soils are thin, sparse, nutrient poor, and tenuous on steep slopes. Plants are generally dwarfed, in dense clumps, and low-lying to reduce exposure to wind and abrading snow and ice; they must also be extremely hardy to survive the many and prolonged rigors of such an environment. Unlike the true Arctic, precipitation is abundant as rain, snow, and dew from the regular cloud cover, even though it may run off the steep slopes quickly. Common here, but very uncommon for the region as a whole, are such arctic species as Bigelow's sedge, alpine bilberry, mountain sandwort, highland rush, and others whose main range is a thousand miles or more to the north.

Living among the plants are very few animals that can make do on the meager food supplies and harsh conditions: mammals such as red-back voles eat seeds and plant materials, and shrews prey on other small mammals and abundant summer insects; migratory birds such as dark-eyed juncos may nest here and eat seeds and fruits on the ground. In the craggy ledges of cliffs near the tundra (and elsewhere high in the mountains), ravens and peregrine falcons, the latter back from the brink of extinction, now nest regularly.

•

Within these and other places, many creatures—be they salamanders of woodland soils or cold rushing streams, insects and other invertebrates of dying trees, decaying logs, or fallen leaves, ferns and mosses of rocky recesses—tuck their lives into the nooks and crannies of the mountains. Their world is wondrous, awaits exploration, and invites discovery.

Charles W. Johnson, Vermont's state naturalist, is author of The Nature of Vermont, Bogs of the Northeast, *and many articles in* Vermont Life. *David Lacy, an archaeologist with the Green Mountain National Forest, wrote portions of the text about native peoples in this chapter.*

TRAIL
DESCRIPTIONS

DIVISION 1

Massachusetts-Vermont
State Line to Vt. 9

Take Note

The southern terminus of the Long Trail is in the woods at the Massachusetts-Vermont boundary northwest of North Adams, Mass. Two hiking trails, the Appalachian Trail and the Pine Cobble Trail, provide the only access to the start of the Long Trail. The Appalachian Trail approach description begins on page 49. The Pine Cobble Trail is found on page 51.

The Long Trail and the Appalachian Trail coincide throughout this division.

Suggested Hikes

PINE COBBLE. This pleasant hike on the Pine Cobble Trail leads to a vista of the tri-state region's rugged terrain. Round trip, 3.0 mi., 2 h.

HARMON HILL. A short, steep climb on the Long Trail south from Vt. 9, this hike boasts expansive hilltop views. A steep rock staircase may be challenging to some hikers. Round trip, 3.6 mi., 2¾ h.

ROARING BRANCH. This hike on the Long Trail north from Mill Road out of Stamford leads to a sizable beaver dam beneath Scrub Hill. Mill Road may not be passable all the way to the LT so some walking along the road may be necessary. Round trip, 5.2 mi., 3½ h.

Camping and Fires

Although the Long Trail in Division 1 crosses the Green Mountain National Forest, it follows a fairly narrow trail corridor surrounded by private property. Camping is allowed only at shelters. Small wood fires, although discouraged, are permitted at shelters in established fire rings. Follow leave-no-trace guidelines (pages 4 to 6) to minimize impact on the Long Trail System.

Winter Use

The steep north slope of Harmon Hill south of Vt. 9 can be treacherous. The Appalachian Trail and Pine Cobble Trail out of Williamstown make good snowshoe hikes.

Access to Long Trail

MILL ROAD. To reach this trailhead turn onto Mill Road from Vt. 8 and Vt. 100, 0.5 mi. north of Billmont's Country Store in Stamford, or 6.8 mi. south of the junction of Vt. 8 and Vt. 100 in Readsboro. Follow the road beyond the last residences at 3.3 mi. where it turns into an unimproved gravel road. In dry conditions the road is driveable another 0.9 mi. west to the Long Trail where there is parking for four cars on the south side just beyond the Trail. If the road is not driveable, park cars so that no woods roads are blocked. This road is not passable from the Pownal side where it is known as County Road. The last mile of Mill Road to the Long Trail is not plowed in winter.

VT. 9. This Long Trail crossing is 5.0 mi. east of U.S. 7 in downtown Bennington or 8.8 mi. west of the junction of Vt. 9 and Vt. 8 South. There is a U.S. Forest Service parking lot on the north side of the highway just west of the Trail.

Approach Trails

APPALACHIAN TRAIL (Blackinton Approach). This trail begins on Mass. 2 opposite Phelps Ave. at a traffic light 3.0 mi. east of the U.S. 7/Mass. 2 traffic circle in Williamstown, and 2.4 mi. west of the center of North Adams. There is no parking at the trailhead, so hikers should obtain permission to park at the Greylock Community Club 0.1 mi. east of the trail on Mass. 2 or at the Holy Family Catholic Church adjacent to the AT.

The white-blazed Appalachian Trail proceeds north from **Mass. 2 (0.0 mi.)** opposite Phelps Ave. east of the church, and crosses over the railroad and Hoosic River on a footbridge. From the AT footbridge, the Appalachian Trail follows Massachusetts Ave. east. Just before reaching a stone bridge, the trail turns left off the road and crosses two footbridges before reaching a small reservoir on Sherman Brook (0.2 mi.). After following Sherman Brook upstream, the trail makes a short, steep ascent away from the brook. Descending, the trail soon reaches **Pete's Spring (1.4 mi.)** on the right and a **spur trail** to the left. This trail leads 0.1 mi. to **Sherman Brook Primitive Campsite** and continues another 0.1 mi. to rejoin the Appalachian Trail.

The AT continues and shortly returns to Sherman Brook at some old bridge abutments. From this point the trail bears northwest and reaches the north end of the campsite spur trail. Ascending, the trail joins an old woods road (1.7 mi.), which it follows for some distance before swinging to the west and making a steep climb through an old rock slide from which there are good views to the south and east (2.3 mi.). There is a bad weather alternate route around the rockfall to the west. The trail then skirts a boggy pond and rises to a rocky knoll where the **Pine Cobble Trail (2.6 mi.)** enters from the left.

This junction is located near the southern end of an extensive area on East Mtn. that is recovering from old forest fires. There are limited views of the Berkshire Hills to the south, including the Hoosac Range (left), the Taconics (right), and, between them, Mt. Greylock (el. 3,491'), Massachusetts' highest peak. Turning right at the Pine Cobble junction, the AT ascends to the north along the ridge, and soon reaches **Eph's Lookout (3.0 mi.)**, named after Ephraim Williams, founder of Williams College. Just beyond, the trail enters the woods and finally comes to the **southern terminus of the Long Trail (3.8 mi.)** at the Massachusetts-Vermont state line. **Mass. 2 to LT, 3.8 mi., 6.1 km, 2⅔ h (Rev. 2 h).**

PINE COBBLE TRAIL **(Williamstown Approach).** From its junction with U.S. 7 in Williamstown, follow Mass. 2 east 0.6 mi. to Cole Ave. Go north 0.8 mi. on Cole Ave. to its end at North Hoosac Road. Turn right onto this road and proceed 0.3 mi. and take a left onto Pine Cobble Road. Follow this road 0.2 mi. to the trailhead. Pine Cobble Road is 2.1 mi. west of the AT on Massachusetts Ave./North Hoosac Road. Parking is available opposite the trail.

From **Pine Cobble Road (0.0 mi.)**, the blue-blazed Pine Cobble Trail slabs the hillside and shortly enters the woods. After passing a side trail on the right leading 350 ft. to Bear Spring in a hollow, the trail rises steeply to the ridge where an orange-triangle-blazed **spur trail (1.4 mi.)** on the right leads 0.1 mi. to the summit of **Pine Cobble**. Here there is a wide view of the Hoosic Valley with Mt. Greylock and other Berkshire and Taconic peaks.

Continuing from its junction with the spur trail, the Pine Cobble Trail follows gentle grades through scrub oak, pitch pine, and stunted white pines to a rocky knob where the trail ends at its junction with the **Appalachian Trail (2.0 mi.)**. From here the Appalachian Trail (described in the Blackinton Approach) leads north (left) to reach the **southern terminus of the Long Trail (3.2 mi.)** at the Massachusetts-Vermont state line. **Pine Cobble Road to LT, 3.2 mi., 5.2 km, 2½ h (Rev. 1¾ h).**

IT'S YOUR DRINKING WATER

Wash dishes and yourself away from the water source. The next person might not like secondhand oatmeal or the taste of detergent.

WINTER HIKING?

- The Long Trail is marked with white blazes, which are difficult to see against a snowy background and frequently buried beneath the snow.

- Deep snow may obscure all signs of the trail. Topographical maps and a compass are helpful.

- Daylight is short in the winter. Darkness may come suddenly.

- Stay alert to the dangers of hypothermia and frostbite. Know the signs and how to treat them.

- Keep group size between four and ten people.

- Be prepared to keep warm and sheltered with nothing more than the equipment you carry. Never count on a campfire or wood stove to keep you warm.

- You may encounter winter weather at higher elevations during the fall and spring.

- Use skis or snowshoes. Post-holing makes the trail unpleasant and dangerous for the next person.

Long Trail Description

From the **Massachusetts-Vermont state line (0.0 mi.)**, the Long Trail descends to a brook crossing (0.4 mi.). It then climbs to the east side of a low ridge, passes over a bedrock ridge (1.7 mi.), and continues to a woods road (2.4 mi.). Crossing the road, the Trail proceeds to a dirt road, which is the **Broad Brook Trail (2.6 mi.)**. This trail leads southwest 4.0 mi. to White Oaks Road in Williamstown.

The LT crosses the road and rises to a junction with a **spur trail (2.8 mi.)**, which leads 300 yds. west to **Seth Warner Shelter**. This frame lean-to was built in 1965 by carpenter trainees of the Manpower Development Training Act. It has space for 8. A brook, which may fail in dry seasons, is 150 yds. to the west. A primitive tenting area is located 400 ft. south of the shelter on a spur trail. **Blackinton to Seth Warner Shelter, 6.7 mi., 10.8 km, 4¼ h (SB 3½ h). Pine Cobble Road to Seth Warner Shelter, 6.1 mi., 9.8 km, 4 h (SB 3¼ h).**

Going north from the junction with the spur trail, the Long Trail soon crosses **Mill Road (3.1 mi.)**, also known as County Road from Pownal, just beyond a power line. Under favorable conditions this road may be driveable 4.2 mi. east to Vt. 8 and 100 in Stamford.

The Trail then begins a steady ascent from the road and, after passing a view south to Mt. Greylock and a spur trail on the right leading 100 ft. to Ed's Spring (4.2 mi.), continues to the south summit, el. 3,025', of a nameless ridge (4.5 mi.). Here there are views to the south and west. Returning to the woods, the Trail continues north along the ridge and, shortly after passing under the **north power line (4.9 mi.)**, begins a steady and sometimes steep descent to an old beaver pond, from which there is a good view of nearby Scrub Hill. It then crosses **Roaring Branch (5.8 mi.)** on a log bridge just below the beaver dam.

Beyond the brook crossing, the Trail passes over several minor knobs and, remaining on or just below the ridge most of the way, continues to the wooded northwest summit of

Consultation Peak (7.0 mi.), so named by volunteer trail workers because of its strategic location for planning maintenance activities. It then descends to a well-travelled woods road (8.0 mi.), which leads 0.1 mi. west to a clearing on the east shore of Sucker Pond. To protect the Bennington public water supply, no swimming or camping is allowed here.

From the woods road crossing, the Long Trail descends gently and soon crosses the **Sucker Pond Outlet Brook (8.4 mi.)**. Then, after passing over puncheon through a wetland, the LT climbs a wooded knoll, on which are located the building foundations of a 19th century tavern (8.9 mi.). Continuing to the ridge and crossing a woods road, the Trail then descends to picturesque Stamford Stream (9.4 mi.), which it parallels downstream for some distance before bearing left to **Congdon Shelter (10.0 mi.)**.

This open-front frame cabin, with bunks for 8, was built by the Long Trail Patrol in 1967. It was named for Herbert Wheaton Congdon, a Long Trail pioneer, trail builder and mapmaker, and was the gift of the Congdon family. A small brook east of the shelter furnishes water, and overflow campsites are located on the ridge west of the LT above the outhouse. **Seth Warner Shelter to Congdon Shelter, 7.3 mi., 11.7 km, 4½ h (SB 4½ h).**

Continuing north from the shelter, the Long Trail ascends the ridge, skirts an area of beaver activity, and then reaches the **Old Bennington-Heartwellville Road (10.6 mi.)**. This woods road can be followed west 4.0 mi. to Vt. 9 via Burgess Road, 1.0 mi. east of U.S. 7 in Bennington. To the east, this road leads to Stamford Stream and the woods roads of Dunville Hollow.

From the woods road, the LT crosses a small stream, climbs steadily past two more woods roads, and then traverses a small clearing (11.4 mi.). Beyond this point, after fairly level going, the Trail crosses a brook and rises to the open summit of **Harmon Hill (12.5 mi.)**, where controlled burns are used as a management tool by the U.S. Forest Service to retain vistas and provide wildlife clearings. From here there is a fine view to the west including Mt. Anthony, the historic village of Bennington, and the monument that commemorates the American Revolution's Battle of Bennington. To the north are limited views of Bald Mtn. and Glastenbury Mtn.

North of Harmon Hill, the Trail bears slightly east across the clearing, enters the woods, and soon begins to descend. After swinging to the left, the Trail bears right (13.7 mi.) and begins a very steep drop, utilizing extensive rock staircases, to **Vt. 9** (Bennington-Brattleboro Highway) **(14.3 mi.)**.

To the west via Vt. 9, it is 5.0 mi. to U.S. 7 in Bennington. Old Bennington, the town center of colonial days, is 1 mi. west of the present center. Many historical buildings and sites, including the Bennington Museum and the Bennington Battle Monument, are located here. To the east via Vt. 9, it is 2.8 mi. to Woodford and 4.8 mi. to Woodford State Park.

Side Trail

BROAD BROOK TRAIL. This trail begins on White Oaks Road in Pownal, Vt., near the state line. Follow the Pine Cobble Trail directions to the junction of Cole Ave. and North Hoosac Road. From here proceed 0.8 mi. west on North Hoosac and Bridges Roads to White Oaks Road. Continue on White Oaks Road 1.2 mi. north to the Vermont border and the crossing of Broad Brook. Parking is available at a small lot opposite a house just south of the brook.

From White Oaks Road (0.0 mi.), the Broad Brook Trail follows the path that is closest to the brook on its south side and then passes through a metal fence. The trail parallels Broad Brook, which it crosses several times along the way. These crossings can be challenging in spring. The trail ascends northeasterly to reach a dirt road (3.7 mi.) and then follows the dirt road east to the Long Trail. White Oaks Road to LT, 4.0 mi., 6.4 km, 2½ h (Rev. 2 h).

DIVISION 2

Vt. 9 to Arlington– West Wardsboro Road

Take Note

The Long Trail and the Appalachian Trail coincide throughout this division.

Suggested Hikes

SPLIT ROCK. This short hike leads to a large glacial erratic on the Long Trail north of Vt. 9. Round trip, 1.4 mi., 1 h.

PORCUPINE LOOKOUT. A full day's trip on the Long Trail north from Vt. 9 to the lookout just north of an un-named summit (el. 2,815') offers fine views. Round trip, 8.8 mi., 5½ h.

GLASTENBURY OVERNIGHT. A challenging overnight backpack, this trip makes a loop of the Long Trail north from Vt. 9 to Goddard Shelter and then to the West Ridge Trail and east branch of the Bald Mtn. Trail back to Woodford Hollow. There is a two-mile road walk between the two trailheads. Round trip, 21.8 mi., 13¼ h.

Camping and Fires

The Long Trail in Division 2 crosses the Green Mountain National Forest. Leave-no-trace camping with small wood fires is allowed. Follow leave-no-trace guidelines (pages 4 to 6) to minimize impact on the Long Trail System.

Exception: Camping between Maple Hill and Porcupine Lookout is prohibited to protect the city of Bennington public water supply (Hell Hollow Brook).

Winter Use

The remoteness of this section of trail cannot be overemphasized. Snowshoeing north from Vt. 9, though steep, provides good views south to Harmon Hill.

Access to Long Trail

VT. 9. Refer to the description on page 49 in Division 1.

ARLINGTON–WEST WARDSBORO ROAD (Kelley Stand Road). *From the west:* This Long Trail crossing is 13 mi. east of U.S. 7A in Arlington. Take exit 3 (Arlington) off U.S. 7 and proceed 0.1 mi. west on Vt. 313 to a right turn onto South Road. Follow South Road 0.6 mi. to its end on Old Mill Road. This junction is 1.8 mi. east of Arlington and U.S. 7A. Turn right again and proceed 0.7 mi. to a fork just after crossing a bridge. The right-hand fork is Kelley Stand Road, which continues east 10.5 mi. to the Long Trail. Parking is on the north side of the road just beyond the East Branch of the Deerfield River.

From the east: From Vt. 100 in West Wardsboro, 8.5 mi. south of East Jamaica and 13.6 mi. north of Wilmington, follow Stratton Ski Area signs west 3.4 mi. to the town of Stratton and another 3.4 mi. further to the Long Trail.

The Arlington–West Wardsboro Road is not plowed between East Arlington and the LT parking lot, when the unmaintained portion of the road is a major snowmobile trail.

Long Trail Description

North of **Vt. 9** (Bennington-Brattleboro Highway) **(0.0 mi.)**, the Long Trail passes to the east of a large, paved parking lot with a trailhead privy on the north side of the highway and immediately crosses **City Stream** on the **William D. MacArthur Memorial Bridge.** The bridge, built by the U.S. Forest Service, honors the memory of a dedicated GMC volunteer trail maintainer who devoted many years to the Long Trail with the Pioneer Valley and Bennington Sections.

From the bridge, the LT follows City Stream's north bank downstream for a short distance and then turns right to begin a steep climb with several switchbacks to a lookout with a view to the northwest, just beyond which it passes between the upright halves of **Split Rock (0.7 mi.)**. After crossing a woods road, the Trail climbs easily for some distance, crosses another woods road, and then continues to a **spur trail (1.6 mi.)** leading right 250 ft. to **Melville Nauheim Shelter**. This frame shelter, constructed in 1977, has bunk space for 8. It was built with funds contributed by Mrs. Melville Nauheim of New York City in memory of her husband. Water is from the stream just north of the spur trail. **Congdon Shelter to Melville Nauheim Shelter, 5.9 mi., 9.5 km, 3¾ h (SB 4 h).**

Continuing north, the Trail climbs gradually and then ascends at a moderate rate to cross a power line on **Maple Hill (2.1 mi.)**. Here there are views of Bennington and Mt. Anthony to the west and of Mt. Snow, Haystack Mtn., and the northern end of the Hoosac Range to the east. After ascending gradually, the LT descends to cross a small stream and then continues with little change in elevation to cross a bridge over **Hell Hollow Brook (3.2 mi.)**. Just beyond, the Long Trail crosses its original route (circa 1920), long since obliterated, which followed Hell Hollow Brook upstream from Woodford Hollow. **Camping is prohibited in this area to protect the Bennington public water supply.**

North of the brook, the LT rises gradually and, after passing through a balsam and spruce swamp over puncheon, climbs steadily to an unnamed summit (el. 2,815'). It then follows the ridge to **Porcupine Lookout (4.4 mi.)**, with views to the east and south, after which it drops to the first of several sags in the ridge. After some gradual climbing, the Trail ascends moderately to the wooded summit of Little Pond Mtn. (5.5 mi.), descends a short distance, and then continues along a narrow ridge to **Little Pond Lookout**

(5.8 mi.). After proceeding with only minor elevation changes, the Long Trail climbs steadily to a point just below the summit (el. 3,331') of an unnamed peak. Remaining somewhat below the ridge to the west, the Trail descends steeply at first and then continues on easier grades for nearly a mile before regaining the ridge a short distance south of **Glastenbury Lookout (7.6 mi.)**, from which there is a view of Glastenbury Mtn. and the connecting ridge to Bald Mtn.

Beyond the lookout, the LT leads to a shallow sag, where it crosses an old woods road (8.1 mi.). From the woods road, the Trail ascends gradually, then climbs steadily to a large rectangular boulder near the summit (el. 3,150') of an unnamed peak (8.8 mi.). It continues along the ridge with little change in elevation, then begins a moderate ascent. The Long Trail then climbs very steeply over rock and log stairs for a short distance, and finally levels off to pass a piped spring and then reaches **Goddard Shelter (10.1 mi.)**, where there are views to the south.

This log lean-to, with space for 12, was completed by the Bennington Section and the U.S. Forest Service in 1985. Some of the materials were airlifted to the site by the Air National Guard. It is named in honor of Ted Goddard, former president and treasurer of the GMC, and past president of the Bennington Section. A spring 150 ft. southbound on the Long Trail provides water. **Melville Nauheim Shelter to Goddard Shelter, 8.5 mi., 13.7 km, 5¾ h (SB 5 h).**

On the west side of the shelter, the **West Ridge Trail** follows Glastenbury Mtn.'s southwest ridge toward Bennington and Woodford Hollow. Combined with one of the branches of the **Bald Mtn. Trail**, this is an alternate route to the summit of Glastenbury Mtn. from the south.

The LT ascends north of Goddard Shelter past the remains of the old fire warden's cabin to the densely wooded summit of **Glastenbury Mtn. (10.4 mi.)**. Here, a fire tower built in 1927 and renovated by the U.S. Forest Service in the 1970s now serves as an observation deck for hikers. It affords a 360-degree view, which includes more wilderness than is to be seen from any other point on the Long Trail. Beyond

LEAVE NO TRACE

Help preserve a piece of the Long Trail as you enjoy it . . . leave no trace.

- Travel only on foot.
- Stay on the footpath.
- If you packed it in, pack it out!
- Use a backpacking stove. Fires are discouraged.
- If you have a campfire, use an established fireplace. Burn only dead and downed wood.
- Travel and camp quietly and in small groups.
- Camp at areas established for overnight use.
- If camping off trail, camp at least 200 feet from any trail, stream, or pond. Camp below 2,500 feet elevation.
- Wash and rinse dishes away from open water.
- Use outhouses. Otherwise, dispose of human and pet waste in a "cat hole" (4 to 6 inches deep) 200 feet from any water source. Bury toilet paper.
- Carry out all tampons and sanitary napkins.
- Don't carve into trees or shelters. People don't care who loves Sally or where Joe stayed when.
- Take only pictures. Leave the lightest of footprints.
- Keep pets on a leash and away from water sources.

the nearby ridges are the Berkshires to the south, the Taconics to the west, Mt. Equinox and Stratton Mtn. to the north, and Somerset Reservoir, Mt. Snow, and Haystack Mtn. to the east.

From the tower, the Trail descends very gradually and then bears northeast along the rugged ridge with minor changes in elevation to **Big Rock (13.7 mi.)**. Dropping steeply the Trail reaches the south end of a loop trail **(14.2 mi.)** leading right 0.1 mi. to **Kid Gore Shelter**. The Long Trail soon reaches the north end of that loop in Glen Haven. Via the north loop it is 60 yds. to **Kid Gore Shelter**. Just beyond and to the left of the Long Trail is **Caughnawaga Shelter (14.4 mi.)**. Kid Gore Shelter is a log lean-to with bunks for 8. It was built in 1971 by Connecticut Section volunteers and Camp Najerog alumni and is named in honor of Harold M. (Kid) Gore, late owner and operator of Camp Najerog. Its water source is a spring 10 yds. north of the shelter (unreliable in dry seasons). The backup source is Caughnawaga's stream. Caughnawaga Shelter, a small log shelter, was built by the boys of Camp Najerog in 1931. It has bunks for 5, and there is a reliable brook 30 ft. in front of the shelter. **Goddard Shelter to Kid Gore and Caughnawaga Shelters, 4.3 mi., 6.9 km, 2½ h (SB 3 h).**

Turning right just south of Caughnawaga Shelter, the LT drops sharply to cross the brook, ascends to a small ridge, and then makes a short, steep descent to a brook. Beyond the brook crossing, the Trail begins a steep ascent and bears to the west of an unnamed summit, el. 3,412' **(15.1 mi.)**. Descending to the west side of the ridge, the Trail eventually crosses two adjacent branches of **South Alder Brook (18.1 mi.)**. Then, after passing several beaver ponds, the Long Trail rises to **Story Spring Shelter (19.0 mi.)**. This frame lean-to with space for 8 was built in 1963 by the U.S. Forest Service. It was named in honor of George F. Story, for many years an active trail worker in the Worcester Section. There is a spring beside the Trail 45 yds. north of the shelter. **Caughnawaga Shelter to Story Spring Shelter, 4.6 mi., 7.4 km, 3 h (SB 3 h).**

Following a rugged climb from the shelter, the Trail soon descends gradually through an old logged-over area to reach **USFS Road 71 (20.6 mi.)**. After crossing the road the LT passes a series of beaver ponds, ascends a low knoll, and descends to a woods road. After crossing a bridge over **Black Brook (21.7 mi.)**, the trail follows a woods road to a clearing with fine views of Little Stratton Mtn. Bearing northeast across the clearing and entering the woods, the Long Trail continues along a low ridge above the Deerfield River. After crossing a brook, the LT gradually ascends to a gravel road. The Trail turns right to follow the road over the East Branch of the Deerfield River. Just beyond the river is trailhead parking on the north side of the **Arlington–West Wardsboro Road** (Kelley Stand Road) **(22.6 mi.)**.

West along the Kelley Stand Road it is 0.9 mi. to Stratton Pond Trail parking, 2.1 mi. to the Branch Pond Trailhead, 4.9 mi. to the site of Kelley Stand, a famous overnight stagecoach stop, and 13 mi. to Arlington on U.S. 7A. To the east it is 6.7 mi. to West Wardsboro and Vt. 100.

Side Trails

WEST RIDGE TRAIL. This trail links the Bald Mtn. Trail to Glastenbury Mtn. and the Long Trail. From the Bald Mtn. Trail (0.0 mi.), the West Ridge Trail passes over the summit of Bald Mtn. (0.1 mi.) with views north to Glastenbury Mtn., Mt. Equinox, and Dorset Peak. The trail descends steeply from the summit, then continues north on or near the ridge toward Glastenbury Mtn. Swinging to the west of an unnamed summit (el. 3,423'), the trail descends to an old woods road (5.3 mi.), which it follows briefly south. The trail re-enters the woods, passes a beaver pond, and after climbing near another unnamed summit (el. 3,365'), slabs the southwest slope of Glastenbury Mtn. to its junction with the Long Trail (7.8 mi.) at Goddard Shelter. Bald Mtn. Trail to LT, 7.8 mi., 12.5 km, 4¾ h (Rev. 4¼ h).

BALD MTN. TRAIL. *West Branch Trailhead:* The west branch of this trail begins at a power line crossing of Branch Street

Extension in Bennington. Go north on U.S. 7 from the junction of U.S. 7 and Vt. 9 in Bennington. At 1.0 mi. turn east on Kocher Drive, then continue straight past a traffic light about 1.0 mi. to the power line crossing (blue-blazed utility pole). The parking space is minimal.

From Branch Street (0.0 mi.) the trail ascends on old woods roads, crosses a brook over a bridge (0.6 mi.), then bears left off the road (0.9 mi.). It crosses and follows several brooks for the next mile before turning right and beginning a steady climb out of the hollow (1.9 mi.). The trail ascends using several long switchbacks, and eventually crosses some old rock slides before reaching White Rocks (2.6 mi.) with a good view to the west. It continues to climb, passing a spring (3.1 mi.), to the junction with the West Ridge Trail (3.5 mi.) just below the summit of Bald Mtn. Branch Street to West Ridge Trail, 3.5 mi., 5.6 km, 2¾ h (Rev. 1¾ h).

East Branch Trailhead: To reach the east branch of the Bald Mtn. Trail, continue 1.0 mi. west of the LT crossing on Vt. 9. From here turn north onto a public road in Woodford Hollow. Continue on the road 0.8 mi. north just past a large water storage tank. There is limited parking near the trail sign. Care should be taken not to block any access roads. From the road (0.0 mi.), the trail ascends a series of old woods roads to a 0.1 mi. spur trail to a spring at Bear Wallow (1.6 mi.), then climbs switchbacks to the junction with the West Ridge Trail (1.9 mi.). Woodford Hollow trailhead to West Ridge Trail, 1.9 mi., 3.0 km, 1½ h (Rev. 1 h).

Additional distances: Branch Street in Bennington to Woodford Hollow via the Bald Mtn. Trail is 5.4 mi.; Branch Street in Bennington to Goddard Shelter on the LT via the Bald Mtn. (west branch) and West Ridge Trails is 11.3 mi.; and Woodford Hollow to Goddard Shelter on the LT via the Bald Mtn. (east branch) and West Ridge Trails is 9.7 mi.

Massachusetts: 36.9 miles   *Canada: 234.6 miles*

DIVISION 3

Arlington–West Wardsboro Road to Mad Tom Notch

Take Note

Vondell and Bigelow Shelters have been replaced by Stratton Pond Shelter.

The Long Trail crosses the Lye Brook Wilderness from the Winhall River to the Trail's junction with the Branch Pond Trail. Refer to wilderness information on page 10.

The Long Trail and the Appalachian Trail coincide throughout this division.

Suggested Hikes

SPRUCE PEAK. This rock outcrop (el. 2,040') with good views of Mt. Equinox and Dorset Peak is located on a spur trail off the Long Trail south from Vt. 11 and 30. Round trip, 4.8 mi., 2½ h.

BROMLEY MTN. This summit (el. 3,260'), reached either south or north on the Long Trail, features good views from its observation tower. LT north from Vt. 11 and 30: round trip, 5.4 mi., 3½ h. LT south from USFS Road 21 in Mad Tom Notch: round trip, 5.0 mi., 3 h.

STRATTON MTN. One of southern Vermont's highest peaks, via the Long Trail north from the Arlington–West Wardsboro Road, Stratton Mtn. (el. 3,936') offers a 360-degree view from the summit fire tower. Round trip, 7.6 mi., 4⅔ h.

LYE BROOK WILDERNESS. The LT/AT and its side trails offer a number of day hike and backpack loop opportunities featuring highland ponds, wetlands, and scenic views. One trip is a circuit using the Stratton Pond, Long, Lye Brook, and Branch Pond Trails, passing Stratton and Bourn Ponds. It requires a 1.2 mi. road walk on the Kelley Stand Road between the Stratton Pond Trail and Branch Pond Trail. This loop is suitable for either a long day hike or a backpack. Round trip, 11.7 mi., 6 h.

3

Camping and Fires

The Long Trail in Division 3 crosses the Green Mountain National Forest. Leave-no-trace camping with small wood fires is allowed. Follow leave-no-trace guidelines (pages 4 to 6) to minimize impact on the Long Trail System. *Exceptions:* In an effort to protect vulnerable vegetation and soils, camping at Stratton Pond is limited to designated sites and is prohibited on Stratton Mtn.

Winter Use

Much of the terrain between Stratton Pond and Vt. 11 and 30 is suitable for intermediate level cross-country skiing. Both Stratton Mtn. and Bromley Mtn. make challenging snowshoe destinations. Spruce Peak via the LT from Vt. 11 and 30 is a good winter destination. It offers fine views without exposing winter hikers to the more severe conditions of the high summits. The Long Trail intersects the Catamount Trail (a cross-country ski trail that runs the length of Vermont) at Stratton Pond. There is a variety of ski-loop combinations in that area. See Catamount Trail information on page 19 to 20.

Access to Long Trail

ARLINGTON–WEST WARDSBORO ROAD (Kelley Stand Road). Refer to the description on page 57 in Division 2.

VT. 11 AND 30. This Long Trail intersection is 5.8 mi. east of Vt. 7A in Manchester Center and 0.5 mi. west of the junction of Vt. 11 and 30 South. There is a large paved parking lot on the north side of the road.

MAD TOM NOTCH, USFS ROAD 21. This Long Trail crossing is 4.0 mi. west of Peru. From Peru's J.J. Hapgood Store (0.3 mi. north of Vt. 11), at a point 3.5 mi. east of the junction of Vt. 11 and 30 South or 4.4 mi. west of the junction of Vt. 11 and 100 South, follow the Hapgood Pond Road 1.0 mi. to North Road. Take North Road 0.7 mi. beyond the end of the pavement to the second left, which is the unpaved Mad Tom Notch Road. Follow this road to the height of land in Mad Tom Notch and the LT. A gravel parking lot on the south side of the road is just beyond the trail crossing. USFS Hapgood Pond campground, a good base for day hikes in the region, is on Hapgood Pond Road, 0.7 mi. north of the road's junction with North Road.

The last mile of USFS Road 21 to the Long Trail is not plowed in winter. A large parking lot is maintained at the end of the plowed portion of the road. It is a popular snowmobile trailhead and is open for all winter recreationists.

Long Trail Description

From the parking lot on **Arlington–West Wardsboro Road** (Kelley Stand Road) (**0.0 mi.**), at the site of Grout Job, an old lumber camp, the Long Trail proceeds north into the woods and continues over gently rolling terrain toward Stratton Mtn. Soon after crossing the gravel International Paper (IP) Road (1.4 mi.), the LT begins to climb gradually, then ascends switchbacks to pass a vista to the right (2.0 mi.).

Climbing to, then following, a level bench, the LT reaches the col (2.7 mi.) between Stratton and Little Stratton Mtns., and then ascends another series of switchbacks. The trail passes a spring (3.2 mi.), and continues its ascent to the fire tower on the southern peak of **Stratton Mtn. (3.8 mi.).** Stratton Mtn. claims a unique role in hiking trail history. James P. Taylor was on the mountain when the idea of the Long Trail was born, and the Appalachian Trail was conceived by Benton MacKaye on its summit.

The fire tower on the summit provides a sweeping view

of the surrounding mountains and countryside. Somerset Reservoir and Mt. Snow are to the south, Glastenbury Mtn. is southwest, and the Taconics, including Mt. Equinox, the highest peak of this range, lie to the west. Mt. Ascutney is to the northeast and Grand Monadnock in New Hampshire is to the southeast. To the north is Stratton's North Peak with its gondola station. On clear viewing days, Killington Peak and the Coolidge Range are visible in the distant north. A GMC summit caretaker may be on duty to assist hikers. **Camping is prohibited on Stratton Mtn. to protect its vulnerable vegetation and soils.**

At the summit, the LT bears left just beyond the tower. Straight ahead, a wide, unblazed, old service road follows the ridge 0.7 mi. to the **North Peak of Stratton Mtn.** Descending a series of switchbacks, the Trail passes a short spur trail (4.0 mi.) to a spring and continues to a fine view (4.5 mi.) west to Stratton Pond, the Lye Brook Wilderness and Mt. Equinox. The Long Trail continues downhill at a gradual grade to recross the IP Road (5.8 mi.). Beyond the road, the LT descends gently, soon reaching a woods road, which it follows for a short distance before crossing a small knoll and then a bridge over a brook (6.4 mi.).

Beyond the brook, the Long Trail rises past a beaver pond, then levels out before reaching its junction with the **Stratton Pond Trail (6.9 mi.).** The Stratton Pond Trail is an alternate route between the Arlington–West Wardsboro Road and Stratton Pond. The side trail to **Stratton Pond Shelter** leaves the Stratton Pond Trail about 50 yds. from the Long Trail. This shelter, built in 1999, has bunks and loft for 16. **Story Spring Shelter to Stratton Pond Shelter, 10.7 mi., 17.2 km, 6¼ h (SB 6 h).**

Descending, the LT shortly reaches **Willis Ross Clearing** at the southeast corner of Stratton Pond and the junction with the **Lye Brook Trail** at the shore of **Stratton Pond (7.0 mi.).** Willis Ross Camp, destroyed by fire in 1972, was located in the clearing on the right.

Stratton Pond is the largest body of water on the Long Trail. It also receives the heaviest annual overnight use of any location on the Trail, with over 2,000 campers at the pond between Memorial Day and Columbus Day. Hikers should stay on the trail to avoid eroding the shoreline. A GMC care-taker stays near Willis Ross Clearing during the hiking season to assist hikers and to maintain the local trails and campsites. Hikers are strongly urged to safeguard this natural area by using the shelters and designated campsites. A fee is charged for overnight use at the shelters and campsites near the pond.

To the left from the clearing, the Lye Brook Trail fol-lows the south shore of the pond to a piped spring (unreli-able in drought) and continues west to Bourn Pond and Manchester.

From Willis Ross Clearing, the Long Trail heads north (right), immediately passes an intermittent spring on the right, and soon reaches its junction with the **North Shore Trail (7.1 mi.)**. West via this trail it is 0.5 mi. to the **North Shore Tenting Area**. From the junction, the LT bears right and leaves the shoreline. After a short distance, it bears left from the woods road, which is the Catamount Trail. The Long Trail continues with minor changes in elevation, before descending to the **Winhall River (8.9 mi.)**. Crossing the river on a bridge, the LT enters the Lye Brook Wilderness and proceeds, again with little change in elevation, along the northeast edge of the plateau above the Winhall River valley. The Trail may be more challenging to follow in the Wild-erness Area due to minimal brushing and blazing. It contin-ues to the junction with the **Branch Pond Trail (11.7 mi.)**, at the northern boundary of the Lye Brook Wilderness. To the left on the Branch Pond Trail, it is 0.5 mi. to **William B. Douglas Shelter**. **Stratton Pond Shelter to William B. Douglas Shelter, 5.3 mi., 8.5 km, 2¾ h (SB 2¾ h).**

The Long Trail continues from the junction, crosses a brook over a bridge and makes a left turn into a clearing. After following the unimproved Rootville Road for nearly a mile, the Trail arrives at a **spur trail (12.6 mi.)** to the left that leads 50 yds. to **Prospect Rock**, perched high above Downer Glen. It commands a fine view of Manchester below and Mt. Equinox. The Trail turns right at the spur trail, climbs a rock staircase out of the roadbed, and proceeds in a northerly direction. The Rootville Road continues downhill 1.8 mi. to a public road, which leads 0.2 mi. to Vt. 11 and 30, 1.8 mi. east of Manchester Center.

After passing west of a summit (14.3 mi.), the LT descends to a **spur trail (14.7 mi.)** that leads left 0.1 mi. to **Spruce Peak Shelter**. This enclosed structure, with bunk space for 16, was built in 1983 by the Brattleboro Section in cooperation with the U.S. Forest Service. A reliable piped spring is located 100 ft. beyond the shelter. **William B. Douglas Shelter to Spruce Peak Shelter, 3.6 mi., 5.8 km, 2¼ h (SB 2¼ h).**

From the shelter spur, the LT continues to a junction where another **spur trail (15.1 mi.)** leads 300 ft. left to **Spruce Peak**. From here is a good view of the Taconic Range and the valley below. The Trail continues from the junction, drops to a brook, crosses a power line, and just beyond, a woods road (15.6 mi.). After a gradual ascent, it reaches the top of a ridge, passes two vistas to the west and begins a winding descent to a stream crossing. A short distance beyond, the LT crosses an abandoned road, old Vt. 30, and a bridge over a stream (17.1 mi.), and then continues through large boulders to **Vt. 11 and 30** (Manchester-Peru Highway) **(17.5 mi.)**. From here it is 5.8 mi. west to U.S. 7A in Manchester Center and 4.1 mi. east to Peru.

The Long Trail crosses the road and bears right through a large, paved parking lot, then onto an abandoned road (Old Vt. 11), which it follows briefly before turning sharply left (17.6 mi.) and entering the woods. The Trail soon crosses a brook over an I-beam bridge, passes under a power line, and rises gently, paralleling Bromley Brook. The LT finally crosses a bridge, and then arrives at **Bromley Tenting Area (18.2 mi.)** on the right. Two tent platforms are located here.

Past the spur trail, the Long Trail ascends gradually for some distance. Then, just before reaching a brook (19.3 mi.), it turns sharply left and climbs steeply. Upon reaching a ski trail (20.0 mi.), the LT bears left and follows this ski trail to the summit of **Bromley Mtn. (20.2 mi.)**. To the right it is 100 ft. to the facilities of Bromley Mtn. Ski Area including an observation tower that offers excellent views, especially toward Stratton Mtn. and Mt. Equinox.

Continuing straight ahead along the west edge of the clearing, the Trail turns sharply left just beyond the chair lift and descends, passing to the left of an outhouse. The LT then drops steeply, and, after crossing the col, climbs over Bromley's northern summit (20.7 mi.). Descending steadily the Trail passes a vista near the northern summit and then continues its descent to USFS Road 21 (Mad Tom Notch Road) at the height of land in **Mad Tom Notch (22.7 mi.)**. A parking area is located just west of the Trail. East from the notch it is 4.0 mi. to Vt. 11 in Peru, reached by taking right turns onto North and Hapgood Pond Roads.

Side Trails

STRATTON POND TRAIL. This trail provides an alternate lowland route between the Arlington–West Wardsboro Road and Stratton Pond. Follow Long Trail directions for the Arlington–West Wardsboro Road. There is parking for the Stratton Pond Trail opposite USFS Road 71, 0.9 mi. west of the LT parking lot and 1.2 mi. east of the Branch Pond Trailhead. In winter the Arlington–West Wardsboro Road is not plowed west of the LT crossing.

Gradually ascending from the Arlington–West Wardsboro Road (0.0 mi.), the trail passes through wetlands over numerous puncheon and crosses a gravel road (2.2 mi.), which is also the Catamount Trail. The trail then travels northeast with little change in elevation over more puncheon to its junction with the Long Trail (3.7 mi.) 0.1 mi. east of Stratton Pond. Arlington–West Wardsboro Road to LT, 3.7 mi., 6.0 km, 2 h (Rev. 2 h).

LYE BROOK TRAIL. Linking Manchester and Bourn Pond to the Long Trail, this trail is within the Lye Brook Wilderness from near its trailhead in Manchester to its crossing of the Winhall River west of Stratton Pond. From U.S. 7A in Manchester Center follow Vt. 11 and 30 1.9 mi. east and then turn right onto East Manchester Road. Follow the road 1.2 mi. to Glen Road and turn left. Continue straight on a short access road to the trailhead where Glen Road bears left. A parking lot and the trailhead are about 500 ft. from that junction. This access road is not plowed in winter.

From the parking lot (0.0 mi.) the trail enters the Lye Brook Wilderness (0.5 mi.) and follows old railroad grades and woods roads along the west side of Lye Brook Hollow. A spur trail (2.3 mi.) to the right leads to a small stream and one of the higher waterfalls in Vermont. From the waterfall to Bourn Pond this trail is minimally maintained. A compass and topographic map (USGS) are strongly recommended. From the spur trail, the Lye Brook Trail continues along an old woods road to its end. From here the grade eases as the trail crosses a series of low ridges. The trail passes some beaver ponds, and eventually reaches its junction with the Branch Pond Trail (7.3 mi.) at a stream crossing just beyond South Bourn Pond Shelter. This shelter, a frame lean-to with space for 8, was built by the U.S. Forest Service in 1966 on a low bluff overlooking the south shore of Bourn Pond. Water is supplied by the stream and a boxed spring located on a spur trail 250 ft. east of the shelter. Manchester to South Bourn Pond Shelter, 7.3 mi., 11.7 km, 4½ h (Rev. 3½ h).

From Bourn Pond, the trail passes over a low ridge and crosses a shallow ford of the headwaters of the Winhall River (8.5 mi.), the eastern boundary of the Lye Brook Wilderness. Soon crossing the outlet stream of Stratton Pond, the trail continues east to its junction with the North Shore Trail (9.1 mi.) at Stratton Pond. Bearing right, the Lye Brook Trail crosses the pond's outlet on puncheon, then follows the south shore of Stratton Pond to piped Bigelow Spring and the GMC caretaker tent platform to its junction with the Long Trail (9.7 mi.) at Willis Ross Clearing. Manchester to LT, 9.7 mi., 15.6 km, 6¼ h (Rev. 5¼ h).

NORTH SHORE TRAIL. This trail links the Lye Brook Trail near the outlet of Stratton Pond with the Long Trail, and together with the Lye Brook and Long Trails completes a 1.4 mi. loop around the pond. Bearing east off the Lye Brook Trail (0.0 mi.), the North Shore Trail follows the shoreline past a clearing (0.1 mi.) with a grand view of Stratton Mtn.

Continuing on the North Shore Trail, a spur trail soon turns left at a beaver-dammed stream to follow puncheon to its headwaters, Stratton View Spring.

The North Shore Trail continues to hug Stratton Pond's shoreline, shortly reaching the North Shore Tenting Area (0.2 mi.), which has tent platforms. The trail follows the increasingly rugged shore, crosses an arm of the pond on a massive double log bridge and ends at its junction with the Long Trail (0.7 mi.), where the Catamount Trail enters Stratton Pond from the east. Lye Brook Trail to LT 0.7 mi., 1.1 km, ½ h (Rev. ½ h).

BRANCH POND TRAIL. Traversing the eastern half of the Lye Brook Wilderness, this trail connects Branch and Bourn Ponds with the Long Trail. Follow Long Trail or Stratton Pond Trail directions to the Arlington–West Wardsboro Road. The trailhead is 1.2 mi. west of the Stratton Pond parking lot, 2.1 mi. west of the LT crossing, and 11 mi. east of East Arlington. There is space for one car on the north side of the road at the trailhead and space for four cars further west on the north side of the road. In winter the Arlington–West Wardsboro Road is not plowed west of the LT parking lot.

From the Arlington–West Wardsboro Road (0.0 mi.), the trail heads north over rolling terrain to a spur trail on the left (1.8 mi.) that leads 0.3 mi. to USFS Road 70 and, just beyond it, the canoe access to Branch Pond. Skirting to the east of Branch Pond, the trail then enters the Lye Brook Wilderness (2.5 mi.), where it remains until its junction with the Long Trail. Traversing Lye Brook Meadows on an old railroad grade, the trail reaches its junction with the Lye Brook Trail (4.3 mi.) at South Bourn Pond Shelter just south of Bourn Pond. Arlington–West Wardsboro Road to South Bourn Pond Shelter, 4.3 mi., 6.9 km, 2¼ h (Rev. 2¼ h).

Passing below the shelter, the trail follows the west shore of Bourn Pond, soon reaching a 300 ft. spur trail that leads east to North Bourn Pond Tenting Area (4.8 mi.). A path leads to the pond where there is a good view of Stratton Mtn. Continuing north, the trail skirts an area of beaver activity and continues along an old lumber railroad grade to a ford of Bourn Brook (5.6 mi.). This crossing can be difficult during snowmelt or heavy rains. After crossing an overgrown clearing (7.0 mi.), the trail passes William B. Douglas Shelter (7.8 mi.). This log lean-to, completed by the Brattleboro Section in 1956, has bunks for 10. There is a spring on the trail 50 ft. to the south. South Bourn Pond Shelter to William B. Douglas Shelter, 3.5 mi., 5.6 km, 1¾ h (Rev. 1¾ h).

The trail follows an old woods road from the shelter to its junction with the Long Trail (8.3 mi.) at the northern boundary of the Lye Brook Wilderness. Arlington–West Wardsboro Road to LT, 8.3 mi., 13.3 km, 4½ h (Rev. 4¾ h).

3

Massachusetts: 59.6 miles　　　　*Canada: 211.9 miles*

DIVISION 4

Mad Tom Notch to Vt. 140

Take Note

A major renovation of Peru Peak Shelter is planned.

From Mad Tom Notch to USFS Road 10, the Long Trail traverses Peru Peak Wilderness and Big Branch Wilderness. Refer to wilderness information on page 10.

From Mad Tom Notch to Bully Brook, the Long Trail passes through the White Rocks National Recreation Area, where the U.S. Forest Service emphasizes management of the forest to provide recreation opportunities.

The Long Trail and the Appalachian Trail coincide throughout this division.

Suggested Hikes

STYLES PEAK. This short but steep hike on the LT north from USFS Road 21 in Mad Tom Notch provides good views of southeastern Vermont from the summit. Round trip, 3.2 mi., 3¼ h.

GREEN MTN. AND LITTLE ROCK POND. A loop using the Long, Green Mtn. and Green Mtn. Connector Trails from USFS Road 10 combines scenic Little Rock Pond with views from the ledges of Green Mtn. Round trip, 7 mi., 4¾ h.

BAKER PEAK. This destination offers fine views from the open summit. This loop hike from U.S. 7 uses the Lake, Baker Peak, and Long Trails. Round trip, 8.1 mi., 5 h.

BIG BRANCH WILDERNESS. The Old Job Trail and the Long Trail create a loop hike to Griffith Lake, Baker Peak, Big Branch, and Old Job Shelter. This circuit is suitable for a long day hike or a moderate backpack. Round trip, 10.4 mi., 6 h.

Camping and Fires

The Long Trail in Division 4 south of White Rocks Mtn. crosses the Green Mountain National Forest. Leave-no-trace camping with small wood fires is allowed. Follow leave-no-trace guidelines (pages 4 to 6) to minimize impact on the Long Trail System. *Exception:* Camping at Griffith Lake and Little Rock Pond is limited to designated sites to protect the vulnerable vegetation and soils in these areas.

North of White Rocks Mtn., the Long Trail traverses some private property; camping and fires are prohibited along this portion of the Trail.

Winter Use

Many of the trails in this division, in combination with the unplowed USFS roads, provide good cross-country ski opportunities. A suggested loop includes USFS Roads 10 and 30 with the Old Job Trail (north branch) and the Long Trail. Griffith Lake via the Lake Trail and Little Rock Pond via the Homer Stone Brook Trail make fine snowshoe destinations. Styles Peak from Mad Tom Notch provides good views for a 5.2 mi. round trip from the winter parking lot on USFS Road 21.

Access to Long Trail

MAD TOM NOTCH, USFS ROAD 21. Refer to the description on page 66 in Division 3.

USFS ROAD 10. Long Trail parking is available at two trailheads, 0.3 mi. apart. From U.S. 7 in Danby, follow USFS Road 10 3.2 mi. to the primary parking lot (paved) at the west trailhead or continue to a smaller, pull-off parking area at the east trailhead. These sites are also accessible from Peru to the east. From the Peru general store (see USFS Road 21 description on page 66 in Division 3), follow the Hapgood Pond/Landgrove Road 3.6 mi. to an intersection. Turn left and continue for 0.6 mi. to USFS Road 10 on the right. Follow USFS Road 10 10.6 mi. north and west to the Trail.

These parking lots are heavily used during the hiking season, particularly on weekends, and cars left overnight are sometimes vandalized. More secure long-term parking is available at the USFS Mount Tabor Work Center in Danby, 2.7 mi. west of the Long Trail. Contact the GMNF Manchester Ranger District at (802) 362-2307 to make arrangements.

USFS Road 10 between the silver bridge over Big Black Branch (0.9 mi. east of Danby) and the Long Trail is not plowed in winter, a distance of 2.3 mi. The road is also not plowed between the LT and Landgrove to the east.

Vt. 140. From U.S. 7 in Wallingford, follow Vt. 140 east past Sugar Hill Road on the right (2.3 mi.). Pass through the Long Trail crossing (2.7 mi.) and then turn sharp left on a paved drive (2.9 mi.). Parking is at the end of the drive (200 ft.). From Vt. 103 and 155 in East Wallingford, the driveway is 3.3 mi. west.

Long Trail Description

From **Mad Tom Notch (0.0 mi.)** at USFS Road 21 the Long Trail enters the Peru Peak Wilderness and the White Rocks National Recreation Area (0.1 mi.) and then climbs steadily to the summit of **Styles Peak (1.6 mi.),** which has views extending from the northeast to the south. Continuing along the ridge, the LT descends steeply and, after passing over several knobs, reaches **Peru Peak (3.3 mi.),** where a short side trail leads east to a lookout.

Beyond the summit, the Trail descends past a piped spring (3.7 mi.) and, eventually, the western boundary of the Peru Peak Wilderness. Just beyond is **Peru Peak Shelter (4.6 mi.).** This log structure, with space for 10, was built in 1935 by the Civilian Conservation Corps and rebuilt by the Youth Conservation Corps and U.S. Forest Service in 1979.

Water is found at the nearby brook. **Spruce Peak Shelter to Peru Peak Shelter, 12.7 mi., 20.4 km, 8 h (SB 7¾ h).**

Proceeding west from Peru Peak Shelter, the Long Trail crosses three bridged streams before arriving at the shore of Griffith Lake, and shortly thereafter **Griffith Lake Tenting Area (5.1 mi.).** To protect this shoreline and preserve its natural beauty, all camping in the vicinity of Griffith Lake is restricted to the tent platforms. A GMC caretaker is usually in residence to assist hikers and help maintain the region's campsites and trails. A fee is charged for overnight use at these designated sites and at Peru Peak Shelter.

Paralleling the shore of the lake 200 ft. to the west along a nearly continuous boardwalk, the LT proceeds to its southern junction with the **Old Job Trail (5.3 mi.),** which leads northeast 3.4 mi. to USFS Road 30. From the trail junction, the Trail continues straight ahead, leaving the northern end of Griffith Lake. It enters the Big Branch Wilderness and then reaches its junction with the **Lake Trail (5.4 mi.),** which descends 3.3 mi. west to a public road 0.5 mi. off U.S. 7.

The Long Trail follows the ridge northward, descending to cross an old woods road (6.2 mi.). After crossing another woods road, the Trail begins its ascent of Baker Peak. Upon reaching its junction with the **Baker Peak Trail (7.2 mi.),** the LT bears right and the two trails coincide for the final scramble up the exposed ledges to the summit of **Baker Peak (7.3 mi.).** Should adverse weather conditions make the ascent over open rocks treacherous, there is a parallel bypass route to the east. Baker Peak offers expansive views of the valley below. Danby is in the foreground with the north-flowing Otter Creek. Directly across the valley is Dorset Peak with its famous marble quarry. Emerald Lake and Mt. Equinox are to the south, and the fire tower on Stratton Mtn. can be seen just behind the ridge of Peru Peak. Pico and Killington Peaks are to the north, and the Adirondacks can be seen, on a clear day, to the northwest.

Leaving the summit of Baker Peak, the LT enters the woods and bears northerly, keeping east of a ridge. After crossing over a height of land (7.8 mi.), the Trail begins a moderate, then gentle, descent on the west side of the ridge.

Reaching a wide, grassy woods road (9.1 mi.), the Long Trail turns right and, after following the road for 250 ft., turns left into the woods. Continuing north on an old woods road, the Trail soon reaches a **spur trail (9.3 mi.)** leading left 100 ft. to **Lost Pond Shelter**. This shelter, a frame lean-to with room for 8, has a unique background. The gift of Louis Stare, Jr., then of Bass River, Mass., it was constructed at Mr. Stare's home on Cape Cod in 1965. After being dismantled into 13 sections, it was trucked 250 mi. to USFS Road 10 and hauled to its present site by volunteers using a tractor and wagon. The lumber, exposed to the salty sea breezes of the Cape, once made this shelter especially popular with the local porcupine population. The water supply is a stream in the ravine below the shelter. **Peru Peak Shelter to Lost Pond Shelter, 4.7 mi., 7.6 km, 2½ h (SB 2¾ h).**

The LT continues north along the woods road from Lost Pond Shelter. Descending steadily, the Trail reaches Big Branch and its northern junction with the **Old Job Trail (10.8 mi.)**. On this trail it is 1.1 mi. southeast to **Old Job Shelter**. Turning left to follow Big Branch, the Long Trail crosses the **Big Branch** over a suspension bridge **(10.9 mi.)**. Continuing alongside Big Branch, the Trail follows an old road, passes the stone foundation of a mill, and reaches **Big Branch Shelter (11.0 mi.)**. This frame lean-to, with floor space for 8, was built by the USFS in 1963. Big Branch furnishes water. The outhouse is up the hill behind the shelter. **Lost Pond Shelter to Big Branch Shelter, 1.7 mi., 2.7 km, 1 h (SB 1¼ h).**

The Long Trail continues downstream for a short distance, then turns right and ascends gradually, crossing the northern boundary of the Big Branch Wilderness (12.0 mi.), finally reaching **USFS Road 10 (12.1 mi.)** and a small parking area. East from this point, it is about 10.6 mi. to public roads in Landgrove and from there 4.6 mi. to Peru. The Trail bears left along the road, descending to **Big Black Branch (12.3 mi.)**. Here the road continues west down the mountain 3.2 mi. to Danby on U.S. 7.

Just west of the bridge over Big Black Branch, the Trail

turns right, leaving the road opposite a paved parking lot. Following an old woods road, it crosses Little Black Branch (12.9 mi.) over an I-beam bridge, then recrosses it over large rocks (13.1 mi.). Continuing over numerous puncheon the LT comes to a **spur trail (14.0 mi.)** on the right leading a short distance uphill to **Lula Tye Shelter**. This frame lean-to, with room for 8, was built by the U.S. Forest Service in 1962. It was moved to its present location from a site on the east shore of Little Rock Pond in 1972. It is named in memory of Miss Lula Tye, who was corresponding secretary for the Green Mountain Club from 1926 to 1955. Water is available from Little Rock Pond's spring on the LT just north of the caretaker tent platform. **Big Branch Shelter to Lula Tye Shelter, 3.0 mi., 4.8 km, 2 h (SB 1¾ h).**

Proceeding northward, the Long Trail soon reaches the southern end of **Little Rock Pond (14.3 mi.)** and the **Little Rock Pond Loop Trail**. Just beyond lies the GMC caretaker tent platform and the **Little Rock Pond Tenting Area** with tent platforms on a rise 100 ft. east of the pond. This popular pond is one of the most heavily used areas on the Long Trail, and careful management is required to preserve its beauty and fragile shoreline environment. Camping in the vicinity of the pond's shoreline is restricted to designated sites. A GMC caretaker is in residence to help hikers protect the resource and to maintain the area's campsites and trails. A fee is charged for overnight use at these designated sites, as well as at Lula Tye and Little Rock Pond Shelters.

The Long Trail follows the east shore of the pond and passes the spring (14.4 mi.), which is the water source for all campsites in the vicinity of Little Rock Pond. It then reaches a trail junction at the pond's outlet. To the left is the **Green**

KEEP IT PEACEFUL
Respect other hikers—and the wildlife—by traveling and camping quietly.

GROUP HIKING?

- **Plan Ahead.** Get information from the *Long Trail Guide* and GMC office. Obtain the GMC's "A Group Hiking Guide for Vermont's Long Trail and Appalachian Trail."
- **Keep Groups Small.** Ten (including leaders) should be the maximum; four to six is ideal.
- **Obtain Group Use Permits.** Groups of eleven or more need a permit to camp on state land. On National Forest land, groups may need an Outfitter-Guide Special Use permit.
- **Use Shelters and Designated Tenting Areas.** Be prepared to tent. Accommodate late arrivals.
- **Use Backpacking Stoves.** Fires are discouraged.
- **Experienced Leaders Are Essential.** There should be one leader for every four campers.
- **Be Courteous to Others.** Share shelter sites, make latecomers welcome, avoid excessive noise.
- **Safeguard Water Supplies.** Wash dishes and bathe at least 200 feet from water supplies.
- **Leave No Trace.** Pack out all trash. Treat all property as if it were your own.

Mtn. Trail (14.6 mi.); just beyond it the **Homer Stone Brook Trail** also bears left. The LT soon reaches a **spur trail (14.7 mi.)** on the right, which leads 100 ft. to **Little Rock Pond Shelter**. Built by the U.S. Forest Service in 1962, this frame lean-to has space for 8. It was moved to its present location from a site on Little Rock Pond's small island in 1972. Water is from the spring 0.4 mi. south on the Long Trail. **Lula Tye Shelter to Little Rock Pond Shelter, 0.7 mi., 1.1 km, ⅓ h (SB ⅓ h).**

North of the shelter, the Trail continues with little change in elevation to the long-abandoned Aldrich Job clearing (15.4 mi.). It then crosses a bridge over **Homer Stone Brook (15.6 mi.)**, before intersecting with the old South Wallingford–Wallingford Pond Road (15.8 mi.). Here it begins to climb, eventually passing just west of the summit of **White Rocks Mtn. (17.8 mi.)**. Shortly thereafter the LT begins a steady descent to the **White Rocks Cliff Trail (18.6 mi.)**, which leads 0.2 mi. to a view from the top of the cliffs. The LT continues to the **Greenwall Spur (18.9 mi.)**, which leads right 0.4 mi. to **Greenwall Shelter** just outside the northern boundary of the White Rocks National Recreation Area. This frame lean-to, with floor space for 8, was built by the U.S. Forest Service in 1962. A spur trail leads 600 ft. northeast behind the shelter to a spring, which may fail in very dry seasons. **Little Rock Pond Shelter to Greenwall Shelter, 4.6 mi., 7.4 km, 3 h (SB 2¾ h).**

From Greenwall Spur, the LT descends steeply to the **Keewaydin Trail (19.5 mi.)**. The LT turns sharply right and crosses **Bully Brook (19.6 mi.)**. Just past the brook, the Trail leaves the White Rocks National Recreation Area, but continues to be in the Green Mountain National Forest. Traveling beside a dramatic gulch to **Sugar Hill Road (20.2 mi.)**, the LT descends quickly to **Roaring Brook** and **Vt. 140** (Wallingford Gulf Road) **(20.3 mi.)**. (Note: A bridge will be built over Roaring Brook. Until then, if the water is too high for a crossing, return to Sugar Hill Road, walk 0.4 mi. west to Vt. 140, and walk 0.4 mi. east to the LT. Be especially cautious of cars on narrow, winding Vt. 140.) To the east, it is 3.5 mi. to East Wallingford, Vt. 103 and Vt. 155; to the west 0.4 mi. to Sugar Hill Road and 2.7 mi. to U.S. 7 in Wallingford.

Side Trails

OLD JOB TRAIL. Formerly the route of the Long Trail, this trail provides an alternate lowland route between Griffith Lake and Big Branch. An old woods road, this trail links the Long Trail at both Griffith Lake and Big Branch with USFS Road 30. Follow USFS Road 10 for 6.9 mi. east out of Danby, pass the Long Trail crossing, and turn right onto USFS Road 30 for 2.3 mi. to its end. USFS Road 30 is not plowed in winter.

South Branch: From the end of USFS Road 30, the Old Job Trail (south branch) bears south (left) onto a separately gated woods road. From the gate (0.0 mi.) the Old Job Trail ascends gradually, paralleling the east side of Lake Brook, crossing two tributary brooks on snowmobile bridges (0.6 mi. and 2.1 mi.) before finally crossing Lake Brook on a large bridge (2.4 mi.). Following a woods road around Long Hole, it joins the Long Trail (3.4 mi.) at the north end of Griffith Lake. USFS Road 30 to LT at Griffith Lake, 3.4 mi., 5.5 km, 2 h (Rev. 1¾ h).

North Branch: From the end of USFS Road 30, the Old Job Trail bears north (right) at the gate (0.0 mi.), descending the road embankment. Following Lake Brook, the trail eventually reaches an extensive clearing where the village of Griffith once stood. Here stands Old Job Shelter (0.9 mi.), a log structure with space for 8, built in 1935 by the Civilian Conservation Corps. Lake Brook provides water.

Crossing Lake Brook on a suspension bridge, the trail trends northwest through the clearing, passing first a large sawdust pile and then an old jeep road on the right (1.1 mi.). Continuing west, the trail enters the Big Branch Wilderness and parallels Big Branch to its junction with the Long Trail (2.0 mi.), 0.1 mi. south of the Big Branch suspension bridge. USFS Road 30 to LT at Big Branch, 2.0 mi., 3.2 km, 1 h (Rev. 1¼ h).

Griffith Lake to Big Branch via the Old Job Trail is 5.4 mi., 8.7 km, 2¾ h (Rev. 3¼ h).

LAKE TRAIL. Take U.S. 7 south from Danby. At 2.1 mi., turn east onto Town Highway 5 and follow the road 0.5 mi. east to a parking lot and the trailhead. This trail was once a bridle path leading from the valley to Griffith Lake (formerly Buffum Pond).

The trail enters the woods (0.0 mi.) from the parking lot and gently ascends the old road. It then switches back to the left and enters the Big Branch Wilderness (0.9 mi.) where the climb becomes steeper. Crossing a bridge (1.5 mi.) anchored to a rock face (the old trestle supports are still visible), the trail soon reaches a spur trail to the right, which climbs to an open rock with fine views of Dorset Peak and the valley below. The trail continues, crossing McGinn Brook at its junction with the Baker Peak Trail (1.9 mi.). From the junction, the ascent moderates, and the trail eventually reaches the Long Trail (3.3 mi.) just north of Griffith Lake. Town Highway 5 to LT, 3.3 mi., 5.3 km, 2½ h (Rev. 1½ h).

BAKER PEAK TRAIL. This trail connects the Lake Trail with the Long Trail near the summit of Baker Peak. From its junction with the Lake Trail (0.0 mi.), the Baker Peak Trail gradually ascends an old woods road before climbing more steeply over ledges to join the Long Trail (0.9 mi.) 0.1 mi. south of the summit of Baker Peak. Lake Trail to LT, 0.9 mi., 1.5 km, 1 h (Rev. ½ h).

Town Highway 5 to Baker Peak via the Lake, Baker Peak and Long Trails is 2.9 mi., 4.7 km, 2½ h (Rev. 1½ h).

LITTLE ROCK POND LOOP TRAIL. This shoreline trail follows the west side of Little Rock Pond. From the Long Trail (0.0 mi.) at the southern end of Little Rock Pond, the trail bears left, and skirts the south shore of the pond. Continuing, the trail climbs away from the shore to pass above the ledges of the west shore and reaches its junction with the Green Mtn. Trail (0.4 mi.), 0.1 mi. west of the Long Trail at the northern end of the pond. LT to Green Mtn. Trail, 0.4 m., 0.6 km, ¼ h (Rev. ¼ h).

GREEN MTN. TRAIL. This trail links USFS Road 10 with the Long Trail at the north end of Little Rock Pond. USFS Road 10 is plowed in winter only to the silver bridge 0.9 mi. west of the picnic area and this trailhead. Follow USFS Road 10 2.7 mi. east from Danby to the USFS Big Branch Picnic Area.

Entering the woods opposite the picnic area (0.0 mi.), the trail ascends to its junction (0.1 mi.) with the Green Mtn. Connector, which leads east paralleling the road 0.6 mi. to the LT parking lot at Big Black Branch. Soon the trail makes a sharp right and ascends to a lookout to the west (0.3 mi.). Continuing its ascent on an old woods road, the trail traverses an impressive, mature stand of hemlock and white pine, before reaching another woods road and crossing a brook (1.3 mi.). The trail ascends to a shallow saddle (2.1 mi.) before climbing a spruce-covered ridge to a spur trail leading 50 ft. to an easterly lookout near the summit of Green Mtn. Crossing ledges, the trail soon reaches another spur trail, which leads 300 ft. to a view of the pond below. Continuing on the mountaintop, the trail reaches yet another spur trail (3.3 mi.), which leads 200 ft. to an outlook with limited views. From here the trail descends steadily to its junction with the Little Rock Pond Loop Trail (4.0 mi.), before continuing to the north end of Little Rock Pond and the Long Trail (4.1 mi.). Big Branch Picnic Area to LT, 4.1 mi., 6.6 km, 2½ h (Rev. 2¼ h).

HOMER STONE BROOK TRAIL. This trail provides an alternate route from the Otter Creek Valley to Little Rock Pond. From U.S. 7 in South Wallingford, just north of Charlie's Market or 4.2 mi. south of Vt. 140 in Wallingford,

---

LEAVE NO TRACE OF YOUR PASSING
• Stay on the footpath.
• If you packed it in, pack it out.
• Use a backpacking stove.

---

turn east onto the southern end of Hartsboro Road and cross
Otter Creek and the railroad tracks, then bear right; park at
the old schoolhouse lot to the left.

The trail leaves the road just after a bridge crossing to
climb a private driveway (0.0 mi.) to the left, and follows a
woods road just to the left of a garage. Climbing steadily, and
keeping to the right at all forks, the trail follows the old
South Wallingford–Wallingford Pond Road until it takes a
right turn off it to ford Homer Stone Brook (1.7 mi.). From
here the trail ascends steeply southeast to its crossing of the
pond's outlet and its junction with the Long Trail (2.3 mi.)
just north of Little Rock Pond. Public road to LT, 2.3 mi.,
3.7 km, 1¾ h (Rev. 1¼ h).

WHITE ROCKS CLIFF TRAIL. This path descends from the
Long Trail to an outlook on the very brink of White Rocks
Cliff. These cliffs, a peregrine falcon nesting site, may be
closed to the public from mid-March to early August if the
peregrines are nesting. Contact the GMNF Manchester
Ranger District at (802) 362-2307 to confirm the status of
the trail during nesting season. Long Trail to White Rocks
Cliff, 0.2 mi., 0.3 km, 10 min. (Rev. 10 min.).

KEEWAYDIN TRAIL. This trail links the USFS White Rocks
Picnic Area with the Long Trail near the summit of White
Rocks Mtn. From Wallingford go 2.3 mi. east on Vt. 140,
turn south on Sugar Hill Road for 0.1 mi., then turn right
onto USFS Road 52. Continue south on this road 0.6 mi. to
the picnic area and parking. Overnight parking at the picnic
area is not permitted. USFS Road 52 is not maintained in
winter.

From the far end of the picnic area parking lot, this trail
climbs steeply to the Long Trail, 0.9 mi. south of the White
Rocks Cliff Trail. USFS White Rocks Picnic Area to LT, 0.4
mi., 0.6 km, ½ h (Rev. ¼ h). Other hiking trails from the picnic area include the White Rocks Trail leading 0.2 mi. to a
viewpoint on a knoll below White Rocks Cliff and the 0.8 mi.
Ice Bed Trail.

DIVISION 5

Vt. 140 to U.S. 4

Take Note

Tenting near Pico Camp and along the ridge of Pico Peak is very limited. Do not plan to camp near the site if the shelter is full.

Governor Clement Shelter is accessible to four-wheel drive and all-terrain vehicles and is frequented by nonhikers. The GMC discourages overnight use of this site.

The Long Trail and the Appalachian Trail coincide throughout this division.

Suggested Hikes

AIRPORT LOOKOUT. This short hike south on the Long Trail from Vt. 103 crosses impressive Clarendon Gorge over a suspension bridge and climbs to a lookout with views to the west. Round trip, 1.6 mi., 1¼ h.

BEACON HILL. This short, rugged hike on the Long Trail north of Vt. 103 passes Clarendon Lookout and then leads to good views from an old hilltop pasture. Round trip, 3.0 mi., 2 h.

SHREWSBURY PEAK. This hike at the southern end of the Coolidge Range combines the Shrewsbury Peak Trail and Black Swamp Trail with a 1.5 mi. walk on the CCC Road for a loop hike over the summit of Shrewsbury Peak, which offers good views. Round trip, 5.4 mi., 3½ h.

PICO PEAK. This destination boasts good views from its summit dome and is climbed via the Sherburne Pass Trail south from U.S. 4 at Sherburne Pass and Pico Link. Round trip, 5.8 mi., 4 h.

KILLINGTON PEAK. With sweeping views from its rocky summit, this peak is directly accessed by the Bucklin and Killington Spur Trails. Round trip, 7.4 mi., 5¼ h. A longer hike with an optional climb of Pico Peak follows the Sherburne Pass Trail south from U.S. 4 to the LT and then to Killington Peak. Round trip, 11.2 mi., 7 h.

Camping and Fires

Except for two areas of state land at Clarendon Gorge and near Killington Peak, the Long Trail in Division 5 traverses both private land and federally owned Appalachian Trail corridor land. Camping is limited to shelters. Small wood fires, although discouraged, are permitted in established fire rings at all shelters with the exception of Cooper Lodge, due to its sensitive high-elevation location. Camping is prohibited in the vicinity of Clarendon Gorge. Follow leave-no-trace guidelines (pages 4 to 6) to minimize impact on the Long Trail System.

Winter Use

All suggested hikes in this division make good winter trips, except for the Shrewsbury Peak loop owing to the CCC Road's unmaintained winter condition. The challenging terrain is suitable only for advanced cross-country skiers.

Access to Long Trail

VT. 140. Refer to the description on page 76 in Division 4.

VT. 103. This road intersects the LT just north of Clarendon Gorge. The road crossing is 2.4 mi. east of U.S. 7, 7.3 mi. south of U.S. 4 East in Rutland, and 6 mi. west of East Wallingford and Vt. 155. There is parking available on the south side of the highway in a large, unpaved lot. Please note that Vt. 103 is prone to vandalism. Parking cars overnight is not recommended.

COLD RIVER (LOWER) ROAD. Take Lincoln Hill Road north from Vt. 103, 0.7 mi. east of the LT crossing. Follow this road 2.5 mi. to Shrewsbury and continue 2.8 mi. more to North Shrewsbury where the Cold River Road turns left opposite an old store. Proceed on Lower Cold River Road (the Upper Road is to the right just beyond the fire station) 2.4 mi. west to the Long Trail. It is another 7.3 mi. west to U.S. 7 in Rutland, 1.5 mi. south of the junction of U.S. 7 and U.S. 4 East. There is limited parking on the north side of the road just east of a bridge. This road is not recommended for winter or mud season use.

U.S. 4. This trail crossing is 8.6 mi. east of U.S. 7 in Rutland and 2.4 mi. west of the junction of U.S. 4 and Vt. 100 North near the Killington Ski Area access road, and 8.7 mi. west of the junction of U.S. 4 and Vt. 100 South. A small, unpaved parking lot is on the south side of the highway. Use caution when crossing U.S. 4.

Long Trail Description

From **Vt. 140** (Wallingford Gulf Road) **(0.0 mi.)**, the LT quickly reaches a paved trailhead parking lot (0.1 mi.). From the lot, the Trail winds up the west flank of Bear Mtn., crossing stone walls and foundations and passing a 300 ft. **spur** to a domed ledge with southern views of White Rocks **(1.0 mi.)** before reaching a **height of land on Bear Mtn. (2.1 mi.)**. The Trail skirts the summit to avoid a beacon tower and descends gradually to a woods road (2.7 mi.). Here hikers may see signs and blazes for a cross-country ski network. The LT turns sharply left off the woods road (3.3 mi.), crosses a power line (3.5 mi.) and reaches a grassy woods road leading right 200 ft. to **Minerva Hinchey Shelter (3.6 mi.)**. This frame structure, with bunk space for 8, was constructed in 1969 by Louis Stare and members of the Killington Section. It is named for Minerva Hinchey in tribute to her 22 years of service as GMC corresponding secretary, 1955–1977. Water can be found at a small spring 150 ft. south. **Greenwall Shelter to Minerva Hinchey Shelter, 5.4 mi., 8.7 km, 3¼ h (SB 3¼ h).**

After ascending the ridge behind the camp, the LT descends to **Spring Lake Clearing (4.2 mi.)**, where there are limited views. At a power line (4.3 mi.) the Trail enters the woods and holds to a narrow ridge for over a mile before reaching **Airport Lookout (5.5 mi.)** on the left. After a steep descent, the Long Trail reaches **Mill River** at the head of the deep and picturesque **Clarendon Gorge (6.2 mi.)**. The Trail crosses the gorge on a suspension bridge, constructed in 1974 to replace a similar structure swept away in the 1973 flood. It is dedicated to the memory of Robert Brugmann. After a short ascent, the LT reaches the parking lot on **Vt. 103** (Rutland–Bellows Falls Highway) and the Green Mountain Railroad **(6.3 mi.)**. West via Vt. 103 it is 2.4 mi. to U.S. 7, 5 mi. south of Rutland. Cuttingsville is 3.3 mi. east.

Crossing the highway and railroad, the LT traverses a small pasture using stiles to negotiate barbed wire fences then turns left to follow a woods road uphill to a power line. Beyond the power line, the Trail climbs steeply on rock stairs through a boulder-filled ravine. At the top of the ravine, the LT bears right and rises gradually along the ridge to Clarendon Lookout (6.7 mi.) where there are views to the south and west, then continues along the ridge, before dropping gradually to an old town road. To the right, the road descends gently 400 ft. to **Clarendon Shelter (7.3 mi.)**. This frame building, with bunks for 12, was constructed in 1952 by the Killington Section. A brook 50 ft. east furnishes water. **Minerva Hinchey Shelter to Clarendon Shelter, 3.7 mi., 6.0 km, 2½ h (SB 2½ h).**

From the old road, the Long Trail continues east across the brook, briefly following it before climbing steeply to the partially open summit of **Beacon Hill (7.8 mi.)**, where there is a view of the nearby countryside. Turning north, the Trail drops down through a sugarbush, crosses a pasture, passes through a gate (the gate should be kept closed so the cows don't escape) and crosses **Lottery Road (8.2 mi.)** west of the village of Shrewsbury. After re-entering the woods (8.3 mi.), the Trail passes Hermit Spring (8.6 mi.), unreliable in dry seasons. The LT ascends a ridge, which it then descends

5

through an old pasture followed by woods to the gravel Keiffer Road (9.9 mi.). Bearing left on Keiffer Road, the LT then enters a field to the right with good views of the Coolidge Range, and re-enters the woods. The Trail soon reaches the west bank of Cold River (10.1 mi.), which it follows left to the paved **Cold River (Lower) Road (10.2 mi.)**, 2.4 mi. west of North Shrewsbury.

The Long Trail turns right on the road to cross the Cold River over a bridge and shortly bears left onto a woods road to pass through an open area. Re-entering the woods, the Trail follows the woods road a short distance, then bears right (10.4 mi.) to ascend a ridge high above the brook. Traversing this ridge and passing a vista of the Coolidge Range, the Trail then makes a short, steep descent to a ford of **Gould Brook (11.0 mi.)**, which can be challenging in high water. The LT parallels Gould and Sargent Brooks the remaining distance to the unpaved **Upper Road (11.7 m.)**, 2.4 mi. west of North Shrewsbury.

Crossing the Upper Road and still paralleling the stream, the LT reaches another road (12.3 mi.). Turning sharply left onto the road, the Trail immediately crosses Sargent Brook on a bridge, and, in 150 ft., turns right into the woods. After ascending a ridge, the Trail passes through an overgrown clearing (12.7 mi.), the site of the former Haley Farm. The GMC's 1920 *Guide Book of the Long Trail* described the farm as providing "good beds and board; telephone" for Trail users. The LT parallels the brook, crosses it on a bridge, immediately crosses a woods road, and soon reaches **Governor Clement Shelter (13.1 mi.)**, located on a dirt road in an overgrown field. This stone structure was built in 1929 by the family of William H. Field of Mendon

OH, THAT WACKY WEATHER

Never underestimate the variability of Vermont weather. Always be prepared for rain and cold.

and named for Percival W. Clement, governor of Vermont, 1919–1921. There is bunk space for 10. Abundant water is available at the brook 200 ft. to the east. Unfortunately, this shelter is subject to unexpected nocturnal visits by uninvited carousers. The GMC discourages the use of this shelter.
Clarendon Shelter to Governor Clement Shelter, 5.8 mi., 9.3 km, 3½ h (SB 3 h).

The Long Trail follows the road behind the shelter to the north, then bears left into the woods (13.4 mi.), and, sometimes following woods roads, climbs steadily to two small brook crossings (15.3 mi.). Slabbing the steep south slope of Little Killington, the LT meets the **Shrewsbury Peak Trail (15.7 mi.)** then continues to the top of **Little Killington Ridge (16.1 mi.)** beyond which the Trail continues by easy grade, skirting the southwest flank of Killington Peak in dense evergreen forest, before reaching **Killington Spur (17.4 mi.)** on the right, which leads 0.2 mi. to the summit of **Killington Peak**.

Killington Peak is the second highest mountain in Vermont; only Mt. Mansfield is higher. It takes its name from the town of Killington in which the mountain is located. Killington Peak is in the Coolidge Range, which also includes Pico Peak, Mendon Peak, Little Killington, and Shrewsbury Peak. From the summit a path descends a short distance east to the facilities of the Killington resort. The summit is on a self-guided Killington Ski Area nature trail that starts near the gondola station.

From the bare rocky summit of Killington Peak there are views in all directions, including all the prominent Green Mountain peaks from Glastenbury Mtn. to Mt. Mansfield. To the southeast is Mt. Ascutney and to the northeast are the White Mountains. To the west are the Taconics, including Bird Mtn. with its precipitous south face, Lake Champlain, and the Adirondacks. To the east is the village of Plymouth where Calvin Coolidge was born and where he was sworn in as president in 1923.

Cooper Lodge is 100 ft. downhill on the LT from the Killington spur junction. Cooper Lodge, of stone and wood construction, with bunks for 12, was erected in 1939 by the Vermont Forest Service. It is located on land given to the state by Mortimer R. Proctor, former president of the Green Mountain Club and later governor of Vermont, and named in honor of Charles P. Cooper, president of the Club when a considerable portion of the Long Trail was completed. It is the highest shelter (el. 3,850') on the LT. There is a spring 100 ft. north on the Long Trail. A GMC roving caretaker may be present to help hikers protect the high-elevation ecosystem around Killington Peak, as well as manage other overnight sites in the Coolidge Range. An overnight fee may be charged at Cooper Lodge. **Governor Clement Shelter to Cooper Lodge, 4.3 mi., 6.9 km, 3 h (SB 2 h).**

From Cooper Lodge, the LT head west, downhill to the **Bucklin Trail (17.5 mi.)** then turns north and holds to a fairly constant elevation, passing well to the west of Snowden Peak and Rams Head. It then junctions with the southern end of the **Sherburne Pass Trail (19.9 mi.).** The Sherburne Pass Trail is the former LT and reconnects with the present LT, via the Appalachian Trail, north of U.S. 4. **Pico Camp** and the **Pico Link**, which leads 0.4 mi. to the summit of Pico Peak, are 0.5 mi. north on the Sherburne Pass Trail. Pico Camp, built by the Long Trail Patrol in 1959, is a frame cabin with bunk space for 12. It offers good views of Killington Peak directly south and Mt. Ascutney to the southeast. A small spring is located 100 ft. north on the Long Trail. A GMC caretaker may be present to protect the high-

TRAIL LOCATIONS MAY CHANGE

Trail and shelter changes are published in *The Long Trail News,* the quarterly membership newsletter of the Green Mountain Club. Become a member and keep your guidebook up-to-date. Guidebook updates may also be obtained by writing to the GMC office.

elevation ecosystem around Pico Peak. An overnight fee may be charged at Pico Camp. **Cooper Lodge to Pico Camp, 3.0 mi., 4.8 km, 1¾ h (SB 2 h).**

From the Sherburne Pass Trail, the Long Trail wraps around the west flank of Pico and descends gradually through open birch forest to a westerly **Mendon Lookout (21.5 mi.)**. Following a series of switchbacks the Trail crosses a **brook (21.9 mi.)** then continues to **U.S. 4 (23.7 mi.)**. East it is 2.2 mi. to the Killington Post Office and west it is 8.6 mi. to U.S. 7 in Rutland.

Side Trails

SHREWSBURY PEAK TRAIL. This trail links the CCC Road south of the Coolidge Range with the Long Trail near Little Killington. The trail starts at a parking lot on the CCC Road 3.0 mi. east of North Shrewsbury, and 3.5 mi. west of Vt. 100. The CCC Road leaves Vt. 100 10.7 mi. north of the junction of Vt. 100 and 103 and 3.1 mi. south of the junctions of Vt. 100 and U.S. 4. The CCC Road is not maintained in winter.

From the parking lot (0.0 mi.) the trail climbs Russell Hill, el. 2540' (0.2 mi.), and briefly descends into a small ravine (0.5 mi.) before first gradually, then steeply ascending to the summit of Shrewsbury Peak (1.8 mi.), where there are good views to the south and east. From the top the trail descends to its junction with the Black Swamp Trail (1.9 mi.) and continues north to a wooded summit (2.0 mi.). It then drops into a swale (3.2 mi.) and climbs to the northwest, crossing a brook just before it turns south, crosses another ski trail, and joins the Long Trail (4.2 mi.). CCC Road to LT, 4.2 mi., 6.8 km, 3¼ h (Rev. 2½ h).

BLACK SWAMP TRAIL. This is an easier route from the CCC Road to Shrewsbury Peak and the Long Trail beyond. It begins at the intersection of the Black Swamp and CCC Roads, 4.5 mi. east of North Shrewsbury, 1.5 mi. east of the Shrewsbury Peak Trail, and 2.0 mi. west of Vt. 100. Because this is a spring feeding area for black bears, the Black Swamp

Road is gated until at least mid-July. The CCC Road is not maintained in winter.

From the CCC Road (0.0 mi.) the trail ascends the gravel Black Swamp Road to its end (0.8 mi.). The blazed trail begins here and climbs steadily on more primitive woods roads to Shrewsbury Peak Shelter (1.7 mi.), a log lean-to with space for 8, built by the Civilian Conservation Corps. A rock-lined spring is located 50 ft. to the south. From here the trail ascends to its junction with the Shrewsbury Peak Trail (2.0 mi.), 0.1 mi. north of Shrewsbury Peak and 2.3 mi. south of the Long Trail. CCC Road to Shrewsbury Peak, 2.1 mi., 3.4 km, 1¾ h (Rev. 1 h).

KILLINGTON SPUR. This trail scrambles up Killington Peak from the LT near Cooper Lodge. The spur bears easterly from the Trail 100 ft. south of Cooper Lodge and then climbs very steeply to the summit. LT to Killington Peak, 0.2 mi., 0.3 km, ⅓ h (Rev. ¼ h).

BUCKLIN TRAIL. This trail ascends the western side of Killington Peak from the town of Mendon. The trail begins at a sharp turn (Brewers Corner) of the unpaved Wheelerville Road 4 mi. south of U.S. 4 and 6½ mi. east of downtown Rutland. From Sherburne Pass follow U.S. 4 west 4.3 mi. then turn south onto the Wheelerville Road. Follow the road 4.0 mi. south to a sharp turn known as Brewers Corner and the beginning of the trail. To reach Brewers Corner from Rutland, turn onto Killington Ave. east from U.S. 7 at Christ the King Church, ½ mi. south of U.S. 7's junction with U.S. 4 East. Follow the road to its end at a "T". Turn right onto the increasingly steep Notch Road. Beyond the end of the pavement, turn left onto Wheelerville Road and follow it 3.1 mi. to the trail. Do not block woods roads when parking. North from Brewers Corner, the old Killington Carriage Road (gated, unmaintained) heads south, then east, rejoining the Bucklin Trail about 0.1 mi. northwest of Cooper Lodge.

From Brewers Corner (0.0 mi.), the trail follows a logging road east for about 2 mi., diverging once for a difficult stream crossing near the bottom of the trail (0.2 mi.). The

Trail, again on the logging road, stays close to the brook except at one point where it ascends to a limited view west and then bears right downhill to the second crossing of Brewers Brook (1.2 mi.). It then continues to follow the brook before turning right (2.0 mi.) to climb steeply out of the valley to meet the LT (3.3 mi.) 0.1 mi. downhill from Cooper Lodge and the Killington Spur. Wheelerville Road to LT, 3.3 mi., 5.3 km, 2¾ h (Rev. 1¾ h).

SHERBURNE PASS TRAIL, SOUTH HALF. The Sherburne Pass Trail, which extends north and south of U.S. 4, is the former route of the Long Trail. Forming a loop with the LT and the AT, it is an alternate route for long-distance hikers. The northern half of the Sherburne Pass Trail is described on page 183.

The trailhead is in Sherburne Pass, 9.3 mi. east of U.S. 7 in Rutland, and 1.4 mi. west of the junction of U.S. 4 and Vt. 100 near the Killington Ski Area Access Road. There is a large unpaved parking lot on the south side of the highway. Use caution when crossing U.S. 4.

South from U.S. 4, the trail crosses the remnants of the original Route 4, then reaches a dirt road (0.1 mi.) leading back to the parking area. The trail climbs steadily, passing Sink Hole Brook (1.1 mi.), to a ski trail (2.1 mi.) which it follows uphill for 300 ft., then reenters the woods to the left. The trail follows a rugged path with little change in elevation to Pico Camp and Pico Link (2.5 mi.). From here, the Sherburne Pass Trail continues across an open swath (2.7 mi.) to a junction with the Long Trail (3.0 mi.). Sherburne Pass to LT 3.0 mi., 4.8 km, 2 h (Rev. 1 h).

PICO LINK. This route provides access to the summit of Pico Peak from the Sherburne Pass Trail. The link enters the woods from the north side of Pico Camp and bears west, climbing steeply to Pico Peak. The open summit offers fine views to the north and toward Killington. Sherburne Pass Trail to Pico Peak, 0.4 mi., 0.6 km, ½ h (Rev. ¼ h).

DIVISION 6

U.S. 4 to
Vt. 73 (Brandon Gap)

Take Note

Water is scarce between Rolston Rest and David Logan Shelters. Hikers should take advantage of the water sources at these two sites.

The Long Trail and the Appalachian Trail coincide in Division 6 for 1.0 mile from U.S. 4 to Maine Junction. Some of the land in Division 6 is managed for silviculture. Please heed posted notices of logging jobs.

Suggested Hike

CHITTENDEN BROOK TRAIL. This pleasant woods walk leads from USFS Road 45 to the Long Trail. Round trip, 7.4 mi., 4⅓ h.

Camping and Fires

The Long Trail in Division 6 crosses federal and state land with scattered private inholdings. Camping is limited to shelters between Sherburne Pass and Wetmore Gap. Small wood fires, although discouraged, are permitted in established fire rings at shelters.

From Wetmore Gap to Brandon Gap the LT crosses the Green Mountain National Forest. Leave-no-trace camping with small wood fires is permitted. Follow leave-no-trace guidelines (pages 4 to 6) to minimize impact on the Long Trail System.

Winter Use

This division offers good hiking with extensive views after the leaves have fallen. Much of the Long Trail in this division is suitable for intermediate cross-country skiers. A good cross-country ski trip is to go south on the Long Trail from Brandon Gap and then follow the same route back to Vt. 73. The LT parking lot on the south side of Vt. 73 is plowed in winter.

Access to Long Trail

U.S. 4. Refer to the description on page 88 in Division 5.

BRANDON GAP, VT. 73. From the junction of Vt. 73 and Vt. 100 just south of Rochester, it is 9.2 mi. west to the LT crossing at Brandon Gap. The Long Trail is 5.2 mi. east of Forest Dale and 8.2 mi. east of Brandon and U.S. 7. There is a parking lot on the south side of the highway.

6

Long Trail Description

North of **U.S. 4 (0.0 mi.)**, the Long Trail climbs gradually to **Maine Junction** at **Willard Gap (1.0 mi.)**. Here the Appalachian Trail bears right toward Deer Leap, Gifford Woods State Park, and Katahdin, while the Long Trail goes north toward Canada. A description of the AT from this junction to the Connecticut River begins on page 178. Trail summaries and maps begin on page 218.

A short distance north of Willard Gap is **Tucker-Johnson Shelter (1.4 mi.)**. This frame shelter, with bunks for 8, was built in 1969 by the Long Trail Patrol, Louis Stare, and members of the Killington Section. It is named for Fred H. Tucker of Boston, a long-time member of the GMC, and for Otto Johnson of Proctor, Vt., who bequeathed funds for its construction. Nearby Eagle Square Brook furnishes water. **Pico Camp to Tucker-Johnson Shelter, 5.7 mi., 9.2 km, 3 h (SB 4 h)**.

The Long Trail continues with minor changes in elevation and occasional stretches of rough footing, to the east side of the ridge, eventually reaching the abandoned **Elbow Road (3.3 mi.)** or Chittenden-Pittsfield Road. The Trail briefly follows a logging road north, turns right and, continuing without much change in elevation, reaches **Rolston Rest Shelter (5.0 mi.)**. This frame lean-to, with space for 8, was built by the Long Trail Patrol in 1966. The shelter was named for Ben Rolston, a former GMC guidebook editor and trail maintainer. A small brook crosses the LT just south of the shelter and provides water for this site. **Tucker-Johnson Shelter to Rolston Rest, 3.6 mi., 5.8 km, 2¼ h (SB 2¼ h).**

A short distance north of the shelter the LT crosses a private road, which descends east to Vt. 100. The Trail climbs moderately to the top of a ridge (5.5 mi.), passes west of an unnamed summit, el. 2,800' (6.2 mi.), and continues northwest on or near the ridgeline with occasional limited views. It leaves the ridge in a shallow gap (7.2 mi.) to slab the west side of the ridge. In a small rocky gap, it crosses the abandoned **Green Road (8.9 mi.)** that runs from Chittenden to Pittsfield, used as early as 1796 (now a snowmobile trail). The Long Trail slabs the western slope and passes about 100 ft. west of an enormous split boulder. There are a few limited views west and one good view of Chittenden Reservoir just north of the road. The Trail finally crosses to the east side of the ridge, drops to a sag known as **Telephone Gap (10.8 mi.)** and, swinging back to the northwest, ascends to the west side of the ridge once again. The Long Trail briefly follows a snowmobile trail (11.9 mi.), ascends the south slope of Mt. Carmel, and then continues with

PETS

Keep pets under control and away from water supplies. Dispose of waste properly.

minor changes in elevation along the ridge to the **New Boston Trail (12.7 mi.)**.

Bearing left on the **New Boston Trail** it is 0.2 mi. to **David Logan Shelter**, a frame lean-to with bunks for 8. This shelter was built with the help of 60 campers from the Vermont Camping Association under the direction of GMC's George Pearlstein, and named in memory of David Logan, an active club member whose family and friends provided funds and assistance. A reliable source of water is located 200 ft. north of the shelter along the New Boston Trail. **Rolston Rest to David Logan Shelter, 7.9 mi., 12.7 km, 5¼ h (SB 5¼ h).**

Continuing north from the New Boston Trail, the LT briefly ascends, then descends the west slope of Mt. Carmel and soon reaches **Wetmore Gap (13.2 mi.)**. The Trail climbs the east ridge of **Bloodroot Mtn. (14.0 mi.)** and then contours along the east slope of the mountain to **Bloodroot Gap (15.7 mi.)** where it crosses another snowmobile trail.

North of the gap, the Long Trail slabs the east ridge of **Farr Peak (16.2 mi.)**, named for Albert G. Farr of Brandon who supplied the funds to complete the LT between Lincoln and Brandon Gaps. The LT continues with little change in elevation around the east slope of the peak until reaching the **Chittenden Brook Trail (17.6 mi.)** on the right. Beyond the junction, the LT begins a gradual descent on an old woods road to **Sunrise Shelter (19.0 mi.)**. This frame shelter was built by the Long Trail Patrol in 1964, a gift of Mortimer R. Proctor, governor of Vermont from 1945 to 1947, and former president of the GMC. The shelter has space for 8, and water is located at a brook 200 ft. south. **David Logan Shelter to Sunrise Shelter, 6.5 mi., 10.5 km, 4 h (SB 4 h).**

From the shelter the LT continues downhill on the old road, passes a clearing from which there is an excellent view of the Great Cliff of Mt. Horrid, and reaches **Brandon Gap** and **Vt. 73** (Brandon-Rochester Highway) **(19.9 mi.)**. To the east it is 9.2 mi. to Vt. 100 just south of Rochester, and 3.7 mi. to USFS 45, which leads 2.3 mi. south to the USFS

6

Chittenden Brook Camping Area. Forest Dale is 5.2 mi. west and Brandon is 8.2 mi. west.

Side Trails

NEW BOSTON TRAIL. From the Civil War monument in Chittenden (0.0 mi.), follow the road to Mountain Top Ski Touring Center and Mountain Top Inn 1.8 mi. north to fork in road. Continue straight ahead on the right-hand fork on the unpaved town road to a small pull-out (2.4 mi.) on the right. Here the road becomes USFS Road 99 and is passable only by high clearance vehicles. The road improves after turning left onto a recently used logging road. It is 1.3 mi. from the pull-out to a primitive campsite and trailhead parking.

From the trailhead the New Boston Trail bears left off the logging road and ascends on a woods road for .75 mi. to a fork. Here the Mt. Carmel snowmobile trail continues on the wide woods road to the right. The New Boston Trail goes straight on an overgrown woods road and climbs steadily to David Logan Shelter (1.0 mi.). Just above the shelter the trail passes a piped spring to the left and then reaches the Long Trail (1.2 mi.). Upper Turnout to David Logan Shelter, 1.0 mi., 1 h; to LT, 1.2 mi., 1.9 km, 1¼ h (Rev. ¾ h).

CHITTENDEN BROOK TRAIL. Located in the Chittenden Brook Recreation Area (named after Vermont's first governor, Thomas Chittenden) this trail offers a pleasant approach to the LT as well as some good hiking and skiing loops with other trails in the recreation area. From its junction with Vt.

WHO WANTS DIRTY WATER?

Proper disposal of human and pet waste prevents the spread of *Giardia* and other diseases. If an outhouse is not available, bury waste in a 4- to 6-inch hole 200 feet (75 paces) from water and 50 feet from trails.

---

100 near Rochester, follow Vt. 73 west 5.5 mi. and turn south onto USFS Road 45. Continue 0.6 mi. on this road to the hikers' parking area. From here along the road it is another 1.7 mi. to the USFS Chittenden Brook Campground. USFS Road 45 is not maintained for winter travel.

From the hikers' parking lot (0.0 mi.), the trail follows the stream on old woods roads and climbs steadily through spruce and fir forest, passes a cross-country trail on the right, and reaches the Beaver Pond Spur Trail (1.7 mi.). This trail leads a short distance to a wetland with the chance to see beaver, tree swallows, and an occasional moose. After crossing a major branch of the brook, the Chittenden Brook Trail passes a short spur trail (1.9 mi.) to the campground on the left, cuts across the last of the cross-country ski loops (2.2 mi.), and then climbs more steeply to its junction with the Long Trail (3.7 mi.). USFS Road 45 to LT, 3.7 mi., 6.0 km, 2⅓ h (Rev. 2 h).

6

DIVISION 7

Vt. 73 (Brandon Gap) to Cooley Glen Shelter

Take Note

The Long Trail remains on or near the ridgeline in this division. Water is scarce and hikers should take advantage of sources noted in the text.

From Middlebury Gap to Cooley Glen Shelter, the Long Trail traverses Breadloaf Wilderness. Refer to wilderness information on page 10.

Suggested Hikes

LAKE PLEIAD. This short hike, following the Long Trail south from Middlebury Gap to the spur trail to Lake Pleiad, is especially suitable for children. Round trip, 1.0 mi., ½ h.

MT. HORRID. This short steep climb on the Long Trail north from Brandon Gap provides excellent views from its precipitous heights. However, the cliffs are closed to the public from March 15 to May 1 because they are a prime peregrine falcon nesting site. If falcons do nest at that site, the cliffs remain closed until August 1. Round trip, 1.4 mi., 1¼ h.

MT. ROOSEVELT. This moderate day hike on the Clark Brook Trail and LT leads to a rock outcrop just north of the summit. Round trip, 6.8 mi., 4½ h.

Camping and Fires

The Long Trail in Division 7 crosses the Green Mountain National Forest from Brandon Gap to Worth Mtn., and from Middlebury Gap to Cooley Glen Shelter. Leave-no-trace camping with small wood fires is allowed. Follow leave-no-trace guidelines (pages 4 to 6) to minimize impact on the Long Trail System. **Exceptions:** Camping within 500 ft. of Skylight Pond is limited to Skyline Lodge (tenting around the pond is prohibited) and wood fires are prohibited within 500 ft. of Skylight Pond to protect the vulnerable soils and vegetation.

Between Worth Mtn. and Middlebury Gap, the Long Trail traverses private property; camping and fires are prohibited along this portion of the Trail.

Winter Use

All suggested hikes in this division make good snowshoe treks. Most of the terrain is too rugged for beginner and intermediate cross-country skiers. The lower portion of the Cooley Glen Trail, however, offers good beginner to intermediate skiing.

Access to Long Trail

BRANDON GAP, VT. 73. Refer to the description on page 97 in Division 6.

MIDDLEBURY GAP, VT. 125. The Long Trail crossing at Middlebury Gap is 2.5 mi. east of the Bread Loaf Campus, 5.6 mi. east of Ripton, and 10.1 mi. east of the junction of Vt. 125 and U.S. 7 (3.8 mi. south of Middlebury). The crossing is 6.4 mi. west of Vt. 100 in Hancock. A large area for pull-off parking is located on the south side of the road.

Long Trail Description

North of **Vt. 73** (Brandon-Rochester Highway) in **Brandon Gap (0.0 mi.)**, the Long Trail ascends steeply on rock staircases to a short 0.1 mi. **spur trail (0.7 mi.)** to the **Great Cliff of Mt. Horrid**. The cliff top, 600 ft. above the road, provides a fine view of the gap and the mountains beyond. The spur trail may be closed between March 15 and August 1 to prevent the disturbance of nesting peregrine falcons. The LT continues west of the ridge to the summit of **Mt. Horrid (1.3 mi.)** and then along the wooded ridge to **Cape Lookoff Mtn. (1.8 mi.)** and **Gillespie Peak (3.3 mi.)**. There are many vistas along this ridge.

North from Gillespie Peak (formerly White Rocks Mtn.) to Mt. Wilson, the Long Trail is mostly on forest land bequeathed to Middlebury College in 1915 by Col. Joseph Battell. The college still owns 700 acres at Lake Pleiad, including 1.8 mi. of the LT; the remainder is part of the Green Mountain National Forest. Col. Battell established the Bread Loaf Inn west of Middlebury Gap, now used as the Bread Loaf Campus of Middlebury College. He also cut a trail from Mt. Abraham north to Mt. Ellen in 1901, possibly the first skyline trail in the Green Mountains.

From Gillespie Peak, the Long Trail traverses the ridge passing a spur trail to a view west just before reaching the east summit of **Romance Mtn. (4.1 mi.)**. It then switches back down to **Romance Gap (4.5 mi.)** and continues west of the ridge to a junction with the **Sucker Brook Trail (5.4 mi.)**, which leads 1.0 mi. west to USFS Road 67. **Sucker Brook Shelter** is located 0.1 mi. down this trail. This frame shelter, which sleeps 8, was built by the U.S. Forest Service in 1963. Water is found at Sucker Brook, 50 ft. further down the Sucker Brook Trail. **Sunrise Shelter to Sucker Brook Shelter, 6.4 mi., 10.3 km, 4 h (SB 4¼ h).**

From the Sucker Brook Trail junction, the LT climbs gradually up the ridge of Worth Mtn. passing by vistas to the south and west. The Trail then ascends moderately, passing two vistas to the east, before reaching the wooded summit of **Worth Mtn. (7.2 mi.)**. Leaving the summit, the Long Trail soon passes Eastern Lookout, then descends moderately, passing over a couple of minor summits until it reaches the upper station of a chair lift for **Middlebury Snow Bowl (8.9** mi.). There are good views to the north and east. The LT passes to the west of the chair lift on a ski trail and continues to follow and cross ski trails several times. Hikers should pay close attention to blazes and signs. Upon finally re-entering the woods, the Trail crosses a small brook at a junction with a **spur trail (9.5 mi.)** leading 0.1 mi. to **Lake Pleiad**. Shortly beyond the junction the Long Trail crosses an abandoned ski trail and reaches the former site of the Lake Pleiad Shelter (9.6 mi.), removed in 1994. Camping is not allowed at this site.

The Trail then passes over a low ridge to **Middlebury Gap** and **Vt. 125** (Middlebury-Hancock Highway) **(9.9 mi.)**. To the west it is 0.7 mi. to the Snow Bowl and 10.1 mi. to U.S. 7, 3.8 mi. south of Middlebury. To the east it is 6.4 mi. to Vt. 100 in Hancock.

Crossing the highway, the Long Trail enters the Breadloaf Wilderness where trail blazing may be sparse. It rises rapidly to a junction with the **Silent Cliff Trail (10.3 mi.)**. North of the trail junction, the LT ascends to the ridge (10.8 mi.), continues along it to Burnt Hill, then descends to a junction with the **Burnt Hill Trail (12.4 mi.)**, which descends west 2.2 mi. to USFS Road 59. From the junction the Trail passes along the rugged west slope of Kirby Peak (12.6 mi.), and continues to **Boyce Shelter (13.0 mi.)**. This frame shelter, with space for 8, was built by the U.S. Forest Service in 1963. Water, not always reliable, is from a small brook 200 ft. north via the LT. **Sucker Brook Shelter to Boyce Shelter, 7.7 mi., 12.4 km, 5¼ h (SB 5½ h).**

Beyond the shelter, the Trail climbs **Mt. Boyce (13.9 mi.)**, continues along the ridge over **Battell Mtn. (14.9 mi.)**, and eventually reaches an established tenting area with a spur trail leading west to a vista at Sunset Rock. Descending, the LT comes to a junction with the **Skylight Pond Trail (15.0 mi.)**, which leads left 2.5 mi. down to USFS Road 59. To the right it is 0.1 mi. to **Skyline Lodge** and **Skylight Pond**.

Skyline Lodge, an enclosed shelter with bunk space for 14, was built by the GMC and U.S. Forest Service in 1987.

The lodge sits on a steep hillside overlooking shallow Skylight Pond, which is not suitable for fishing or swimming. Water is available from a spring 250 ft. north or from the pond in dry seasons. The area around the pond is very sensitive to resource damage. A caretaker is in seasonal residence to educate hikers and help them minimize their impact. A fee is charged for overnight use of the shelter. There is no tenting allowed in the vicinity of the pond, but there is an established tenting area just south on the Long Trail on Battell Mtn. A no-wood-fire zone extends 500 ft. from the pond to permit the surrounding forest to recover from years of indiscriminate cutting of vegetation by campers. **Boyce Shelter to Skyline Lodge, 2.4 mi., 3.9 km, 1½ h (SB 1¼ h).**

Continuing north from the junction, the Long Trail soon begins a steep ascent to the top of the ridge on **Bread Loaf Mtn. (16.2 mi.)**, which it follows to a sharp turn to the east. Here a spur trail leads left 0.1 mi. to a lookout providing an extensive view over the Champlain Valley. The LT descends gradually along the ridge to **Emily Proctor Shelter** and the **Emily Proctor Trail (16.8 mi.)**, which descends 3.5 mi. west to USFS Road 201 out of South Lincoln.

Emily Proctor Shelter, a log shelter built by the Long Trail Patrol in 1960 and rebuilt in 1983, has space for 5. Water is from the brook crossed by the LT 20 ft. to the south. **Skyline Lodge to Emily Proctor Shelter, 1.9 mi., 3.1 km, 1¾ h (SB 1¼ h).**

The Long Trail turns sharply right at the southern end of the shelter and ascends steadily to the ridge. It continues

---

LEAVE NOTHING BUT THE LIGHTEST OF FOOTPRINTS

- Remove all litter from trails.
- Clean campsites and carry trash home.
- Help keep woodlands clean.
- Stay on the footpath.

along the crest to **Mt. Wilson** (17.7 mi.) where a short spur trail leads right to a vista to the south and east. Leaving the summit the Trail bears left and descends steeply to a sag between Mt. Wilson and Mt. Roosevelt, then continues to a junction with the **Clark Brook Trail** (18.5 mi.). This trail descends 3.0 mi. east to USFS Road 55.

From the side trail junction the Long Trail ascends quickly to the summit of **Mt. Roosevelt** (18.9 mi.); just beyond is a rock outcrop, **Killington View**, with spectacular views to the south and east. From here the Trail descends a short distance, then traverses a series of knobs along the northeast ridge of Mt. Roosevelt before dropping to a sag where it crosses a small seep. It then ascends to a minor peak (20.3 mi.) before dropping steadily and then making a rough climb to the wooded summit of **Mt. Cleveland** (22.0 mi.). After descending gradually to a sharp turn to the right (22.4 mi.), the LT drops steeply to a junction with the **Cooley Glen Trail**, which leads 3.2 mi. west to USFS Road 201 and the Emily Proctor Trail. A short distance from the junction, the Long Trail arrives at **Cooley Glen Shelter** (22.5 mi.).

A frame lean-to with room for 8, Cooley Glen Shelter was built by the U.S. Forest Service in 1965. A spring is located 600 ft. west on the Cooley Glen Trail. **Emily Proctor Shelter to Cooley Glen Shelter, 5.7 mi., 9.2 km, 3¾ h (SB 3¾ h).**

Side Trails

Sucker Brook Trail. This trailhead is reached by following USFS Road 67 (Goshen Brook Rd.) 3.8 mi. south from Vt. 125. USFS Road 67 is 3.5 miles east of Ripton or 0.5 mi. east of the Bread Loaf Campus of Middlebury College, and 8.5 mi. west of Vt. 100 in Hancock or 2.1 mi. west of the LT crossing in Middlebury Gap. The road may be gated near its beginning during spring and fall mud seasons. There is parking for several cars at a USFS primitive campsite at the end of the road where the trail begins.

Sucker Brook Trail ascends easily and then more steadily on an old logging road to Sucker Brook Shelter (0.9 mi.).

Just beyond the shelter the trail climbs to its junction with the Long Trail. USFS Road 67 to LT, 1.0 mi., 1.6 km, ¾ h (Rev. ½ h).

SILENT CLIFF TRAIL. This spur trail leaves the Long Trail 0.4 mi. north of Vt. 125 and Middlebury Gap and leads east 0.4 mi. to Silent Cave and Silent Cliff. From the cliff there is an excellent view south of Middlebury Gap with Monastery Gap and the Green Mountains beyond. LT to Silent Cliff, 0.4 mi., 0.6 km, ¼ h (Rev. ¼ h).

BURNT HILL TRAIL. This trail starts on the east side of USFS Road 59, 1.1 mi. north of Vt. 125. USFS Road 59 is 2.7 mi. east of Ripton and 0.2 mi. west of Bread Loaf Campus. Parking in a grassy lot is available at the trailhead.

The Burnt Hill Trail coincides with the Norske Ski Trail, then turns left at an intersection (0.7 mi.) and follows an old logging road into the Breadloaf Wilderness (1.0 mi.). The trail then ascends more steeply to its junction with the Long Trail. USFS Road 59 to LT, 2.2 mi., 3.5 km, 1¾ h (Rev. 1 h).

SKYLIGHT POND TRAIL. This trail starts at a primitive campsite on the east side of USFS Road 59 (follow the directions to the Burnt Hill Trail), 3.6 mi. north of Vt. 125. There is a large gravel parking lot at the trailhead. USFS Road 59 is not plowed north of the Burnt Hill Trail in winter.

The trail ascends easily on an old woods road, crosses two small streams (the upper crossing over a bridge), before entering Breadloaf Wilderness (0.4 mi.). The trail meanders by long, sweeping switchbacks, ascending moderately to the Long Trail (2.5 mi.), 0.1 mi. west of Skyline Lodge. The trail continues down the east side of the ridge to Skylight Pond and Skyline Lodge. USFS Road 59 to Skyline Lodge, 2.6 mi., 4.2 km, 2 h (Rev. 1¼ h).

EMILY PROCTOR TRAIL. This trailhead (shared with the Cooley Glen Trail), is reached via USFS Roads 54 and 201. Follow USFS Road 54 south off the Lincoln-Warren Road, 1.2 mi. east of Lincoln and 3.5 mi. west of the LT crossing in Lincoln Gap. Continue through South Lincoln, then bear left onto USFS Road 201, 4.2 mi. from the Lincoln-Warren Road. Follow USFS Road 201 0.3 mi. to the trailhead and a USFS primitive campsite where there is parking at a turn-around. USFS Road 201 is not maintained in winter.

From the trailhead (0.0 mi.), the Emily Proctor Trail turns right and ascends on a logging road (0.0 mi.), crosses the edge of a clear-cut, and follows an older woods road, entering Breadloaf Wilderness (0.6 mi.). At 1.4 mi., the trail leaves the old road, staying on the west side of the New Haven River, before crossing it on some large rocks. After crossing two small streams, the trail makes a steep and rocky ascent, and enters the clearing in front of Emily Proctor Shelter (3.5 mi.) at the Long Trail. USFS Road 201 to LT, 3.5 mi., 5.6 km, 2¾ h (Rev. 1¾ h).

CLARK BROOK TRAIL. From the northern end of Upper Granville Village take the only road leaving west off Vt. 100. At 0.5 mi., take a left-hand fork onto USFS Road 55. Continue on this road 1.3 mi., ignoring three right-hand turns, until reaching the trailhead shortly after a sharp left turn over a bridge above Clark Brook. There is roadside parking adjacent to a USFS primitive campsite. USFS Road 55 is not plowed in winter.

The trail ascends easily along Clark Brook, crossing it on bridges twice, enters Breadloaf Wilderness (1.1 mi.) and, after crossing a small brook (2.5 mi.), becomes steeper and rockier before reaching its junction with the Long Trail. USFS 55 to LT, 3.0 mi., 4.8 km, 2¾ h (Rev. 1½ h).

COOLEY GLEN TRAIL. This trail begins at the same parking area as the Emily Proctor Trail. From the trailhead (0.0 mi.), the Cooley Glen Trail follows the extension of USFS Road 201 to a bridge crossing of the New Haven River (0.4 mi.). It passes through a clearing and then stays on the north bank of the river. A tributary brook is crossed shortly before entering Breadloaf Wilderness (1.6 mi.). The trail ascends the western flank of Mt. Cleveland and, after passing a spring that is the Cooley Glen Shelter water supply, it meets the Long Trail just south of the shelter. USFS Road 201 to LT, 3.2 mi., 5.1 km, 2½ h (Rev. 1¾ h).

DIVISION 8

Cooley Glen Shelter to Birch Glen Camp

Take Note

The Long Trail traverses a narrow ridgeline through most of this division. Water is scarce and hikers should take advantage of sources noted in the text. Minor relocations are planned between Mt. Abraham and Mt. Ellen.

The LT crosses Mt. Abraham in this division. It is one of three sites in Vermont with alpine vegetation. Please take care to do the "rock walk" and tread only on the rocks, not the plants.

From Cooley Glen Shelter to Lincoln Gap the Long Trail traverses the Breadloaf Wilderness. Refer to wilderness information on page 10.

From Lincoln Gap north to the Winooski River, the LT is called the Monroe Skyline in honor of Prof. Will S. Monroe who built this section.

Suggested Hikes

BIRCH GLEN CAMP. This short hike passes through pleasant woods on the Beane Trail. Round trip, 1.8 mi., 1¼ h.

MOLLY STARK'S BALCONY. This hike leads north on the LT from Appalachian Gap to a lookout with fine views to the north. This is a challenging short hike with some steep ups and downs. Round trip, 2.6 mi., 2 h.

MT. ELLEN. South on the Long Trail from Appalachian Gap, this wooded summit has fine views from its upper slopes. This hike features difficult, steep climbs. Round trip, 10.6 mi., 6½ h. A shorter route to Mt. Ellen uses the Jerusalem Trail and the Long Trail. Round trip, 8.4 mi., 5½ h.

Camping and Fires

The Long Trail in Division 8 crosses the Green Mountain National Forest from Cooley Glen Shelter to the national forest boundary just north of Mt. Ellen. Leave-no-trace camping with small wood fires is allowed. Follow leave-no-trace guidelines (pages 4 to 6) to minimize impact on the Long Trail System. *Exceptions:* Wood fires are prohibited within 500 ft. of Battell Shelter to protect the high-elevation forest at this site. Camping is prohibited on the summit of Mt. Abraham to protect the alpine plant community.

North of Mt. Ellen the LT crosses state and private land. Camping is limited to shelters. Wood fires are prohibited at Glen Ellen Lodge and Theron Dean Shelter due to their sensitive, high-elevation nature. Small wood fires, although discouraged, are permitted at Birch Glen Camp.

Winter Use

The suggested hikes for the northern end of this division make good snowshoe treks. The summit of Mt. Abraham is more readily accessible from the Battell Trail to the west than the Long Trail because the road through Lincoln Gap (access to the LT) is not maintained in winter. Although the Long Trail crosses the Catamount Trail in Lincoln Gap, the rugged terrain here is not suitable for beginner or intermediate cross-country skiers. See Catamount Trail information on page 19.

Access to Long Trail

LINCOLN GAP, LINCOLN-WARREN HIGHWAY. The Long Trail crosses this steep, winding gravel road in Lincoln Gap, 4.7 mi. east of Lincoln, 10.0 mi. east of the junction of Vt.

17 and 116 in Bristol. The crossing is 4.7 mi. west of Vt. 100 in Warren. There is roadside parking at the crossing and a large secondary parking lot just east of the Trail on the highway's south side. This trailhead is heavily used during the hiking season, and cars left overnight are sometimes vandalized. Long-term parking is not recommended. The road through Lincoln Gap is closed during winter.

APPALACHIAN GAP, VT. 17. This road intersects the LT at the summit of Appalachian Gap, 1.4 mi. west of Mad River Glen Ski Area, 6.0 mi. west of Vt. 100 in Irasville, and 8.9 mi. east of the northern junction of Vt. 17 and Vt. 116. There is a large parking lot on the north side of the road just west of the Long Trail. Vt. 17 is open year-round.

Long Trail Description

From **Cooley Glen Shelter (0.0 mi.)** the Long Trail ascends northwest to the summit of **Mt. Grant (0.8 mi.)**, where there is a good view south into the heart of the Breadloaf Wilderness. From the summit the Trail descends steadily to the ridge, which it follows through a hardwood forest before switchbacking down to a sag (2.9 mi.). Climbing out of the sag, the LT crosses some open areas with views to the south and east, then traverses a short ridge and drops down to another sag. After ascending to a smaller open area with views to the south, the Long Trail reaches Sunset Ledge (3.6 mi.), which has an expansive western vista. The LT continues to traverse the ridge until reaching Eastwood's Rise (4.3 mi.), then drops steeply to the northern boundary of the Breadloaf Wilderness at **Lincoln Gap (4.7 mi.)**, through which passes the **Lincoln-Warren Highway**. To the west it is 10.0 mi. to Bristol. To the east it is 4.7 mi. to Warren and Vt. 100.

After climbing out of Lincoln Gap, the Trail, bearing to the west of a knoll, begins a moderate ascent, passing en route the "Carpenters" (5.9 mi.), two huge boulders named after a pair of trail workers. Soon after crossing a brook the LT reaches a junction where the **Battell Trail (6.4 mi.)** descends west 2.0 mi. to USFS Road 350. Here the LT turns right and climbs to **Battell Shelter (6.5 mi.)**. This shelter was built in 1967 by campers from Farm and Wilderness Camp using materials airlifted to the site. It sleeps 8. Water is from a small spring 100 ft. to the east. A caretaker may be in seasonal residence to assist and educate hikers and help protect the resources of the site and the summit of Mt. Abraham. A fee is charged for overnight use. Wood fires are not allowed within 500 ft. of this high-elevation site. Tenting near Battell Shelter is very limited. **Cooley Glen Shelter to Battell Shelter, 6.5 mi., 10.5 km, 4¼ h (SB 4¼ h).**

Bearing north in front of the shelter and following an old road, the Trail begins the gradual, then steep, ascent of Mt. Abraham. The trail scrambles up bare ledge in places; extra care should be used in wet weather. The alpine summit of **Mt. Abraham (7.3 mi.)**, the southernmost peak of Lincoln Mtn., offers one of the best panoramas on the entire Long Trail, ranging from houses nearby in the valleys to the White Mountains of New Hampshire, 80 miles east. Due west is Mt. Marcy and its Adirondack neighbors. To the south may be seen the Green Mountains as far as Killington Peak. To the north, though partly hidden by nearby higher peaks, the same range is visible as far as Belvidere Mtn.

The summit of this mountain is above treeline and supports a small community of alpine vegetation, one of only three such communities in Vermont. These plants do not tolerate foot traffic; they have been damaged by hikers straying from the trail. *Note: Above treeline, take care to walk only on the rocks, not the fragile alpine plants. Please leash dogs. Camping is prohibited on the summit of Mt. Abraham.*

Entering the woods and crossing a sag, the LT soon reaches Little Abe (8.0 mi.), a minor summit, just beyond which is **Lincoln Peak (8.1 mi.)**. Here is an observation platform, built by Sugarbush Valley Resort and the U.S. Forest Service, which offers wide views.

At the clearing, the Trail bears sharply left, enters the woods and swings north, following the wooded ridge of Lincoln Mtn. After passing over **Nancy Hanks Peak**

8

(8.7 mi.), the LT continues along the ridge to the upper station of the **Castlerock Chair Lift (9.4 mi.)**. Turning left and passing behind the lift station, it follows a ski trail to **Holt Hollow (9.5 mi.)**, where water may be found 200 ft. to the west.

Continuing along the skyline, the Long Trail ascends gradually to **Cutts Peak (10.6 mi.)**, where there are distant views. From this point it is very easy going to the wooded summit of **Mt. Ellen (11.0 mi.)**, tied with Camel's Hump for the third-highest mountain in Vermont (el. 4,083'). Leaving the summit, the LT joins a ski trail descending from the upper station of the Sugarbush North summit chair lift, located to the right. Descending on the ski trail for 150 ft., the LT veers left, enters the woods, and drops, steeply at first and then more moderately, to the marked **north boundary of the Green Mountain National Forest (11.4 mi.)**. After winding back and forth across the ridge, and passing several limited lookouts, the Trail reaches a junction with the **Jerusalem Trail (12.8 mi.)**, which descends 2.4 mi. west to the Jim Dwire Road.

Just beyond the junction are Orvis Lookout (50 ft. left), and the **Barton Trail (12.9 mi.)**, which branches right and descends 0.3 mi. to **Glen Ellen Lodge**. Built in 1933 by the Long Trail Patrol, the lodge is of log construction with bunks for 8. Water source for the lodge is an unreliable spring lo-

---

BEWARE OF TRAILHEAD VANDALISM

If you're leaving your car overnight, park away from the trail near major public transportation routes. Police and service stations often provide a place to park (the latter for a small fee). Reach the Long Trail by walking or arranging for other transportation.

cated to the west of the Long Trail near the junction, before descending the Barton Trail. A second intermittent water source is a brook that may be found by following the contour beyond the outhouse. Wood fires are prohibited at the lodge. There are views to the east from the Glen Ellen Lodge. Beyond the Mad River Valley are the Northfield Mountains, the Granite Mountains and, on the horizon, several ridges of the White Mountains. **Battell Shelter to Glen Ellen Lodge, 6.7 mi., 10.8 km, 4 h (SB 4 h).**

From the Barton Trail junction, the LT ascends steeply to the ridge of **General Stark Mtn.** After passing General Stark's **highest summit (13.2 mi.)**, the Trail continues along the ridge and soon joins a ski trail, which it follows for 600 ft. to the northern peak and **Stark's Nest (13.8 mi.)**, a Mad River Glen Ski Area warming hut. There are views to the east and limited views of Lake Champlain and the Adirondacks to the west.

Passing to the west of the summit building, the Long Trail enters Camel's Hump State Forest, follows a ski trail through some trees, then enters the woods to the left. After 200 ft., the LT rejoins the ski trail and then cuts back into the woods again, before continuing along the ridge and then descending steeply, utilizing a ladder at one point (14.3 mi.), to **Theron Dean Shelter (14.5 mi.)**, located 25 ft. to the west.

This small log shelter, with space for 5, was built in 1966 by the Long Trail Patrol. It is named for Theron Dean, an energetic promotor of the GMC in its early years and a close friend of Will S. Monroe. A small spring west of the shelter is unreliable. Wood fires are prohibited at Theron Dean Shelter. **Glen Ellen Lodge to Theron Dean Shelter, 1.9 mi., 3.1 km, 1¼ h (SB 1¼ h).**

At the shelter, one trail leads right, back to the LT, while a short, alternate route leads straight ahead to **Dean Panorama** where there is a view north. This trail then drops and switchbacks to the right, passing through **Dean Cave**, before rejoining the Long Trail route 150 ft. from the shelter.

The Trail continues its steep descent, passing the upper station of another chair lift (14.7 mi.), and then leveling out as it continues along the ridge. Descending sharply once again, the LT passes a vista to the north, leads over a knoll, then drops into **Appalachian Gap** and crosses **Vt. 17** (Bristol-Irasville Highway) **(16.3 mi.).** To the east it is 1.4 mi. to Mad River Glen Ski Area and 6 mi. to Irasville and Vt. 100. To the west it is 2.5 mi. to the Huntington Road. There is a parking lot west of the LT at the summit of the highway with a fine western vista. At "App." Gap, the Long Trail enters Camel's Hump State Park, which it passes in and out of until entering it on Mts. Ira and Ethan Allen for the remainder of the route north over Camel's Hump to River Road.

At Appalachian Gap the Long Trail turns right and follows the road east for 100 ft. The LT then ascends the northern embankment of the road, climbing rather steeply, passes a spur trail (16.4 mi.) to the Mad River Glen Lookout, and reaches its highest point on the east slope of **Baby Stark Mtn. (16.7 mi.).** Descending, steeply in places, it reaches a brook (16.9 mi.), and then ascends to the ridgeline. The Trail then passes over **Molly Stark Mtn. (17.3 mi.)** and continues to **Molly Stark's Balcony (17.6 mi.)** where there is a fine view of Camel's Hump and the intervening peaks, with the Worcester Mountains standing out boldly toward the northeast. After following a circuitous route around the cliff below the Balcony, the LT descends moderately, passing west of Beane Mtn., and reaches a junction with the **Beane Trail (18.9 mi.),** which leads 1.5 mi. west to Carse Road. Via this trail it is 100 ft. to **Birch Glen Camp.**

This log structure, built in 1930 by GMC volunteers, has an open front "living room" and semi-enclosed sleeping quarters with bunk space for 12. The water source is a brook 100 ft. south. **Theron Dean Shelter to Birch Glen Camp, 4.4 mi., 7.1 km, 2¾ h (SB 3¼ h).**

Side Trails

BATTELL TRAIL. From Lincoln turn north off the Lincoln-Warren Road by the general store. At 0.7 mi. turn right onto USFS Road 350 (Elder Hill Rd.). Continue on this road (with signs to the trail) 1.9 mi. to a left turn, which continues

0.1 mi. to the Battell Trail and a small parking lot. The final 0.1 mi. is not maintained in winter.

From the road (0.0 mi.), the trail climbs steadily through a sugar bush for almost a mile. After crossing two small streams and an old woods road (1.0 mi.), and then another woods road (1.2 mi.), the trail ascends more steeply to its junction with the Long Trail (2.0 mi.) just south of Battell Shelter. Trailhead to LT, 2.0 mi., 3.2 km, 2 h (Rev. 1 h).

JERUSALEM TRAIL. In South Starksboro turn south off Vt. 17 onto the Jerusalem Road, 3.2 mi. east of Vt. 116 and 6.6 mi. west of the Long Trail crossing at Appalachian Gap. After 1.2 mi. on Jerusalem Rd. bear left onto Jim Dwire Rd. and follow it 0.5 mi. to the trailhead on the right. Roadside parking space is limited.

From the road (0.0 mi.), the trail ascends easily through open hardwoods, crosses a logging road and finally ascends more steeply to its junction with the Long Trail (2.4 mi.) just south of the Barton Trail. Jim Dwire Road to LT, 2.4 mi., 3.9 km, 2¼ h (Rev. 1¼ h).

BEANE TRAIL. At a point 2.7 mi. west of the LT crossing at Appalachian Gap and 6.7 mi. east of Vt. 17's northern junction with Vt. 116, take the Huntington Road north from Vt. 17. Follow this road 2.4 mi. through Hanksville and then take a public road east 0.1 mi. north of the village (at a large sign for the Huntington River Tree Farm), cross a bridge and at 0.5 mi., turn right and then immediately left onto Carse Road. At 1.5 mi. there is parking on the north side of the road (large bend) before the farmhouse (old Beane Farm).

The Beane Trail begins at a gate (0.0), then follows an old, grassy road before turning right and ascending into the woods. The trail climbs moderately and crosses two brooks before reaching Birch Glen Camp with the Long Trail junction (1.5 mi.) 100 ft. beyond. Carse Road to LT, 1.5 mi., 2.4 km, 1¼ h (Rev. 1 h).

DIVISION 9

Birch Glen Camp to Bolton Mountain

Take Note

In this division the Long Trail crosses Camel's Hump, the state's highest undeveloped mountain. It is one of three sites in the state with alpine vegetation. Please take care to do the "rock walk" and walk only on the rocks, not the plants. See pages 120 to 121 for information about Camel's Hump.

Backpacking groups camping on Camel's Hump should use the Hump Brook Tenting Area to minimize impact on the mountain's heavily used shelter sites.

From Lincoln Gap to the Winooski River, the Long Trail is called the Monroe Skyline in honor of Prof. Will S. Monroe who led the efforts to build this section of the Trail.

Side trails in this division are numbered to correspond with the Mt. Mansfield/Camel's Hump pocket map at the back of the book.

The Long Trail now follows the route of the Bamforth Ridge Trail from Gorham Lodge to a parking lot on River Road. Due to this relocation the former Long Trail route through Honey Hollow and the Honey Hollow Tent Site are now closed.

Suggested Hikes

DUCK BROOK SHELTER. This short but rugged hike north on the Long Trail from U.S. 2 offers several good views of the Winooski Valley. Round trip, 3.4 mi., 2¼ h.

MT. ETHAN ALLEN. This moderate ascent of the north peak of Mt. Ethan Allen (el. 3,680') via Forest City and Long Trails offers good views. Round trip, 6.4 mi., 4¾ h.

BAMFORTH RIDGE. This rewarding, but challenging, climb of Camel's Hump is the longest and most difficult ascent of the mountain. Follow the Long Trail south from the River Road over the Bamforth Ridge to the summit. There are excellent views along the way. Round trip, 12.4 mi., 8½ h.

Camping and Fires

The Long Trail in Division 9 south of the Winooski River primarily traverses state land of Camel's Hump State Park. North of the Winooski River the Trail crosses private property. Camping is allowed only at shelters and tenting areas. Tenting at shelters is permitted only if a shelter is filled to capacity. Small wood fires, although discouraged, are permitted in established fire rings at some shelters and the tenting areas. Follow leave-no-trace guidelines (pages 4 to 6) to minimize impact on the Long Trail System. *Exception:* Fires are prohibited at Montclair Glen and Gorham Lodges to protect the vulnerable vegetation at these sites.

Winter Use

Camel's Hump is a challenging winter ascent. Its gentle lower slopes, particularly on the east side with open hardwood forest, are popular with skilled backcountry skiers. The LT crosses the Catamount Trail in Huntington Gap. A section of the Catamount Trail passes through the Honey Hollow area of Camel's Hump State Park.

9

Access to Long Trail

RIVER ROAD. From Jonesville cross the bridge over the Winooski River (0.0 mi.) and take the first left onto the River Road. Continue east until reaching a large parking lot maintained year-round by the state on the south side (right) of

River Road (3.2 mi.). From the junction of U.S. 2 and Vt. 100 South in Waterbury, follow Vt. 100 South (0.0 mi.), take the first right, continue straight through a small intersection and follow the River Road west to the lot (7.7 mi.).

U.S. 2. The Long Trail crosses this highway in Jonesville next to the post office opposite the bridge over the Winooski River, 3.5 mi. east of Richmond and 10.0 mi. west of Vt. 100 North in Waterbury. There is limited parking opposite the post office by the railroad tracks.

BOLTON NOTCH ROAD. From Jonesville, follow U.S. 2 east 1.0 mi. and turn north (left) on the Bolton Notch Road. There is limited parking at the Long Trail crossing, 2.7 mi. north of U.S. 2.

Camel's Hump Area

The ridgeline of Camel's Hump makes the mountain one of the most distinctive peaks in the Green Mountains. It ties with Mt. Ellen (4,083') for Vermont's third highest mountain.

The Abenaki called Camel's Hump the "saddle mountain," and Samuel de Champlain's explorers named it *le lion couchant*, translated "the couching [not crouching] lion" or, in more contemporary language, "the sleeping lion." Either name is more descriptive of the mountain's profile seen from the east or west than is Camel's Hump, a name amended by Zadock Thompson in 1830 from the less genteel "Camel's Rump" listed on Ira Allen's 1798 map.

Camel's Hump is the only undeveloped peak over 4,000' elevation in Vermont. State land acquisition began in 1911 with a gift of 1,000 acres, including the summit, from Col. Joseph Battell of Middlebury, Vt. The present size of Camel's Hump State Park is 20,315 acres. In 1965 the summit area was designated a State Natural Area; in 1968 it was designated a National Natural Landmark; and in 1969 the Vermont General Assembly expanded this protected zone, making the mountain itself the focal point of Camel's Hump Forest Reserve.

The summit of Camel's Hump supports one of three communities of alpine vegetation in the Green Mountains. Several of these tiny flowers and grasses growing above tree-line are listed on the endangered plant list in Vermont.

Note: Although these plants are hardy to the weather, they are extremely fragile to foot traffic. Please take special care to do the "rock walk" and walk only on the rocks, not the plants. Above treeline, walk only on marked trails. Please leash dogs. Camping is not permitted in the alpine zone of Camel's Hump. For information about alpine areas turn to pages 44 to 46.

Camel's Hump is one of the most heavily visited peaks in the Northeast. Each year 20,000 people and hundreds of dogs hike to the summit. This use has severely damaged the alpine ecosystem. GMC summit caretakers are on duty at or near the summit to aid hikers and explain the fragile nature of the alpine area. The caretaker program on Camel's Hump is sponsored by the GMC and the Vermont Department of Forests, Parks, and Recreation.

Long Trail Description

From the **Beane Trail (0.0 mi.)** junction, 100 ft. from **Birch Glen Camp,** the Long Trail contours around the north side of Beane Mtn., crosses two woods roads, and soon reaches **Huntington Gap (1.5 mi.).** Long ago a road passed through the gap. Today both a snowmobile trail and the Catamount Trail run through the gap.

The LT climbs northwesterly to the west side of the ridge, which it then crosses (2.0 mi.) to slab the east slope through mature woods to **Cowles Cove Shelter (2.9 mi.).** This log lean-to, with space for 8, was named for Judge Clarence Cowles of Burlington, a charter member of the GMC who helped build many trails, especially in the Monroe Skyline section. It was built in 1956 by the New York Section under the direction of Prof. Roy O. Buchanan. The brook 100 ft. south is a dependable water source. Nearby stands the remains of the old Cowles Cove Shelter, built in 1920 by Professor Monroe. **Birch Glen Camp to Cowles Cove Shelter, 2.9 mi., 4.7 km, 1¾ h (SB 1½ h).**

9

From the shelter the Trail rises gradually and, soon after gaining the crest of the ridge, reaches **Hedgehog Brook Trail (1) (3.8 mi.)** on the right, which descends 2.0 mi. east to a public road 5.0 mi. from Vt. 100.

Beyond the junction, the Long Trail becomes increasingly rugged and more interesting. Soon a spur trail (4.0 mi.) leads left a short distance to a small glacial pothole, one of the highest of its kind in New England. Shortly beyond the spur trail the LT emerges from the woods and begins an up-and-down scramble over bare rocks and cobbles to the summit of **Burnt Rock Mtn. (4.4 mi.)**. The summit provides views in nearly every direction. North are views of Mts. Ira and Ethan Allen and Camel's Hump, to the west lies Lake Champlain, to the east are the Northfield Mountains and Granite Mountains, and to the south stands Lincoln Mtn.

North of the main summit lie several other knobs. The Trail uses a ladder to drop into Ladder Ravine (4.8 mi.), and then begins a steady ascent along the "Paris Skidway," an old logging sluiceway (5.5 mi.). After some rough going the LT finally reaches **Mt. Ira Allen (5.9 mi.)** about 100 ft. below the summit, which is at the top of the cliff west of the Trail. Slabbing the sidehill and slowly descending, the Long Trail passes Rock Refuge, a shallow cave in the rocks to the left of the Trail. This point of interest is one of many named by Professor Monroe.

After more rough scrambling but little ascent, the LT begins a short, steep climb to the south peak of **Mt. Ethan Allen** (6.9 mi.) and, after a small dip, reaches the **north peak (7.0 mi.)**. Here there is a good lookout facing east. Descending, a small rocky area is reached (7.2 mi.) from which Camel's Hump seems to loom to the north. A fairly steep descent to a more moderate grade brings the hiker to a junction **(7.8 mi.)** with the south end of the **Allis Trail (2)**.

At the junction, the Long Trail turns left, dropping to **Montclair Glen Lodge (8.0 mi.)**, a log cabin with bunks for 10, built in 1948 by the Long Trail Patrol for the New York Section. There is a brook 80 ft. east. During the hiking season a GMC caretaker is in residence to assist hikers and maintain the site and nearby trails. A small fee is charged for overnight use. Wood fires are prohibited at Montclair Glen Lodge. **Cowles Cove Shelter to Montclair Glen Lodge, 5.1 mi., 8.2 km, 3¼ h (SB 3¼ h).**

From Montclair Glen Lodge, north via the Long Trail, it is 200 ft. to the site of the original Montclair Glen Shelter where the **Forest City Trail (3)** descends westerly to a road leading to Huntington Center. The LT soon reaches **Wind Gap (8.2 mi.)**, with the north end of the **Allis Trail (2)** leading to the right and, just beyond, the **Dean Trail (4)**, which heads east 0.8 mi. to **Hump Brook Tenting Area** and joins the Monroe Trail 1.0 mi. from the Long Trail.

In Wind Gap the craggy cliffs of the mountain's southernmost ridge rise above the hiker, but the LT turns to the west, then east, to ascend the ridge by a more moderate route. Breaking into the open, the Trail follows the eastern slope of the ridge, with views of the beaver ponds alongside the Dean Trail. Clambering over rocks and through thickets of scrub, the LT then turns left into the woods.

Reaching the west side of the ridge, the LT skirts two minor knobs with intermittent views. After a steep ascent the Trail reaches, at treeline, the south end of the yellow-blazed **Alpine Trail (5) (9.7 mi.)**, which diverges right to circle the east side of the summit cone to its northern terminus at the Long Trail (a good way around the summit in inclement weather).

Note: Above treeline, walk only on the rocks, not the fragile alpine plants. Please leash dogs. Above the Alpine Trail junction the LT bears west around the forbidding south wall of the cone, climbs the exposed western face, and arrives at the **summit of Camel's Hump (9.9 mi.)** from the southwest.

The views from the summit are extensive and remarkable. To the south, beyond the Allens, General Stark Mtn. can be identified by its wide ski trails. Next is Lincoln Mtn. and far beyond, to the left, are Killington and Pico Peaks. To the north, the Bamforth Ridge leads to the Winooski Valley. Beyond the valley Mt. Mansfield stands out, with the Sterling Range and the Worcester Range to its right. Farther north is Belvidere Mtn., distinguished by the white scar of its asbestos mine, and just to the right of it is Owl's Head in Canada. Mt.

MUD SEASON

The Green Mountain Club encourages hikers to avoid higher-elevation trails during the spring "mud season" (late March through the end of May). Snow melt creates extremely muddy trails and makes them vulnerable to damage from foot traffic, which is often compounded when hikers walk beside the trail to avoid the mud.

Spring and Fall Hiking Guidelines

- If a trail is so muddy that you need to walk on the vegetation beside it, turn back, and seek an alternative area to hike.

- Hike in the hardwood forest at lower elevations.

- The State of Vermont closes trails in the Camel's Hump and Mt. Mansfield areas from mid-April until Memorial Day weekend. Please do not hike here. Also avoid Stratton Mtn., the Coolidge Range (Killington to Pico Peaks), Lincoln Ridge (Lincoln Gap to Appalachian Gap), and Jay Peak.

- Late fall and winter thaws can present similar conditions.

Washington is a little south of east, dominating the White Mountains' Presidential Range, with the Franconia Ridge and Mt. Moosilauke nearer and to the south. Much nearer are the Granite Mountains in Vermont and just across the valley are the Northfield Mountains. Mt. Marcy is somewhat south of west, surrounded by a contingent of Adirondack peaks, while Whiteface stands alone to the north of the High Peaks. Lake Champlain is visible for much of its length, with the Champlain Valley and its many small eminences in the foreground.

Heading north from the summit, the LT drops down to **Camel's Hump Hut Clearing (10.2 mi.)**. This was the site over a century ago of a rustic frame hotel (summit house), which failed financially and finally burned down in 1875. The clearing was later adopted by the Camel's Hump Club of Waterbury as a location for three tin huts that provided shelter for hikers from 1912 until the early 1950s. West from the clearing the **Burrows Trail (6)** descends 2.1 mi. to a road leading to Huntington Center. To the east the **Monroe Trail (7)** leads 3.1 mi. to the parking area at the Couching Lion Farm site.

Beyond the clearing, the Long Trail enters the woods and descends steeply to a junction with a **spur** leading 100 ft. to **Gorham Lodge (10.6 mi.)**.

Gorham Lodge, a log cabin with bunks for 12, was built in 1950 by the Long Trail Patrol in memory of H. W. Gorham, with funding from the New York Section. The lodge was extensively rebuilt in 1981 by the patrol and GMC volunteers. A brook to the east provides water. A seasonal GMC caretaker educates and assists hikers and maintains the site and nearby trails. A small overnight use fee is charged. Wood fires are prohibited at Gorham Lodge. **Montclair Glen Lodge to Gorham Lodge, 2.6 mi., 4.2 km, 2¼ h (SB 1¾ h).**

From Gorham, the Long Trail descends Camel's Hump via the former Bamforth Ridge Trail, the original Trail route built by Prof. Will Monroe in the early 1920s. In 1996, the Long Trail Patrol and Montpelier Section volunteers returned the Long Trail to the Bamforth Ridge and closed

9

both the old route through Honey Hollow and the Honey Hollow Tent Site. The ridge is named for dedicated GMC trail maintainer Eugene Bamforth.

North of the Gorham spur junction, the Long Trail soon leaves the woods and reaches the north end of the **Alpine Trail (11.0 mi.)** on the right. From here the LT descends steeply over rocks and continues over the ridge, in and out of woods, with fine views in various directions. Descending steeply, the Long Trail re-enters the woods and goes over several prominent knobs until reaching **Spruce Knob (14.2 mi.).** Beyond Bolton Lookout (14.3 mi.), the Trail drops to Duxbury Window (14.5 mi.). The Trail descends the ridge until it reaches the former site of Buchanan Lodge (15.2 mi.). From here, the LT follows abandoned logging roads until it crosses **Gleason Brook (15.5 mi.).** After a moderate descent through open glades, the Long Trail reaches **River Road (16.1 mi.)** where there is a large parking lot. Vt. 100 in Waterbury is 7.7 mi. east. The Trail turns left onto this dirt road and follows it along the Winooski River, then turns right (19.2 mi.) at a stop sign onto another road, which leads north to the Winooski River Bridge, a crossing of the New England Central Railway, and **U.S. 2** (Burlington-Montpelier Highway) in **Jonesville (19.3 mi.). Gorham Lodge to Jonesville, 8.7 mi., 14.1 km, 4½ h (SB 6½ h).**

East from Jonesville on U.S. 2 it is 10.0 mi. to Waterbury. West it is 3.5 mi. to Richmond. Jonesville (el. 326') is the lowest elevation on the LT. The Jonesville post office is located just west of the Long Trail on U.S. 2. Mail may be sent here in care of General Delivery, marked "Hold for Long Trail Hiker." See page 226 for more information.

From Jonesville the Long Trail proceeds directly north on a narrow dirt road and, after passing beneath Interstate 89, soon reaches a power line crossing. Here the Trail leaves the road and turns east to ascend along the power line. Bearing north from the power line (21.0 mi.), the Trail climbs to a lookout with fine local views of the Winooski Valley and enters the woods (20.5 mi.), eventually reaching **Duck Brook Shelter (21.0 mi.).**

This open-front frame shelter, with space for 12, was built by the Long Trail Patrol for the Burlington Section in 1966. Duck Brook, in a deep ravine below the shelter, is the best water supply. **Gorham Lodge to Duck Brook Shelter, 10.4 mi., 16.7 km, 6 h (SB 7½ h).**

From the shelter the LT follows an old woods road a short distance, crosses a brook, then turns sharply left, leaving the road. Heading north and climbing steadily, the Trail passes three lookouts and descends gradually, then steeply, before ascending to the top of the ridge, from which there is a limited view to the west. The Long Trail then begins a gradual descent to a logging road (23.5 mi.), crosses Duck Brook (24.0 mi.) and continues to the unpaved **Bolton Notch Road (24.3 mi.),** along which it is 2.7 mi. south to U.S. 2. From the road this crossing is very hard to see; on the east side of the Bolton Notch Road the Trail coincides with an abandoned road that splits off from the start of a driveway. There is limited parking on the east side of the road.

Crossing Bolton Notch Road, the Long Trail begins its ascent. The LT here is difficult to follow along a series of woods roads. Continuing, the Trail crosses several unreliable small brooks, passes through a logged-over area, and finally reaches the top of Oxbow Ridge (25.2 mi.), which it follows north. After passing several lookouts to the east, then one to the west (25.5 mi.) that offers a good view of Lake Champlain and the Adirondacks, the LT climbs along the ridge to yet another lookout (25.9 mi.) with views of Camel's Hump, Honey Hollow, and Robbins Mtn. to the south, and the Adirondacks to the west.

Continuing from the lookout, the Trail reaches the highest point on the ridge and, bearing easterly, reaches a spur trail (26.0 mi.) that leads right 120 ft. to a lookout, with Bolton Valley in the distance. The LT bears left, descends, crosses a brook (26.5 mi.) and reaches a **spur trail (26.6 mi.)** on the right leading 0.3 mi. to **Buchanan Shelter.**

Buchanan Shelter, named for Prof. Roy O. Buchanan, founder of the Long Trail Patrol and for 36 years its leader, was built in 1984 by the Burlington Section. This shelter has an open-front porch and enclosed bunkroom with space for

9

16. Water is located 100 ft. to the north. **Duck Brook Shelter to Buchanan Shelter 5.9 mi., 9.5 km, 4 h (SB 3½ h).**

The long climb from Buchanan Shelter to Bolton Mtn. is characterized by numerous ups and downs. From the shelter spur trail, the LT continues with minor changes in elevation to reach another **spur trail (27.6 mi.)** leading 150 ft. to **Harrington's View**, named after its discoverer, Jack Harrington of the Burlington Section. It offers exceptional views of Mt. Mansfield, Bolton Mtn., Bolton Valley, and Ricker Mtn.

After a short descent the Trail continues in an easterly manner, crosses a small brook (28.2 mi.), and makes a zigzag ascent to a wooded, unnamed summit, el. 3,236', (29.0 mi.) with a good view south to Camel's Hump. From this summit the LT descends gradually to a saddle (29.7 mi.) and then climbs to the wooded summit of **Bolton Mtn. (30.3 mi.).**

GROUP HIKING—CAMEL'S HUMP

Groups backpacking near Camel's Hump are asked to use the designated group tenting area. The lodges are small, heavily used, and not designed for groups. Please use:

- *Hump Brook Tenting Area:* on the Dean Trail near Hump Brook.

- Tent platforms, communal fireplace, and outhouse are provided. No overnight fee.

- If you are planning a group hike, contact the GMC for guidebook updates and assistance in planning.

Side Trails

Refer to the Mt. Mansfield/Camel's Hump pocket map in the back of this book or the division map on page 207 for the location of numbered trails. (The Hedgehog Brook Trail is not included on the pocket map.) All of the Camel's Hump side trails are marked with blue blazes, with the exception of the Alpine Trail, which is marked in yellow.

1. HEDGEHOG BROOK TRAIL. Hikers are allowed to use the trail because of the generosity of the private landowners. Please stay on the trail and respect all lands. Watch for signs. Drive north on Vt. 100 from Waitsfield (0.0 mi.) to the North Fayston Road at 5.0 mi. Turn left (west) on this road. At 7.5 mi. this road turns to dirt. At a four-way intersection (9.2 mi.) continue on the middle route, Big Basin Road, until it ends (10.2 mi.) at a metal gate with designated parking for about 8 cars.

The start of the trail has been relocated; please do not follow the old woods road. The trail now leaves the parking lot at the trail sign and then immediately crosses a branch of Shepard Brook. After again crossing the branch of Shepard Brook, (0.9 mi.), the trail rises gradually through hardwoods, steepens as it enters the softwoods, then slabs left and finally right to the ridge (2.0 mi.) and the Long Trail. Big Basin Road to LT, 2.0 mi., 3.2 km, 1¾ h (Rev. 1 h).

2. ALLIS TRAIL. The southern end of this short loop trail begins on the Long Trail at a junction 0.2 mi. south of Montclair Glen Lodge. From this junction it is 300 ft. north to a view south to Mt. Ethan Allen. Allis Lookout is another 100 ft. further, with views to the north. The trail continues north, returning to the Long Trail (0.3 mi.) at Wind Gap.

3. FOREST CITY TRAIL. From Huntington Center follow the Huntington Road to the Camel's Hump Road, 6.1 mi. north of Vt. 17 and 2.5 mi. south of the post office in Huntington. Continue 2.8 mi. east on the Camel's Hump Road to a road junction and the trailhead. There is limited parking at the trailhead. To the left the road continues 0.7 mi. to the beginning of the Burrows Trail and a larger parking lot. The Forest City–Burrows Connector (8) joins these two trails.

9

From the road junction (0.0 mi.) the trail follows a logging road, crosses Brush Brook, and reaches Forest City, the site of a former CCC camp, (0.3 mi.). Continuing on the logging road, the trail recrosses Brush Brook, reaches a junction with the Forest City–Burrows Connector (9) (0.8 mi.), and soon bears right, leaving the road. Climbing gradually, with several brook crossings, the Long Trail is reached (2.0 mi.) 200 ft. north of Montclair Glen Lodge. To the left it is 1.9 mi. to Camel's Hump on the Long Trail. Camel's Hump Road to LT, 2.0 mi., 3.2 km, 1¾ h (Rev. 1¼ h). Camel's Hump Road to Camel's Hump, 3.9 mi., 6.3 km, 3½ h (Rev. 2¼ h).

4. DEAN TRAIL. This trail diverges left (south) from the Monroe Trail (7) 1.3 mi. from the Couching Lion Farm site and makes a popular day hike loop with that trail and the LT over Camel's Hump. From the Monroe Trail (0.0 mi.), the Dean Trail heads west, crosses Hump Brook (0.2 mi.), and reaches a spur on the left (0.3 mi.), which leads 0.1 mi. to Hump Brook Tenting Area, with tent platforms and campsites. The trail continues to an area of extensive beaver activity (0.7 mi.) with fine views of Camel's Hump. Just beyond the beaver ponds is Wind Gap (1.0 mi.), where the Dean Trail ends at a junction with the Long Trail and the Allis Trail (2). South on the LT, it is 0.2 miles to Montclair Glen Lodge and a junction with the Forest City Trail. The Allis Trail, which goes off to the left, or southeast, rejoins the LT 0.3 mi. south of this junction. To the right (north) on the Long Trail, it is 1.5 mi. to a junction with the Alpine Trail and 1.7 mi. to Camel's Hump summit. Couching Lion parking lot to Montclair Glen Lodge, 2.5 mi., 4.0 km, 2 h (Rev. 1¼ h). Parking lot to summit, 4.0 mi., 6.4 km, 3½ h (Rev. 2 h).

5. ALPINE TRAIL. Named by Will S. Monroe for one of his Saint Bernard dogs, the yellow-blazed Alpine Trail skirts the east side of the Camel's Hump summit cone and is rarely in deep woods. Its southern end at the LT (0.0 mi.) is 0.2 mi. south of the summit. Descending moderately, the Alpine Trail crosses the Monroe Trail (7) (0.5 mi.) and then proceeds, mostly in the open with views to the summit and with little change in elevation, to a brook crossing (1.0 mi.). Continuing northward over Basque Ledges, the trail then descends to its northern end at the Long Trail (1.7 mi.) at a point 0.4 mi. north of Gorham Lodge and 1.1 mi. north of the summit of Camel's Hump. LT south of Camel's Hump to LT north of Camel's Hump, 1.7 mi., 2.7 km, 1 h (Rev. 1½ h).

6. BURROWS TRAIL. Follow the directions to the Forest City Trail (3). From the Forest City trailhead continue on the Camel's Hump Road 0.7 mi. The trail begins at a large gravel parking lot at the end of the road (3.5 mi. east of Huntington Center). The Forest City–Burrows Connector (8) leaves south from the trailhead to the Forest City Trail.

Entering the woods (0.0 mi.), in what is recognized internationally as a site for research on acid deposition, soils, insects, and other forest health issues, the trail soon crosses a brook, ascends moderately to the ridge between Camel's Hump and Bald Hill (1.7 mi.) and follows the ridge to the Long Trail at the Camel's Hump Hut Clearing (2.1 mi.). To the right it is 0.3 mi. to the summit. Camel's Hump Road to LT, 2.1 mi., 3.4 km, 2¼ h (Rev. 1 h). Camel's Hump Road to Camel's Hump, 2.4 mi., 3.9 km, 2½ h (Rev. 1½ h).

7. MONROE TRAIL. This trail begins at the west end of the Couching Lion Farm site parking lot. At the junction of U.S. 2 and Vt. 100 South in Waterbury (0.0 mi.), turn south on Vt. 100 and then take the first right. Continue straight on this road through a small intersection and follow the River Road west. At 5.1 miles turn south (left) onto the Camel's Hump Road. There are several side roads off the Hump Road so be sure to stay on the main road. At 6.5 mi. bear left at a fork and cross a bridge. At 8.6 mi. reach a large parking lot at the Couching Lion caretaker cabin. This is a very popular trailhead and parking space is at a premium on weekends. The final 0.4 mi. of this road is not maintained in winter, but the state maintains a winter recreation (and summer overflow) parking area to the east on a spur road opposite the last

9

house on the road. From the Jonesville bridge, the Camel's Hump Road is 5.8 mi. east on the River Road.

Couching Lion Farm was left to the State of Vermont by the estate of Prof. Will S. Monroe, who planted, along with white spruce, red and Scotch pines, Douglas fir, Japanese and eastern larch trees, the Norway spruces from which the caretaker cabin was built in 1973. Professor Monroe, his sister Katherine, and his beloved dogs are buried in a small cemetery 100 ft. north of the parking lot.

From the parking lot (0.0 mi.) the Monroe Trail immediately enters the woods, turns sharp left, and continues a short distance before beginning a moderate ascent. The Dean Trail (4) diverges to the left (1.3 mi.) and then, continuing to climb, the Monroe Trail crosses Hump Brook (2.1 mi.), where a spur trail leads left 50 ft. to a good lookout.

Recrossing the brook, turning north and ascending more steeply, the trail crosses the Alpine Trail (5) (2.5 mi.) and continues to the Long Trail (3.1 mi.) at the Camel's Hump Hut Clearing. Camel's Hump summit is 0.3 mi. south on the Long Trail. Couching Lion parking lot to LT, 3.1 mi., 5.0 km, 2¾ h (Rev. 1½ h). Parking lot to Camel's Hump, 3.4 mi., 5.5 km, 3 h (Rev. 1¾ h).

8. FOREST CITY–BURROWS CONNECTOR. This trail starts at the Burrows Trail (6) trailhead and connects with the Forest City Trail to eliminate a road walk in the Burrows –Forest City circuit over Camel's Hump. It bears to the right off the Burrows Trail just beyond the parking lot and heads south, crossing a small brook on a wooden bridge. A few hundred feet farther it crosses a larger bridge over an impressive gorge of Brush Brook and at 0.1 mi. reaches the Forest City Trail. Burrows Trail to Forest City Trail, 0.8 mi., 1.3 km, ½ h. (Rev. ½ h.).

LEAVE NO TRACE

Help preserve a piece of the Long Trail as you enjoy it . . . leave no trace.

- Travel only on foot.
- Stay on the footpath.
- If you packed it in, pack it out!
- Use a backpacking stove. Fires are discouraged.
- If you have a campfire, use an established fireplace. Burn only dead and downed wood.
- Travel and camp quietly and in small groups.
- Camp at areas established for overnight use.
- If camping off trail, camp at least 200 feet from any trail, stream, or pond. Camp below 2,500 feet elevation.
- Wash and rinse dishes away from open water.
- Use outhouses. Otherwise, dispose of human and pet waste in a "cat hole" (4 to 6 inches deep) 200 feet from any water source. Bury toilet paper.
- Carry out all tampons and sanitary napkins.
- Don't carve into trees or shelters. People don't care who loves Sally or where Joe stayed when.
- Take only pictures. Leave the lightest of footprints.
- Keep pets on a leash and away from water sources.

9

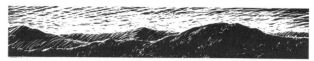

DIVISION 10

Bolton Mountain to Vt. 15 (Lamoille River Bridge)

Take Note

The Long Trail travels mostly above treeline on Mt. Mansfield for 2.3 mi. from the Forehead to the Adam's Apple and is exposed to strong winds and sudden storms. The portions of the LT south from the Forehead and north from the Chin can be treacherous in poor weather. Hikers should be familiar with the side trails (particularly the Forehead Bypass (8) and the Profanity (25) Trails) that can be used to avoid or leave the exposed summit ridge.

Mt. Mansfield, Vermont's highest summit, is one of three sites in the state with alpine vegetation. Take care to do the "rock walk" and walk only on the rocks, not the plants. For more information on Mt. Mansfield, see pages 137 to 139.

Plans are underway to relocate the southern trailhead of the Long Trail in Smugglers' Notch, as well as the Trail through the notch.

Backpacking groups camping on Mt. Mansfield should use the Twin Brooks Tenting Area to minimize impact on the mountain's heavily used shelter sites.

Side trails in this division are numbered to correspond with the Mt. Mansfield/Camel's Hump pocket map in the back of the book.

Due to stricter federal standards for exposure to radio frequency radiation, the Nose is temporarily closed.

Suggested Hikes

NEBRASKA NOTCH. This short and sometimes steep climb on the Lake Mansfield Trail through a glacial cirque features views of the northern wall of the notch, a large beaver pond, and a fine view of Lake Mansfield from Taylor Lodge. Round trip, 3.2 mi., 2 h. Continuing on the Clara Bow Trail (filled with boulders and rock crevices) and returning to Taylor Lodge via the Long Trail adds 0.8 mi.

BEAR HOLLOW. This woods walk on the LT south of Vt. 15 leads to Bear Hollow Shelter. Round trip, 5.2 mi., 3¼ h.

BUTLER LODGE LOOP. This hike, with fine views to the west from Butler Lodge, follows the Nebraska Notch, Long, and Butler Lodge Trails from the Stevensville Road. Round trip, 6.0 mi., 4 h.

MANSFIELD TRAVERSE. Ascending through the picturesque forest of the Haselton Trail, the Nose Dive Ski Trail and the Toll Road under Mt. Mansfield's Nose, this route features a 2.0 mi. alpine ridge walk along the Long Trail north to the Chin, Vermont's highest point (el. 4,393'). A descent on the Long Trail passes Taft Lodge and returns to Vt. 108, less than a mile north of the gondola parking lot (parking for the Haselton Trail). Round trip, 6.5 mi., 4¾ h.

ELEPHANT'S HEAD LOOP. This loop takes the Elephant's Head Trail to Sterling Pond and the LT south to Vt. 108 in Smugglers' Notch, and returns to the trailhead via one of New England's most scenic road walks. The spur trail to the cliffs above Smugglers' Notch is closed to the public from mid-March until mid-August because it is a prime peregrine falcon nesting area. Round trip, 6.5 mi., 4 h.

BEAVER MEADOW. Featuring fine views from the Sterling Range, this rugged trip utilizes the Beaver Meadow, Chilcoot, Long, and Whiteface Trails. This circuit passes Beaver Meadow Lodge and Whiteface Shelter and makes a fine backpack. Round trip, 8.7 mi., 6 h. A climb of Whiteface Mtn. via the LT north lengthens this trip to 9.7 mi., 7 h.

10

Camping and Fires

The Long Trail in Division 10 south of Smugglers' Notch crosses state and University of Vermont land. North of the notch it crosses state and private land. Camping is allowed only at shelters (tenting is allowed only if a shelter is filled to capacity) and tenting areas.

Wood fires are prohibited in Division 10 at all shelters south of Smugglers' Notch to protect the vulnerable vegetation at these sites. Small wood fires, although discouraged, are permitted in established fire rings at Twin Brooks Tenting Area and shelters north of Smugglers' Notch. Follow leave-no-trace guidelines (pages 4 to 6) to minimize impact on the Long Trail System.

Winter Use

All suggested hikes in this division make good snowshoe trips, although some may be longer than indicated owing to unplowed approach roads. The Chilcoot Trail may be too steep for all but the expert snowshoer. Much of the terrain of this division is too difficult for beginner and intermediate cross-country skiers. Vt. 108 through Smugglers' Notch (closed to vehicles in winter) and the Nebraska Notch Trail out of Stevensville make challenging trips for intermediate skiers. Beaver Meadow offers easier terrain for skiing.

Access to Long Trail

SMUGGLERS' NOTCH, VT. 108. There are two LT trailheads on this road. The southern trailhead (where the LT reaches Vt. 108 after descending from Mt. Mansfield) is 8.2 mi. north of Vt. 100 in Stowe and 9.6 mi. south of Vt. 15 in Jeffersonville. A large parking lot on the west side of the road is just north of the trailhead. The northern trailhead (where the LT goes north to Sterling Pond) is opposite a small parking lot just west of the height of land in Smugglers' Notch, 9.8 mi. from Vt. 100 in Stowe and 8 mi. south of Vt. 15 in Jeffersonville.

During the winter a 3.5 mi. stretch of Vt. 108 through Smugglers' Notch between the Mt. Mansfield Ski Area maintenance entrance (0.3 mi. south of the Long Trail) and the Smugglers' Notch Ski Area upper parking lot (1.3 mi. north of the notch height of land) is not plowed. Vt. 108 is designated a Scenic Highway by the Vermont state legislature.

VT. 15. Because the Long Trail follows Vt. 15 east 0.6 mi. over the Lamoille River Bridge (1.8 mi. west of Johnson), there are two trailheads on this road. There is parking at both ends of the Lamoille River Bridge and limited parking at the junction of Vt. 15 and Hogback Road (where the LT heads north, see Division 11).

To avoid a considerable road walk on the LT south, take Vt. 15 west from Johnson. At 2.4 mi., after crossing the bridge, turn south (left) onto a private road. Follow this road to parking at the gated end (3.1 mi.). Be sure to park so as not to block the gate. The private road is 6.7 mi. east on Vt. 15 from Jeffersonville and Vt. 108.

Mt. Mansfield Area

Vermont's highest mountain, Mt. Mansfield (el. 4,393') is known for its distinctive ridgeline, which resembles the profile of a human face, especially when viewed from the east. The names of its more prominent south-to-north features reflect this: Forehead, Nose, Upper and Lower Lips, Chin, and Adam's Apple. The Abenaki called the mountain *Moze-o-de-be-Wadso* (mountain with the head of a moose), and it received its present name from the town of Mansfield, disestablished and divided among adjacent towns over one hundred years ago.

The Mansfield summit ridge supports the largest community of alpine tundra found in Vermont. This unique and delicate plant life is a remnant of the era when ice sheets covered northern New England. Few species are able to survive the extreme conditions of the summit ridge; those that do grow very slowly, and hang in a delicate balance. Mt. Mansfield is the most frequently visited mountain in

10

Vermont with nearly 40,000 visitors walking its upper reaches every year. This use has severely affected its fragile alpine ecosystem.

Note: Although these plants are hardy to the weather, they are extremely fragile to foot traffic. Take special care to do the "rock walk" and walk only on the rocks, not the plants. Above treeline, walk only on marked trails. Please leash dogs. Camping is not permitted in the alpine zone of Mt. Mansfield. For more information about alpine areas, turn to pages 44 to 46.

GMC summit caretakers are stationed on the summit ridge to aid hikers and other visitors and explain the fragile nature of the alpine ecosystem. The summit ridge of Mt. Mansfield, owned and managed by the University of Vermont as a Natural Area, has been declared a State Natural Area and National Natural Landmark. The university, the Stowe Mountain Resort, and the Vermont Department of Forests, Parks and Recreation help fund the caretaker program.

Although most people hike the mountain via a few heavily used trails and the auto Toll Road, the many other trails on the mountain are exciting and challenging. Hikers using these side trails should be in good physical condition and have sturdy boots. Backpackers may not enjoy some of these trails as many of them have ladders and tight squeezes through crevices and ledges.

Base camping or lodging facilities in the area can be found at Smugglers' Notch and Underhill State Parks. Overnight facilities can also be found at hotels and other tourist lodgings in the surrounding area. GMC lodges are often overcrowded and should not be used as "base camps."

PROTECT MT. MANSFIELD'S ALPINE PLANTS. DO THE ROCK WALK!

- Walk only on the rocks, not the plants.
- Leash your dogs and keep them off the plants.

Groups in particular should use Twin Brooks Tenting Area or the group camping area at Underhill State Park. Information is available from the Department of Forests, Parks and Recreation, Essex Junction Regional Office, 111 West Street, Essex Junction, Vermont 05452; (802) 879-6565.

Long Trail Description

From the summit of **Bolton Mtn. (0.0 mi.)** the Long Trail heads easterly, then turns northward as it descends a rugged stretch to **Puffer Shelter (0.5 mi.)**. This shelter was built in 1975 by the Burlington Section, with the help of over one hundred volunteers who carried the materials over Bolton Mtn. to the site. It replaced a log cabin that burned in 1974 and is named in honor of Louis B. Puffer, long active in many capacities with the GMC. There is space for 6. A small brook to the west is an unreliable water source. Wood fires are prohibited at Puffer Shelter. **Buchanan Shelter to Puffer Shelter, 4.5 mi., 7.2 km, 3 h (SB 2½ h).**

After dropping to a sag, the LT ascends the wooded summit of **Mt. Mayo (1.4 mi.)**. Descending, it passes several interesting views of Mt. Mansfield and, after reaching the Mayo-Clark col (2.0 mi.), begins a short climb to the south ridge of **Mt. Clark**. Slabbing the ridge, the Trail passes east of the **summit (2.8 mi.)** and gains a lookout (3.0 mi.) with Lake Mansfield below and the Worcester Range beyond. Heading east, the LT drops steeply over rugged terrain, passes a beaver pond on the right, crosses a beaver dam, and descends moderately to a trail junction **(3.9 mi.)**. To the right, the **Lake Mansfield Trail (1)** leads a short distance to **Taylor Lodge** at the east end of Nebraska Notch, then descends 1.6 mi. to Lake Mansfield and the Nebraska Valley Road. Also to the right, the **Clara Bow Trail (2)** leaves the Lake Mansfield Trail just behind Taylor Lodge.

Taylor Lodge, named after James P. Taylor, founder of the GMC, was constructed in 1978 by members of the Burlington Section, replacing a structure that burned in 1977. The lodge, with an open front "porch," has an enclosed bunkroom with space for 15. Water runs from a

10

Protect and Preserve Hiking Opportunities in Vermont

Join the Green Mountain Club!

Your membership or gift:

- Protects Vermont's high-mountain country.
- Supports trail and shelter maintenance.
- Educates hikers.
- Creates hiking opportunities for you and for generations to come.

To join or make a gift to support the Long Trail, contact the GMC at 4711 Waterbury-Stowe Road, Waterbury Center, Vermont 05677; (802) 244-7037 or www.greenmountainclub.org. Thank you!

reliable spring 0.2 mi. down the Lake Mansfield Trail. Wood fires are prohibited at Taylor Lodge. **Puffer Shelter to Taylor Lodge, 3.5 mi., 5.6 km, 2 h (SB 2¾ h).**

Turning sharply left at the Lake Mansfield Trail junction the LT climbs moderately up a fairly smooth treadway, then descends steeply before passing by the north end of the **Clara Bow Trail (2) (4.3 mi.)**. The Long Trail continues west until it approaches a large, shallow beaver pond, where it turns right and climbs shortly to the **Nebraska Notch Trail (3) (4.6 mi.),** which descends 1.5 mi. west to the Stevensville Road leading to Underhill Center.

The LT continues from the junction and slabs the west slope of Mt. Dewey, crossing two brooks (5.8 and 5.9 mi.). Beyond this second brook, the Long Trail reaches a **spur trail (6.0 mi.)** on the left, which leads 100 ft. west to the **Twin Brooks Tenting Area**. Tent platforms are provided, and small wood fires are permitted in the established fireplaces. The water supply is a brook 0.2 mi. south via the LT.

Continuing northward from the junction, the Trail crosses another brook (6.2 mi.), then crosses the Underhill Cross-Country Ski Trail (6.3 mi.), which can be followed east to a rock feature called the Devil's Dishpan near the ridgeline, before climbing to the ridge (6.8 mi.). The LT reaches the **Wallace Cutoff (5) (7.2 mi.)** and the **Butler Lodge Trail (4) (7.3 mi.)**, which both lead about 0.1 mi. west to **Butler Lodge**.

Butler Lodge, of log construction, was erected by the Long Trail Patrol in 1933. It is named for Mabel Taylor Butler, who was a member of the Burlington Section and a lover of the Green Mountains. There are bunks and loft space for 14.

Water, though unreliable in late summer, is available at a small brook 75 ft. to the east. During the hiking season a GMC caretaker is in residence to educate and assist hikers and maintain the site and nearby trails. A small fee is charged for overnight use. Wood fires are prohibited at Butler Lodge. **Taylor Lodge to Butler Lodge, 3.5 mi., 5.6 km, 2½ h (SB 2 h).**

From the lodge there are impressive views of the Green Mountain peaks to the south, the Champlain Valley and Adirondacks to the west, and the south escarpment of the Forehead of Mt. Mansfield to the north and east. From the Lodge the **Butler Lodge Trail (4)** continues 1.9 mi. west to the Stevensville Road leading to Underhill Center. The **Rock Garden Trail (7)** heads north from the Lodge to the **Maple Ridge Trail (9)**. The **Wampahoofus Trail (10)** climbs north for 0.8 mi. to the Long Trail at the Forehead.

Just past the Butler Lodge Trail junction the LT passes through the **Needle's Eye** and reaches the south end of the **Forehead Bypass (8) (7.4 mi.)**. This trail is the recommended route in stormy weather.

Note: Above treeline, take care to walk only on the rocks, not the fragile alpine plants. Please leash dogs. The Trail takes the left fork and begins a steep and rough climb over rocks and ledges, using ladders in some places. Presently the LT reaches the highest point of the **Forehead (8.1 mi.), Mt. Mansfield's southernmost peak**, and the junction of the **Wampahoofus Trail (10)**, which leads west and south 0.2 mi. to the Maple Ridge Trail and 0.8 mi. to Butler Lodge.

Heading north from the Forehead, the LT soon enters the woods and arrives at the north end of the **Forehead Bypass (8)**, an alternate route in stormy weather. Just beyond lies the **TV Road (8.4 mi.)**, which leads right 300 ft. to two television station buildings.

The Long Trail bears left along the TV Road and in 150 ft. passes the south end of the **Lakeview Trail (13)** on the left. After following the **TV Road** a short distance, the LT diverges right into the woods **(8.6 mi.)** and then reaches the end of the Toll Road and the site of the Mt. Mansfield Summit House, now occupied by the Summit Station, and television and radio transmitters. The **Mt. Mansfield Visitor Center** occupies part of the Summit Station and contains displays on the mountain's natural history, research efforts, and ways the public can help protect the rare alpine ecosystem. It is open from Memorial Day to Columbus Day.

One of the last of the famous mountain hotels, the Mt. Mansfield Summit House burned down in 1964 after more than one hundred years of operation. The Toll Road is open during the tourist season and provides automobile access to this point on the Long Trail from Vt. 108. From the Summit Station the Toll Road descends ¼ mi. to a spring and ½ mi. to a spur leading left to the Octagon and the upper station of the Mt. Mansfield quad chair lift. At the spur to the Octagon the **Haselton Trail (14)** bears left down the Nose Dive ski trail. From here the Toll Road descends 4.0 mi. to Vt. 108.

The Long Trail continues past the Summit Station where the coinciding **Lakeview (13)** and **Canyon (17) Trails** lead left. The LT then crosses the **TV Road (8.8 mi.)** where to the right along the road is the south end of the **Amherst Trail (15)**. Also to the right is the **Cliff Trail (16)**, which bears right off the Amherst Trail and follows the east slope of the mountain. Beyond the TV Road the Trail breaks out in the open on the rocky ridge of the mountain. From this point north over the ridge, hikers must take special care to protect the alpine tundra by walking only on the marked trail. The LT passes the **Halfway House Trail (21) (8.9 mi.)** on the left, which descends to a road leading to Underhill Center, and then makes a short ascent to Frenchman's Pile, a cairn marking the spot where a traveller was killed by lightning many years ago. Electrical storms on the exposed ridge of Mt. Mansfield are sudden and severe. Hikers are strongly urged to take shelter on any side trail leading off the ridge for any thunderstorm (they are usually brief). To the east, use the Profanity, Cliff, or Amherst Trails; to the west, the Laura Cowles or Halfway House Trails. Fissures and overhanging rocks along the open ridge do not provide adequate shelter from lightning strikes.

Continuing north from Frenchman's Pile, the Long Trail reaches Drift Rock and the north end of the **Amherst Trail (15) (9.2 mi.)** on the right, a junction with the **Canyon North Trail (18)** on the left, and then ascends the **Upper Lip (9.4 mi.)**. The Trail passes left of the **Lower Lip**

10

(9.6 mi.) (with its Rock of Terror) and reaches the north end of the **Cliff Trail (16) (9.7 mi.)**, which descends to the Cave of the Winds and the upper station of the gondola. To the left at this junction are the **Canyon North Extension (19)** and the **Subway (20)**.

After passing the north end of the Subway, the LT soon comes to another junction **(9.9 mi.)** where the **Sunset Ridge Trail (24)** bears left to descend to Underhill State Park, and the **Profanity Trail (25)** bears right and drops steeply to Taft Lodge. (This is the recommended bad weather alternative route to the precipitous descent on the LT down the Chin.) Straight ahead, the Trail climbs to the **Chin (10.1 mi.)**, Mt. Mansfield's highest peak **(el. 4,393')**.

The view from the Chin is dramatic. East of north lie the Sterling Range, Laraway Mtn., the Cold Hollow Mountains, Belvidere Mtn., Big Jay, and Jay Peak. In Canada Mt. Pinnacle is just east of north and, under extremely favorable conditions, Mt. Royal in Montreal is visible to the northwest. To the east is the Worcester Range and beyond it the Granite Mountains extending northward to the many jumbled peaks of the Northeast Kingdom. Mt. Washington, in New Hampshire, is south of east, and to its left are many summits ranging north to the Connecticut Lakes. Right of Mt. Washington lie the Franconia and Kinsman Ranges and Mt. Moosilauke. To the south the Green Mountains may be seen as far as Killington Peak and include Bolton Mtn., Camel's Hump, Lincoln, and Bread Loaf Mtns. To the west is lofty, pointed Whiteface, which lies to the north of the dense cluster of Adirondack peaks surrounding Mt. Marcy.

From the Chin's highest point, the Trail continues north to an escarpment where there is a view of the Adam's Apple, the Lake of the Clouds, and the northern ridges of the mountain. Across Smugglers' Notch to the east beckons the Sterling Range. Dropping steeply from the Chin on precipitous ledges, the LT levels off at **Eagle Pass (10.4 mi.)**, where the **Hell Brook Trail (29)** bears left to the Lake of the Clouds, then drops precipitously to Vt. 108 in Smugglers' Notch. Descending this trail is not recommended. The **Adam's Apple**

Trail (27) cuts over the **Adam's Apple** to rejoin the Hell Brook Trail near the Lake of the Clouds.

Bearing sharply right, the LT descends through scrub to a junction with the lower end of the **Profanity Trail (25)**. The Trail then reaches a **spur trail (10.7)**, which leades 200 ft. to **Taft Lodge,** perched on a shelf below the Chin, with a view east. This log shelter, the largest of the LT shelters, sleeps 24. Originally built in 1920 by the Burlington Section, it was a gift of Judge Elihu B. Taft of Burlington. In 1996 a large corps of volunteers, spearheaded by the Burlington Section, reconstructed the lodge. Daan Zwick, Taft caretaker from 1938 to 1940, funded the project. Water is found in a reliable brook on the Profanity Trail, approximately 100 yds. from the LT. A GMC caretaker is in residence during the hiking season to assist and educate hikers and maintain the site and nearby trails. A small fee is charged for overnight use. Wood fires are prohibited at Taft Lodge. **Butler Lodge to Taft Lodge, 3.5 mi., 5.6 km, 2¾ h (SB 2¼ h).**

Heading north from the spur junction the LT reaches the **Hell Brook Cutoff (28)**, which contours north to the **Hell Brook Trail (29)**. The Trail then descends moderately, levels slightly at 11.3 mi. to the left of the Chin Clip ski trail, then continues down to **Vt. 108** (Stowe-Jeffersonville Highway) in **Smugglers' Notch (12.4 mi.)**. To the right Vt. 108 leads downhill 0.5 mi. to the Spruce Peak Ski Area, 0.6 mi. to Smugglers' Notch State Park Campground and the Mt. Mansfield Ski Area, 0.8 mi. to the State Ski Dorm and Hostel, and 8.2 mi. to Vt. 100 in Stowe.

Bearing left along the road the Long Trail soon reaches, on the right, **Smugglers' Notch Picnic Area** and the south end of the **Elephant's Head Trail (30) (12.6 mi.)**. The LT continues along the road to **Big Spring** on the right **(13.3 mi.)** and 150 ft. beyond on the left, the **Hell Brook Trail (29)**. Farther along the road follows a zigzag course under Elephant's Head (above right), passes several huge boulders that have fallen from the cliffs above (including "King Rock," which fell in 1910—look for the placard high on the boulder), and ascends to the **Smugglers' Notch height of land**

10

(13.8 mi.). Just beyond, to the left of a large parking area and behind an information booth, is the jumble of boulders known as the Smugglers' Caves (13.9 mi.), the alleged hiding places for smuggled goods during the War of 1812. From here Vt. 108 descends 2.9 mi. to stores in Smugglers' Village and 8 mi. to Jeffersonville and Vt. 15.

Opposite the parking area the **Long Trail** turns right from the road **(13.9 mi.)**, climbs steeply at first on rock steps built by the Long Trail Patrol, then more moderately, and reaches the ski trail connecting the Spruce Peak and Smugglers' Notch Ski Areas (15.0 mi.). The LT turns left onto the ski trail and drops down to the **Sterling Pond Outlet (15.1 mi.)**, which it crosses, then ascends to another junction with a ski trail (15.2 mi.). From the junction the Long Trail follows high ground to **Sterling Pond Shelter (15.3 mi.)** and a junction with the **Elephant's Head Trail (30)**.

This frame shelter, built by the Montpelier Section in 1972, has space for 8. There is a small, unreliable spring 300 ft. east of the shelter on the Elephant's Head Trail (30). A GMC caretaker is on duty during the summer to assist and educate hikers and maintain the site and nearby trails. A small fee is charged for overnight use. Wood fires are prohibited at the shelter. **Taft Lodge to Sterling Pond Shelter, 4.6 mi., 7.4 km, 3 h (SB 3¼ h).**

A second overnight facility, **Watson Camp**, is located a short distance further. It is south of Sterling Pond Shelter on

---

PURIFY YOUR WATER!

Any water supply can become contaminated.

The purity of water supplies cannot be guaranteed.

Filter, boil, or chemically treat water before drinking.

Keep water clean—wash self and dishes away from the source.

---

a short spur trail off the Elephant's Head Trail. This frame camp was donated to the GMC in 1980 by Thomas J. Watson, Jr. of IBM. It has bunk space for 8. The GMC Sterling Pond caretaker is in seasonal residence, and a small fee is charged for overnight use.

From Sterling Shelter, the Long Trail passes over a knob, "the sawtooth," and climbs steadily to the ridge of the Sterling Range, which includes Spruce and Madonna Peaks, and Morse and Whiteface Mtns., and is named for the now-defunct town of Sterling. After crossing one ski trail the LT reaches another, which it follows uphill to the summit of **Madonna Peak (16.5 mi.)**, where open areas afford good views in all directions. The LT passes under the chair lift in back of a warming hut and continues east down a ski trail. The Trail then bears north (left) (16.6 mi.) into the woods and crosses a ski trail before descending to **Chilcoot Pass** and the **Chilcoot Trail (32) (17.3 mi.)**.

From the pass, the Chilcoot Trail bears right, descending steeply 0.8 mi. to **Beaver Meadow Lodge** and the **Beaver Meadow Trail (31)**.

Beaver Meadow Lodge, a log cabin built by the Sterling Section, was completed in 1947. It has space for 15. Water is found in several adjacent brooks. **Sterling Pond Shelter and Watson Camp to Beaver Meadow Lodge, 2.8 mi., 4.5 km, 1¾ h (SB 2½ h).** From Beaver Meadow Lodge the **Whiteface Trail (33)** ascends 1.0 mi. to the Long Trail at Whiteface Shelter.

From Chilcoot Pass, the LT climbs gradually and soon reaches **Hagerman Overlook (17.7 mi.)**, named in memory of Robert L. Hagerman, an active member of the Sterling Section, author of a detailed history of Mt. Mansfield, and former editor of *The Long Trail News*. This overlook affords a unique view of Mt. Mansfield and the Sterling Range. Continuing to climb, steeply at times, the LT passes just east of the summit of **Morse Mtn. (18.0 mi.)** and reaches an overlook of the beaver meadow below. The Trail then bears easterly and descends gradually to **Whiteface Shelter (18.8**

10

GROUP HIKING—MT. MANSFIELD

Groups backpacking in the Mt. Mansfield area are asked to use designated group tenting areas. The lodges are heavily used and not designed to accommodate large groups.

- *Twin Brooks Tenting Area:* South of Butler Lodge on the Long Trail. Tent platforms, communal fireplaces, and toilet facilities are provided. No overnight use fee.

- *Underhill State Park Youth Camping Area, Smugglers' Notch State Park,* and the *State Ski Dorm and Hostel* are also available for use by groups. (Addresses and phone numbers can be found on page 224.)

If you are planning a group hike in the Mt. Mansfield area, contact the Green Mountain Club for updates and assistance in planning.

mi.). Here the **Whiteface Trail (33)** drops to Beaver Meadow Lodge.

Whiteface Shelter, a log lean-to with space for 5, was built by the Long Trail Patrol in 1958. There is a brook 150 ft. east on the Whiteface Trail. From the shelter, Madonna Peak's cone is visible above the Beaver Meadow Basin. To the right of it, the Nose of Mansfield can be seen above Chilcoot Pass and, farther along beyond a shoulder of Morse Mtn., is the Chin. **Sterling Pond Shelter and Watson Camp to Whiteface Shelter, 3.5 mi., 5.6 km, 2¼ h (SB 2¾ h). Beaver Meadow Lodge to Whiteface Shelter, 1.0 mi., 1.6 km, 1 h (Rev. ½ h).**

At Whiteface Shelter, the Long Trail heads north and climbs steeply and circuitously to the wooded summit of **Whiteface Mtn. (19.3 mi.).** A spur trail leads straight ahead to several open spots, which permit views in almost every direction, including vistas of Mt. Mansfield and the west wall of Smugglers' Notch.

Turning north from the summit, the Trail descends moderately following the summit ridge and reaches a shelf with views of the Lamoille River Valley below. Descending steeply along an exposed ridge the LT bears right, passing along an exposed rock outcrop, then crosses Waterman Brook at an overhanging rock. Following the brook the Trail soon reaches a scenic cascade beyond which the LT leaves the brook, enters open hardwoods, then crosses a major logging road. After several minor brook crossings the Long Trail bears right onto an old woods road and descends to **Bear Hollow Shelter (22.4 mi.)** perched on a rocky knoll above the Trail.

Built by Bob Lindemann and the Sterling Section in 1991, this open-faced frame shelter sleeps 12. The water supply is a brook just south of the shelter along the LT. **Whiteface Shelter to Bear Hollow Shelter, 3.6 mi., 5.8 km, 2¼ h (SB 3 h).**

Beyond Bear Hollow Shelter the LT soon crosses French Hill Brook (22.8 mi.), enters a logged area, and follows old logging roads north. After crossing Smith Brook the Trail enters a clearing, turns right, and follows a gravel road. The Long Trail passes an iron gate (25.0 mi.), where parking is available in dry seasons, and continues to an intersection with a narrow public road (25.3 mi.) where there is limited parking. The Trail follows this road north to the **Lamoille Valley Railroad** and, just beyond, **Vt. 15** (Burlington-Morrisville Highway) **(25.7 mi.)**. Jeffersonville and Vt. 108 and 109 are 6.7 mi. west.

Turning right, the LT follows Vt.15 to the east end of the **Lamoille River Bridge (26.3 mi.)**, from which it is another 1.8 mi. east to the village of Johnson.

Side Trails

Refer to the Mt. Mansfield/Camel's Hump pocket map in the back of this book for the location of numbered trails. Many of the side trails are steep and rough. Rugged footwear, planning, and adequate time are recommended.

1. LAKE MANSFIELD TRAIL. This trail begins on private land of the Lake Mansfield Trout Club. Please be considerate of club guests, stay on the trail, and respect all lands and buildings while in this area. To reach this trailhead next to the Lake Mansfield Trout Club, turn west onto the Moscow Road from Vt. 100, 2.5 mi. south of Stowe. Continue on this road, which eventually turns into the Nebraska Valley Road, to its end at the Trout Club, 6.7 mi. west from Vt. 100. Day use parking is available at a large lot just before the Trout Club. The land around the lake and for approximately ¼ mi. beyond is private property.

From the parking lot to the right of the Trout Club buildings (0.0 mi.), the Lake Mansfield Trail parallels the woods road that follows the northern shore of the lake. Near the west end of the lake (0.5 mi.), the trail turns right into the woods, to steadily ascend on an old logging road. The road bears right near the top of the rise and narrows, to stay to the north of a brook in a narrow gorge. The trail passes a spring and gently climbs to a beaver meadow with striking views of the north wall of Nebraska Notch. It crosses the brook and ascends to the Long Trail (1.6 mi.) just beyond Taylor Lodge. Trout Club to LT, 1.6 mi., 2.6 km, 1¼ h (Rev. 1 h).

2. CLARA BOW TRAIL. This trail provides a short, interesting alternate route through Nebraska Notch just north of Taylor Lodge. From behind the lodge (0.0 mi.), the Clara Bow Trail travels north of the Long Trail through the floor of Nebraska Notch and its jumble of enormous boulders. At one point the trail passes under a large rock (tight!) and a vertical drop is negotiated with a ladder. It rejoins the Long Trail 0.4 mi. north of Taylor Lodge. Taylor Lodge to LT, 0.4 mi., 0.6 km, ¼ h (Rev. ¼ h).

3. NEBRASKA NOTCH TRAIL. From Underhill Center take the Pleasant Valley Road north 0.2 mi. and turn east (right) onto the Stevensville Road. Continue east on this road, passing a winter parking lot on the left (Maple Leaf Farm is visible off to the left) at 1.1 mi. and reaching the parking area at the end of the road at 2.8 mi. Although the road is plowed beyond the winter parking area, there is no adequate winter parking beyond the lot.

From the parking area (0.0 mi.), the trail bears right, climbs at an easy grade to an area of beaver activity (1.4 mi.) and bears left to join the Long Trail (1.5 mi.) at the west end of Nebraska Notch. From here it is 0.7 mi. to Taylor Lodge via the LT south. Stevensville Road to LT, 1.5 mi., 2.4 km, 1¼ h (Rev. 1 h).

4. BUTLER LODGE TRAIL. Follow directions to the Nebraska Notch Trail (3). From the parking area, this trail follows a logging road straight ahead from where the Nebraska Notch Trail (3) bears right. After 0.2 mi., the Butler Lodge Trail and Frost Trail (6) leave the road to the left.

From the logging road (0.0 mi.), the Butler Lodge Trail bears right from the Frost Trail and soon begins a steady ascent, eventually passing the Wallace Cutoff (5) (1.6 mi.) 100 ft. before Butler Lodge. Passing right of the lodge, the trail ascends steeply another 0.1 mi. to the Long Trail (1.7 mi.). Parking area to LT, 1.9 mi., 3.0 km, 1½ h (Rev. 1 h).

10

5. WALLACE CUTOFF. From the Long Trail, 0.1 mi. south of the Butler Lodge Trail, the cutoff bears left 0.1 mi. to Butler Lodge, providing a shortcut for the northbound hiker.

6. FROST TRAIL. Follow directions to the Nebraska Notch Trail (3). From the parking area, this trail follows a logging road straight ahead from where the Nebraska Notch Trail bears right. After 0.2 mi., the Butler Lodge Trail (4) and Frost Trail leave the road to the left.

From the logging road (0.0 mi.), the Frost Trail bears left from the Butler Lodge Trail and crosses Stevensville Brook. Climbing steadily, the trail reaches the southernmost knob of Maple Ridge (0.7 mi.), then ascends the ridge to its terminus at the Maple Ridge Trail (9) (1.2 mi.). From here, via the Maple Ridge (9) and Wampahoofus (10) Trails, it is 1.1 mi. to the Forehead. Parking to Forehead, 2.5 mi., 4.0 km, 2½ h (Rev. 1½ h).

7. ROCK GARDEN TRAIL. This trail branches right from the Maple Ridge Trail (9) 0.8 mi. from the start of that trail on the old CCC Road. From this junction (0.0 mi.) the Rock Garden Trail follows the south side of the ridge, mostly in the woods, and eventually reaches the Wampahoofus Trail (10) (0.6 mi.), which it follows to Butler Lodge (0.7 mi.). Underhill State Park to Butler Lodge, 3.6 mi., 5.8 km, 2¼ h (Rev. 1¾ h).

8. FOREHEAD BYPASS. Leaving the Long Trail (0.0 mi.) just north of the Needle's Eye, the Forehead Bypass bears right and slabs the east slope of the Forehead. After the South Link (11) diverges right (0.9 mi.) the bypass climbs to the ridge and joins the Long Trail (1.2 mi.) just south of the TV Road. This trail is less exposed than the LT over the Forehead. However, it is rough and slippery when wet. Hiking time is about the same for both routes. The bypass is recommended during unfavorable conditions. Needle's Eye to TV Road, 1.2 mi., 1.9 km, 1⅓ h (Rev. ¾ h).

9. MAPLE RIDGE TRAIL. From Underhill Center, take the Pleasant Valley Road 1.0 mi. north and turn east onto the Mountain Road (Town Highway 2). Follow the road 2.7 mi. to its end at Underhill State Park (nominal fee for parking). The Mountain Road is 3.8 mi. east of Vt. 15. The upper 1.5 mi. of the Mountain Road to the state park is not plowed in winter.

From the park, the old CCC Road leads uphill past a gate and continues past the start of the Sunset Ridge Trail (24) at a sharp right hand turn 1.0 mi. from the park. The CCC Road then follows a gentler grade and the Halfway House Trail (21) is reached at 1.2 mi. The road then tapers to a trail and, at 2.1 mi. from the park, the Maple Ridge Trail begins (0.0 mi.).

The trail climbs steeply over a rough footpath, then comes out into the open (0.3 mi.), and meets the Frost Trail (6) (0.4 mi.) to the right. It then continues to a junction with the Rock Garden Trail (7) (0.8 mi.), also on the right. The Maple Ridge Trail then climbs steeply over open ledges to its end at the junction with the Wampahoofus Trail (10) (1.3 mi.). Use caution in wet weather, especially if descending. It is another 0.2 mi. via the Wampahoofus Trail to the Long Trail at the Forehead. Underhill State Park to Forehead, 3.6 mi., 5.8 km, 2¾ h (Rev. 2 h).

10. WAMPAHOOFUS TRAIL. This rugged trail heads north from Butler Lodge (0.0 mi.) and for a short distance coincides with the Rock Garden Trail (7), which soon diverges to the left (0.1 mi.). The Wampahoofus Trail continues, ascending over rocks, through crevices and caves, to a point where a large rock overhangs the trail. The Long Trail Patrol thought this rock resembled the open jaws of the mythical "Sidehill Wampahoofus." About 20 ft. beyond, the Maple Ridge Trail (9) comes in on the left (0.6 mi.). Bearing right the Wampahoofus Trail follows the open ridge to the Long Trail at the Forehead. Butler Lodge to Forehead, 0.8 mi., 1.3 km, 1 h (Rev. ½ h).

11. SOUTH LINK. This trail links the Toll Road with the Forehead Bypass (8). From a parking area on the Toll Road opposite the spur to the Octagon, the South Link follows an

10

LEAVE NO TRACE

- Travel only on foot and stay on the trail.
- If you packed it in, pack it out!
- Use a backpacking stove. Fires are discouraged.
- Travel and camp in small groups.
- Camp at areas established for overnight use.
- Wash and rinse dishes away from open water.
- Use outhouses. Otherwise, dispose of waste in a "cat hole" (4 to 6 inches deep) 200 feet from any water source. Bury toilet paper.
- Carry out all tampons and sanitary napkins.
- Please don't carve into trees or shelters.
- Take only pictures. Leave the lightest of footprints.
- Travel and camp quietly.
- Keep pets on a leash and away from water sources.

up-and-down course through the woods for 0.6 mi., reaching its end at the Forehead Bypass, 0.3 mi. south of that trail's northern end at the TV Road.

12. TRIANGLE TRAIL. This trail is temporarily closed.

13. LAKEVIEW TRAIL. Beginning on the TV Road near its southern junction with the Long Trail, the Lakeview Trail soon leaves the woods and emerges on an open shelf. Next it descends over and between large boulders using an underpass, several switchbacks, and a ladder. Following a shoulder of the mountain, this trail offers nearly continuous views of the Champlain Valley and Adirondacks. Re-entering the woods, it joins the Canyon Trail (17) and, crossing the TV Road, ends on the Long Trail at the Summit Station. TV Road to Summit Station, 0.8 mi.

14. HASELTON TRAIL. This trail, named after Judge Seneca Haselton of Burlington, the first vice-president of the GMC and a great lover of Mt. Mansfield, is one of the mountain's oldest trails. This trail begins at the far end of the Mt. Mansfield Ski Area Gondola Base Lodge parking lot (the upper lot), 0.6 mi. south of the Long Trail on Vt. 108. From the parking lot adjacent to the base lodge, pass under the gondola and then follow a ski service road on the left (south) of the Midway Lodge. The trail begins on the left about 50 yds. from where the road enters the woods.

Upon entering the woods (0.0 mi.), the trail climbs steadily. After following a hogback separating two brooks (0.6 mi.) the trail crosses the south brook (0.7 mi.) and ascends steeply to join the Nose Dive Ski Trail (1.3 mi.), which it follows to the Toll Road (1.6 mi.) near the Octagon. From here via the Toll Road, it is 0.5 mi. to the Summit Station and the Long Trail. Parking to LT, 2.1 mi., 3.2 km, 2¼ h (Rev. 1¼ h).

15. AMHERST TRAIL. This trail offers fine views to the east of Mt. Mansfield. The trail begins at the TV Road crossing of the LT (0.0 mi.) north of the summit station. After following the TV Road east for 200 ft., the Amherst Trail then bears left into the woods. The Cliff Trail (16) bears off to the right. The Amherst Trail continues straight, where it passes through a shallow chute, then follows an open shelf before ducking into scrub to meet the Long Trail at Drift Rock. Length, 0.3 mi.

16. CLIFF TRAIL. This trail is not recommended with a large pack. The trail bears right off the Amherst Trail's (15) southern end, 200 yds. from the TV Road crossing of the LT north of the Summit Station. The Cliff Trail begins a series of ascents and descents on the east side of the summit ridge, some involving ladders and cables. After passing through two "caves" and "Wall Street" (0.7 mi.) a spur trail is reached (0.8 mi.) leading right 0.1 mi. to the Cliff House. The Cliff Trail goes straight ahead, passing over and under rocks to another spur on the left (1.0 mi.), leading to the Cave of the Winds where there may be snow as late as July or August. Inside the "cave" (actually a large joint in the bedrock which has closed at the top), there is a sixty-foot descent that should only be attempted by experienced parties with ropes. Beyond the spur trail the Cliff Trail ascends to join the LT just north of the Lower Lip. Length, 1.1 mi., 1¼ h (Rev. 1¼ h).

17. CANYON TRAIL. This trail passes through the Canyon, a large joint in the mountain wall. Beginning on the Long Trail at the Summit Station, it coincides with the Lake View Trail (13) for a short way, then emerges from the woods, and follows an open shelf with views to the west. After squeezing through narrow passages (a backpack won't fit), the trail enters the Canyon, a large chamber overhung by the mountain wall. After climbing ladders and passing through a second chamber, the trail ends at the Halfway House Trail (21), 0.1 mi. west of the Halfway House Trail junction with the Long Trail. Summit Station to Halfway House Trail, 0.6 mi.

18. CANYON NORTH TRAIL. This is a continuation of the Canyon Trail (17) and begins on the Halfway House Trail (21) a few feet west of its junction with the Canyon Trail. Crossing an open shelf, this trail offers fine views to the west before beginning its journey through a series of crevices and caves (tight squeeze!). Regaining the shelf it reaches the Canyon North Extension (19), then bears right, and climbs to its northern end at the Long Trail just south of the Upper Lip. Length, 0.6 mi.

19. CANYON NORTH EXTENSION. This continuation of the Canyon North Trail (18) leaves that trail near its northern end at the LT just south of the Upper Lip. Climbing steadily with fine views to the west, the trail then passes through a crevice and emerges on a narrow ledge, with outstanding views of Sunset Ridge. After another crevice, the trail bears right, passing the start of the Subway (20), and ends on the LT opposite the north end of the Cliff Trail (16). Length, 0.6 mi.

20. THE SUBWAY. Leaving the LT across from the Cliff Trail (16) junction, and joining the Canyon North Extension for a short way, the Subway bears right to a ladder and drops steeply into a maze of crevices, boulders, and caves, which require some agile maneuvering. It is not recommended in unfavorable weather. Leaving the boulders, a steep, winding climb in the open leads back to the LT only a few hundred feet from the starting point. Length, 0.3 mi.

21. HALFWAY HOUSE TRAIL. This trail once served as a bridle path from the old Halfway House to the ridge. Follow the road directions to the Maple Ridge Trail (9) to get to Underhill State Park. This trail branches left from the CCC Road, 0.2 mi. beyond the Sunset Ridge Trail (24) junction and 1.2 mi. from the park. From the road (0.0 mi.) the Halfway House Trail enters the woods and begins a winding course with switchbacks. While ascending steeply over ledges, the Canyon Trail (17) (0.9 mi.) bears right and the Canyon North Trail (18) heads off to the left while the Halfway House Trail continues to the Long Trail (1.1 mi.) on the ridge just south of Frenchman's Pile. From here the Summit Station is 0.2 mi. south and the Chin is 1.2 mi. north. Underhill State Park to Summit Station, 2.5 mi., 4.0 km, 2¼ h (Rev. 1¼ h).

22. LAURA COWLES TRAIL. This trail is named for the first woman president of the Burlington Section and built by her husband, Judge C. P. Cowles, a charter member of the GMC. Follow the road directions to the Maple Ridge Trail (9). This trail branches right from the Sunset Ridge Trail (24) 0.1 mi. above the CCC Road at a point 1.1 mi. from the park. From this junction (0.0 mi.) the Laura Cowles Trail follows a brook, crosses it on a bridge, and climbs the hollow to the south of Sunset Ridge. After passing a small ledge (0.9 mi.), the trail continues in the open and ends on the Sunset Ridge Trail (24) (1.4 mi.) 250 ft. west of the LT. Underhill State Park to Chin, 2.7 mi., 4.3 km, 2¾ h (Rev. 1½ h).

23. CANTILEVER ROCK TRAIL. Cantilever Rock is a horizontal blade of rock 60 ft. above the ground wedged into the vertical face of a 100 ft. cliff, as if thrust there by some angry stone-age Goliath. It is 40 ft. long, 31 of which extend beyond the cliff. Branching left from the Sunset Ridge Trail (24), 0.7 mi. above the CCC Road, the trail leads 0.1 mi. to the scene of this striking phenomenon.

24. SUNSET RIDGE TRAIL. Follow the road directions to the Maple Ridge Trail (9). This trail starts 1.0 mi. above Underhill State Park at a sharp right turn on the CCC Road.

From the CCC Road (0.0 mi.), the trail bears left into the woods and soon reaches the Laura Cowles Trail (22) to the right (0.1 mi.). Continuing past the Cantilever Rock Trail (23) on the left (0.7 mi.), the Sunset Ridge Trail then assumes an easterly course and ascends to the exposed ridge. The trail is marked with cairns (rock piles) in addition to blazes above treeline. An active effort is underway to better delineate the treadway and protect the fragile vegetation it traverses. The trail passes the Story Trail (26) (1.9 mi.) on the left, then the Laura Cowles Trail on the right just below the Long Trail, and finally reaches the LT (2.1 mi.) at a point opposite the Profanity Trail (25), 0.2 mi. south of the Chin. Underhill State Park to Chin, 3.3 mi., 5.3 km, 3 h (Rev. 1¾ h).

25. PROFANITY TRAIL. This trail connects the ridge just south of the Chin with the Long Trail near Taft Lodge and provides a good route around the Chin in unfavorable conditions. Although it is steep (hence the name!), it is fairly sheltered and not as exposed as the LT north off the Chin. There is, however, some exposure close to the summit, and from this trail one cannot see oncoming storms from the west. Note that dogs should be leashed on the lower part of the trail to protect the Taft Lodge water supply. LT to LT, 0.5 mi., 0.8 km, ¼ h (Rev. ½ h).

26. STORY TRAIL. This trail is closed to protect alpine vegetation.

27. ADAM'S APPLE TRAIL. From the junction of the LT and Hell Brook Trail (29) in Eagle Pass this short trail climbs 0.1 mi. to the open summit of the Adam's Apple, where there are impressive views of the Chin, the east wall of the mountain, and the Lake of the Clouds. It then descends 0.1 mi. to rejoin the Hell Brook Trail. Length, 0.2 mi.

28. HELL BROOK CUTOFF. Leaving the Hell Brook Trail (29) 0.9 mi. above Vt. 108, this trail contours south 0.7 mi. to the Long Trail.

29. HELL BROOK TRAIL. This trail starts on Vt. 108 in Smugglers' Notch, 9.1 mi. north of Vt. 100 in Stowe and 8.7 mi. south of Vt. 15 in Jeffersonville, 150 ft. north of and across the road from the Big Spring pullout, which provides limited parking for hikers. Vt. 108 is not plowed beyond the ski area maintenance entrance, 1.2 mi. south, in winter. Descending this trail is not recommended.

From the highway (0.0 mi.) the trail climbs steeply to the ridge, frequently on precipitous ledges, through woods with several spectacular views of the cliffs on the east side of the notch. At 0.9 mi. the Hell Brook Cutoff branches left while the Hell Brook Trail continues steeply to another junction (1.3 mi.) where the Adam's Apple Trail (27) bears left.

10

It then curves around the west side of the Adam's Apple to reach the Long Trail (1.5 mi.) in Eagle Pass. Vt. 108 to LT, 1.5 mi., 2.4 km, 2 h (Rev. 1 h).

30. ELEPHANT'S HEAD TRAIL. This trail begins on Vt. 108 in Smugglers' Notch, 8.4 mi. north of Vt. 100 in Stowe and 9.4 mi. south of Jeffersonville and Vt. 15, at the south end of the Smugglers' Notch State Picnic Area (east side of road). In winter, Vt. 108 through Smugglers' Notch is not plowed beyond the Mt. Mansfield Ski Area maintenance entrance, 0.5 mi. south.

From the picnic area (0.0 mi.), the trail heads south, crosses Notch Brook, and turns right before starting a steep switchbacking ascent to the ridge south of Spruce Peak, crossing and recrossing a slide with views of Mt. Mansfield. It continues to ascend at a more moderate grade, leveling off and then dropping to a 0.1 mi. spur trail (2.3 mi.) on the left that leads to the top of Elephant's Head, a towering cliff on the east side of the notch. This spur trail is closed during the peregrine falcon nesting season (generally mid-March to mid-August, posted by the State of Vermont) to keep from disturbing these rare, magisterial birds. Across the notch more precipitous cliffs form the western wall of the defile, while a thousand feet below the highway winds like a thread.

Beyond the outlook spur trail the Elephant's Head Trail turns easterly, climbing gradually to a service road (3.0 mi.) that leads right 0.2 mi. to the top of the Spruce Peak chair lift. The trail crosses this road and continues to the eastern shore of Sterling Pond and a short spur trail to Watson Camp, before reaching the Long Trail (3.7 mi.) at Sterling Pond Shelter. Vt. 108 to LT, 3.7 mi., 6.0 km, 2¾ h (Rev. 2 h).

31. BEAVER MEADOW TRAIL. From Morrisville follow Vt. 100 south 1.0 mi. and turn right on Morristown Corners Road (0.0 mi.), then immediately bear left to Morristown Corners and a four-way stop sign (0.7 mi.). Continue straight on Walton Road, pass Cote Hill Road by bearing to the left on Walton Road, and then pass Cole Hill Road on the left, before turning left on Mud City Road (1.7 mi.). There may be no sign here or a sign for Mud City Loop. From Mud City Road, turn left on Bryan Road (3.5 mi.) at a T-intersection, and follow it to a fork (4.1 mi.) at an active dairy farm. Bear left to continue to Beaver Meadow Road (signed) on the right (4.4 mi.). Turn right by the machinery shed and follow this road 0.7 mi. to wet weather/winter parking (5.1 mi.), or on an unimproved road to a small clearing on the right opposite an iron gate where the trail begins (5.7 mi.).

Passing the iron gate (0.0 mi.), the Beaver Meadow Trail climbs gradually on old logging roads to an intersection with the Beaver Meadow Bypass Trail (1.8 mi.). Here the trail turns sharp left, leaves the logging road, and crosses Beaver Meadow Brook (1.9 mi.) before following the beaver pond to Beaver Meadow Lodge (2.3 mi.). The Beaver Meadow Bypass Trail to the right loops around the pond, passing the Whiteface Trail (33), then crosses the inlet, and also reaches the lodge. Iron gate to Beaver Meadow Lodge, 2.3 mi., 3.7 km, 1½ h (Rev. 1¼ h).

32. CHILCOOT TRAIL. This short connector leaves Beaver Meadow Lodge and climbs very steeply to the Long Trail at Chilcoot Pass. Beaver Meadow Lodge to LT, 0.8 mi., 1.3 km, ¾ h (Rev. ½ h).

33. WHITEFACE TRAIL. Leaving the Beaver Meadow Bypass Trail just east of Beaver Meadow Lodge, this trail climbs a moderately steep drainage to the Long Trail (1.0 mi.) at Whiteface Shelter. Beaver Meadow Lodge to LT, 1.0 mi., 1.6 km, 1 h (Rev. ½ h).

10

DIVISION 11

Vt. 15 (Lamoille River Bridge) to Tillotson Camp

Take Note

From the Lamoille River to Belvidere Mtn., the LT is named for Marjorie Hulburd whose father, the Hon. R.W. Hulburd, funded the original trail construction.

Suggested Hikes

PROSPECT ROCK. The short, abrupt climb on the Long Trail north from the Ithiel Falls Camp Meeting Ground on Hogback Road is a good beginning hike for people with children. Round trip, 1.6 mi., 1 h.

LARAWAY LOOKOUT. This moderate hike north on the Long Trail from Codding Hollow to Laraway Lookout passes impressive cliffs and features a splendid view. Round trip, 3.6 mi., 2½ h.

RITTERBUSH/BIG MUDDY POND LOOP. This enjoyable trip passes Ritterbush and Big Muddy Ponds, two scenic bodies of water. The loop includes the Long Trail south from Vt. 118, the Babcock Trail, and a short road walk on Vt. 118 to return to the car. Round trip, 3.9 mi., 2½ h.

DEVIL'S GULCH. This pleasant hike on the LT south from Vt. 118 features Ritterbush Lookout and Pond. Except for a short, steep climb on the return trip it is an easy hike to an interesting fern-filled defile. Round trip, 5 mi., 2¾ h.

BELVIDERE MTN. This challenging hike offers sweeping views from the summit fire tower. One route takes the LT north from Vt. 118 and follows the Forester's Trail right to the summit of Belvidere Mtn., el. 3,360'. Round trip, 5.6 mi., 3¾ h. A second option is a loop hike that follows the Frank Post, Long, and Forester's Trails past Tillotson Camp and the summit of Belvidere Mtn. This trip is suitable for backpacking. Round trip, 7.1 mi., 4½ h.

LARAWAY LOOP. This circuit traverses Laraway Mtn., featuring Laraway Lookout, and uses the Davis Neighborhood Trail, Long Trail south, and the old road from Codding Hollow back to Davis Neighborhood. A short road walk at Davis Neighborhood to the first driveable road to the left is needed to return to the trailhead. Round trip, 8.2 mi., 5 h.

Camping and Fires

The Long Trail in Division 11 crosses private and state land. Camping is allowed only at shelters. Small wood fires, although discouraged, are permitted at shelters in established fire rings. Follow leave-no-trace guidelines (pages 4 to 6) to minimize impact on the Long Trail System.

Winter Use

The suggested hikes for Division 11 make good snowshoe trips. The Codding Hollow Road east of the LT and the Davis Neighborhood Trail are suitable for intermediate cross-country skiers.

Access to Long Trail

VT. 15 AND HOGBACK ROAD. The Long Trail leaves Vt. 15 just east of the Lamoille River Bridge, 1.8 mi. west of Johnson and 7.3 mi. east of Jeffersonville and Vt. 108 and 109, and follows the Hogback Road north toward Waterville. The LT leaves Hogback Road 0.9 mi. north of Vt. 15 and 4.5 mi. southeast of Vt. 109 in Waterville. There is parking on both sides of the Lamoille River and limited parking at the Hogback Road trailhead.

11

PLOT ROAD. The LT crosses this road, also known as the Johnson-Waterville Upper Road, 4.2 mi. west of Johnson and Vt. 15. From Johnson (0.0 mi.) take Vt. 15 west to Foot Road (1.2 mi.). Turn right (north) onto Foot Road and continue to an off-set intersection (2.7 mi.), then turn left onto Plot Road. Continue on this road to the Long Trail (4.6 mi.). From Waterville follow Vt. 109 0.3 mi. south and turn east on the Plot Road. Follow it 3.1 mi. to the trailhead. There is limited parking along the road. A parking lot is planned for the south side of the road near the trail crossing.

CODDING HOLLOW ROAD. From Waterville (0.0 mi.) take Vt. 109 north to Codding Hollow Road (1.8 mi.). Turn east on this road and after crossing the North Branch of the Lamoille River through a covered bridge, continue, bearing left at the only fork, to the last farm where the road becomes a narrow, unimproved country lane. At 2.5 mi. the LT enters the road from the south to follow it briefly before turning north onto a short road leading into a clearing where there is parking. To the east from the turnout it is 1.9 mi. by unimproved road (impassable to vehicles), footpath, and then better road to the public road at Davis Neighborhood.

EDEN CROSSING, VT. 118. The LT crosses this road 4.8 mi. west of Eden and Vt. 100, and 6.1 mi. east of Belvidere Center on Vt. 109. There is an off-road parking area on the north side of the highway. Access to it is found a short distance west of the Long Trail crossing.

Long Trail Description

Making a sharp left turn on **Vt. 15** at the east end of the **Lamoille River Bridge (0.0 mi.)** the Long Trail follows the paved Hogback Road northwest along the Lamoille River to the **Ithiel Falls Camp Meeting Ground (0.9 mi.)**. Here the LT turns to the right off the paved road, makes a short ascent up a gravel driveway, and then bears left into the woods onto an old logging road, which it follows for a short distance. Leaving the road, the Trail ascends more steeply to **Prospect Rock (1.7 mi.)**, which it approaches from the northwest.

From this point there is a broad view south of the pastoral Lamoille River Valley and the Sterling Range.

Heading north on an old road, the Long Trail soon reaches the **Ed Derby Road (2.0 mi.)**, which it follows a short distance to the left before turning right (2.1 mi.). Entering the woods the Trail soon begins a gradual ascent to the broad summit of Roundtop before dropping down to **Roundtop Shelter (3.6 mi.).**

This unique log shelter, with space for 10, was built in 1994 by Todd and Wendy Jenner with the Laraway Section and many other volunteers. It is dedicated to Todd's brother Jeff. The logs were cut on Roundtop and skidded to the site by hand the previous winter. Water, obtained from a hand pump, is found at the end of a 150 yd. spur trail which leaves the LT a short distance north of the shelter. Pump water, like all water along the Long Trail System, should be treated. The quality and quantity of water cannot be guaranteed. In case of pump failure, water might be found in a seep just beyond the pump. This source is unreliable. **Bear Hollow Shelter to Roundtop Shelter, 7.6 mi., 12.1 km, 4½ h (SB 4¼ h).**

From the shelter the LT follows the ridge north before dropping to the **Plot Road** (Johnson-Waterville Upper Road) **(4.5 mi.).** To the east it is 4.2 mi. to Johnson and Vt. 15; to the west, 3.1 mi. to Vt. 109, 0.3 mi. south of Waterville.

After crossing Plot Road the Trail rises to a shallow saddle (5.5 mi.), then descends into Codding Hollow. Turning right, over a stone wall, it soon reaches the unpaved **Codding Hollow Road (6.9 mi.).** To the west this road leads 2.5 mi. to Vt. 109, 1.8 mi. north of Waterville. To the east it is 1.9 mi. by old road and footpath to a public road at Davis Neighborhood.

The Long Trail follows this road to the right (east) about 200 ft., then turns left onto a short road, which crosses a brook into a clearing where there is parking. The LT enters the woods at the far north end of the clearing, follows old logging roads, crosses several small brooks, then a major one (7.1 mi.). Finally leaving a logging road, the LT bears left

11

and upon reaching some impressive cliffs continues beneath them for some distance before climbing to **Laraway Lookout (8.7 mi.)**.

From this relatively low vantage point, (el. 2,620'), there is a broad view from southeast to northwest, including Mt. Mansfield from an unusual angle. Continuing north, then east, along the ridge, the Trail reaches the summit of **Laraway Mtn. (9.0 mi.)** with a limited view.

Following the ridge as it goes east, then southeast, the LT descends at a moderate grade, then begins a steeper descent (11.3 mi.) onto a woods road into the Laraway-Butternut saddle and on to **Corliss Camp** and the **Davis Neighborhood Trail (11.7 mi.)**, which leads 1.5 mi. south to a public road at Davis Neighborhood.

Corliss Camp, a frame cabin, was built in 1989 by the Laraway Section and named for Robert Corliss of St. Albans. It has sleeping space for 14. Water is found at a small brook about 350 ft. from the camp at the end of a spur trail to the left off the Davis Neighborhood Trail. **Roundtop Shelter to Corliss Camp, 8.1 mi., 13.1 km, 5½ h (SB 5¼ h)**.

From Corliss Camp the Long Trail follows an easterly course, climbing rather steeply to the highest peak of **Butternut Mtn. (12.9 mi.)** where a small opening provides a limited view. From here the LT descends moderately, eventually reaching a branch of **Basin Brook (14.7 mi.)**. The Trail crosses and follows several woods roads, then enters a gravel road, which it follows for 0.2 mi., then turns right off the road and ascends to the lower of two southerly summits of **Bowen Mtn. (15.9 mi.)**.

Continuing along a ridge with easy grades the LT

MANY THANKS

The Green Mountain Club thanks private landowners for allowing portions of the Long Trail and side trails to cross their land. Please respect private land!

reaches a northerly summit of **Bowen Mtn. (17.4 mi.)** from which it descends gradually, then begins a steep descent to a **spur trail (18.3 mi.)** on the right leading 830 ft. uphill to **Spruce Ledge Camp.** This frame camp with space for 8 was built in 1998 by the Laraway Section. Water sources are the small stream crossed at the beginning of the spur trail and at a spring 250 ft. behind the camp. Devil's Perch Outlook just beyond the camp affords a view to the northeast of Ritterbush Pond and Belvidere Mtn. **Corliss Camp to Spruce Ledge Camp, 6.7 mi., 10.8 km, 4 h (SB 4 h.).**

From the spur trail junction the LT descends to **Devil's Gulch (18.7 mi.).** Turning right in this fern-filled defile the Long Trail follows along a floor of jumbled rocks then continuing northeast reaches a junction with the **Babcock Trail (19.3 mi.)** on the left, crosses a brook, then climbs steeply on a series of stone steps to **Ritterbush Lookout (19.6 mi.)** on a cliff overlooking Ritterbush Pond.

The Long Trail continues to the top of a low ridge (20.2 mi.), drops, and passes under a power line. Re-entering the woods the LT soon reaches **Vt. 118** (Eden-Belvidere Highway) at **Eden Crossing (21.3 mi.).** Eden and Vt. 100 are 4.8 mi. to the east. To the west, via Vt. 118 and Vt. 109, it is 6.1 mi. to Belvidere Center.

After crossing the highway at an angle to the left, the LT drops down to an off-road parking area. From the parking area, the Babcock Trail Extension leaves to the west and the Long Trail to the north. The LT soon crosses Frying Pan Brook (21.5) then climbs steadily at moderate and steep grades to **Belvidere Saddle (23.9 mi.)** between the two summits of Belvidere Mtn. where there is a trail four-corners. To the right, the **Forester's Trail** comes down from the main summit, and straight ahead it descends the mountain's east side. There is an old spring 50 ft. down this trail. To the left, the Long Trail proceeds north.

Via the Forester's Trail it is 0.2 mi. to the summit of Belvidere Mtn. where there is a fire tower maintained by the GMC. From the tower, the Green Mountains are seen to the south to Camel's Hump, the nearby Cold Hollow Mountains

11

are to the west, Big Jay and Jay Peak are prominent to the north and, to their right, stand Owl's Head and other Canadian mountains in Québec near Lake Memphremagog. On a clear day the White Mountains of New Hampshire are visible to the east. A seldom-used asbestos mine lies at the eastern base of the mountain, and another mine, long unused, on the south slope.

Left from Belvidere Saddle, the LT follows the ridge with easy grades, curves from northwest to northeast, and reaches a sag in which Lockwood Pond is located. Skirting the pond and some extensive ongoing beaver activity by bearing right, the LT reaches the **Frank Post Trail (26.7 mi.)** leading about 50 ft. east to **Tillotson Camp** and 2.0 mi. further to a public road.

This camp, built in 1939, is a frame cabin with bunks for 8. Brook water, draining beaver ponds, is 100 ft. to the north on the LT. From the front of the camp there is a limited view to the east. **Spruce Ledge Camp to Tillotson Camp, 8.5 mi., 13.7 km, 6 h (SB 5 h).**

Side Trails

DAVIS NEIGHBORHOOD TRAIL. This trail utilizes a Class 4 town road and an old logging road in the so-called Davis Neighborhood, north of Johnson (see map on pages 214 and 215). Take the Foot Road north off Vt. 15, 1.2 mi. west of Johnson and 0.4 mi. east of the Lamoille River. Drive through two off-set intersections to the trailhead and limited roadside parking at 4.0 mi. Summer parking is also located 0.2 mi. in on the trail (woods road) to the right.

From the road (0.0 mi.), the trail follows a woods road and ascends moderately in a northerly direction, reaching the Long Trail (1.5 mi.) at Corliss Camp. Public road to LT, 1.5 mi., 2.4 km, 1½ h (Rev. 1 h).

BABCOCK TRAIL EXTENSION. This trail leaves the parking area at Eden Crossing in a westerly direction, crosses a small brook, and soon reaches a dirt road, which it follows to the left for slightly over 0.1 mi. The trail then leaves the road on the left and makes a short climb to Vt. 118 directly across the highway from the north end of the Babcock Trail. Parking area to Vt. 118, 0.4 mi., 0.6 km., ¼ h.

BABCOCK TRAIL. Leaving Vt. 118 across the highway from the Babcock Trail Extension, the trail makes an easy ascent on old logging roads to a point near the north end of Big Muddy Pond (0.5 mi.) where it turns right abruptly, makes a short, steep ascent, then, turning southerly again, stays above the pond and to its west. At the south end of the pond (1.1 mi.) the Babcock Trail begins a fairly steep descent on an old logging road to its junction with the Long Trail (1.4 mi.). Vt. 118 to LT, 1.4 mi., 2.3 km, 1 h (Rev. 1 h).

FORESTER'S TRAIL. This trail, relocated in 1993, leaves left off the Frank Post Trail, 0.6 mi. from the trailhead.

From the Frank Post Trail (0.0 mi.), the Forester's Trail, ascending gradually at first, crosses a small brook and then the larger Lockwood Brook. It crosses several more small brooks and old woods roads, and then winds and switchbacks to Belvidere Saddle and the Long Trail (2.1 mi.), 0.2 mi. below the summit of Belvidere Mtn. to which it continues. Public road to Belvidere Mtn., 2.9 mi., 4.7 km, 2½ h (Rev. 1½ h).

FRANK POST TRAIL. This trail honors the memory of Frank Post, a former Boy Scout leader and Burlington Section member. From Eden Mills, follow the North Road north. At 5.2 mi. turn left (northwest) onto Tillotson Rd., a gravel public road. Follow Tillotson Rd. to its end and the trailhead (5.8 mi.). Tillotson Rd. is 3.1 mi. south of Vt. 58 west of Lowell.

Entering the woods at the parking area (0.0 mi.) the Frank Post Trail soon joins a logging road. At 0.6 mi. the Forester's Trail bears left and the Frank Post Trail continues straight ahead, crosses a brook, and, remaining on the logging road and an older woods road, climbs to a right turn (1.6 mi.) where it begins a steeper ascent to Tillotson Camp, and 50 ft. beyond, the Long Trail (2.0 mi.). Public Road to LT, 2.0 mi., 3.2 km, 1½ h (Rev. 1 h).

11

DIVISION 12

Tillotson Camp to the Canadian Border

Take Note

Much of the Long Trail remains on or near the ridgeline in this division. Water is scarce and hikers should take advantage of sources noted in the text. Hazen's Notch Camp was moved to its present site in 1997.

The northern terminus of the Long Trail is in the woods at the Canadian border west of North Troy. The Journey's End Trail, which approaches the border from the east, is the only approach trail to the northern terminus. It is described on page 177 and included in the division summary on page 216.

Suggested Hikes

CARLETON MTN. This easy climb on the LT north from Vt. 105 leads to a lookout. Round trip, 2.4 mi., 1¼ h. A hike further north to the Canadian border features fine ridge walking and views into Québec from the boundary slash at Post 592. Total round trip, 5.2 mi., 3¼ h.

JAY PEAK. This steady ascent via the Long Trail north from Vt. 242 features extensive views from northern Vermont's highest summit (el. 3,861'). Round trip, 3.4 mi., 2½ h.

JAY PEAK (FROM VT. 105). This ascent via the LT south from Vt. 105 features the rugged ridgeline of North Jay Peak. This route passes Shooting Star and Laura Woodward

Shelters and makes a fine backpack trip as well as a very long day hike. Round trip, 15.2 mi., 9½ h.

HAYSTACK MTN. A steep climb on the Long Trail south from Vt. 58 in Hazen's Notch, this rugged hike rewards hikers with views from the summit (el. 3,223') lookouts. Round trip, 4.0 mi., 2¾ h.

Camping and Fires

The Long Trail in Division 12 crosses state and private land. Camping is allowed only at shelters. Small wood fires, although discouraged, are permitted at shelters in established fire rings with the exception of Atlas Valley Shelter where wood fires are prohibited. Atlas Valley Shelter is not intended for overnight use. Follow leave-no-trace guidelines (pages 4 to 6) to minimize impact on the Long Trail System.

Winter Use

The suggested hikes from Jay and North Jay Passes make good snowshoe trips. This division's terrain is not suitable for beginner and intermediate cross-country skiers.

Access to Long Trail

HAZEN'S NOTCH, VT. 58. The LT crosses unpaved Vt. 58 just west of the height of land 5.5 mi. east of Montgomery Center and 5.5 mi. west of the junction of Vt. 58 and Vt. 100 near Lowell. A picnic area on the south side of the road provides parking. This road is not plowed in the winter when it is part of the Catamount Trail. Refer to Catamount Trail information on page 19.

JAY PASS, VT. 242. The Long Trail crosses this highway at Jay Pass, 5.1 mi. west of Jay Village and 6.7 mi. east of Montgomery Center. There is a large parking lot on the south side of the highway.

12

NORTH JAY PASS, VT. 105. This road intersects the LT at North Jay Pass, 8 mi. west of North Troy and 11 mi. east of Richford. Parking is on the north side of the road.

Long Trail Description

From the **Frank Post Trail (0.0 mi.)**, 50 ft. west of **Tillotson Camp**, the Long Trail heads north and ascends wooded **Tillotson Peak (0.6 mi.)**, passing just east of the top. After a short descent, the LT rises gradually to **Haystack Mtn. (2.7 mi.)**. A spur trail goes left 0.2 mi. to the summit knob where there are lookouts. From here the LT descends at a moderate, though uneven, grade along the ridge, then drops steeply on a rugged and rocky trail to a brook (4.4 mi.) and soon reaches **Hazen's Notch (4.6 mi.)** through which passes unpaved **Vt. 58** (Lowell–Montgomery Center Highway or the Hazen's Notch Road).

The Notch was named after Gen. Moses Hazen who with Gen. Jacob Bailey in 1778–1779 built a military road, originally intended to reach Canada, from Peacham, Vt. to this point. A granite marker just east of the LT commemorates this bit of history. To the north the face of Sugarloaf Mtn. rises 700 ft. almost vertically above the road. Just to the east is a highway picnic area with parking space. Lowell and Vt. 100 are 5.5 mi. east; Montgomery Center and Vt. 118 are 5.5 mi. west.

After crossing the highway, the LT descends gradually then turns right to climb steeply over the west shoulder of Sugarloaf Mtn. Keeping west of the summit the LT descends moderately and soon reaches a spur trail **(6.1 mi.)** leading west 0.1 mi. to **Hazen's Notch Camp.** Built by the Long Trail Patrol in 1948 at a site nearer the highway, the camp

TRAILHEAD PARKING

Please avoid obstructing traffic or blocking access to homes, farms, or woodlots. Park efficiently so others have a place to park. Remember to remove valuables from your car to avoid theft and vandalism.

was dismantled, hand-carried, and reassembled at this site in 1997. The work was done by the Vermont Youth Conservation Corps, GMC staff, and volunteers. There are bunks for 8. Water may be found at a small brook crossed by the spur trail in front of the camp. An open view to the north includes Bruce Peak, Buchanan Mtn., Big Jay, and Jay Peak. **Tillotson Camp to Hazen's Notch Camp, 6.1 mi., 9.8 km, 4 h (SB 4½ H).**

From the spur trail, the LT crosses several ravines where there may be water, then ascends to the skyline at **Bruce Peak (7.5 mi.).** A short distance beyond, the summit of **Buchanan Mtn. (8.4 mi.)** (formerly called Old Splatterfoot) is reached, where there is a view of Jay Peak and Big Jay. Buchanan Mtn. is named in honor of Prof. Roy Buchanan of Burlington, long-time GMC Trails and Shelters chairman, founder and leader of the Long Trail Patrol for many years. Bruce Peak is named for Bruce Buchanan who, with his brother Roy, laid out the route of the final miles of the LT from Jay Peak to Canada in 1930.

On the north slope of Buchanan Mtn. is **Chet's Lookout (8.6 mi.)** on a boulder reached by a log ladder. The lookout is named for one of Roy Buchanan's sons who also worked with the Long Trail Patrol. The view is to the north along the ridge. The Trail then descends into a saddle and, following the ridge, climbs to the summit of **Domey's Dome (9.6 mi.),** named after Capt. R. H. Domey of St. Albans, long-time trail maintainer in this area. Just before reaching this summit the LT passes an open area on the right where there are views to the east and south. From Domey's Dome the Trail descends unevenly to a sag (10.2 mi.), then climbs the ridge to the south summit of **Gilpin Mtn. (10.6 mi.)** where there is a lookout with limited views to the east. Gilpin Mtn., formerly called Double Top, is named in honor of the Gilpin brothers, northern Vermont newspaper editors. Following the ridge the LT soon begins a descent, steep at times, to the west of the north summit and, after passing a spring on the right, immediately reaches **Jay Pass (11.4 mi.),** and **Vt. 242** (Jay–Montgomery Center

12

Highway). East it is 1.3 mi. to the Jay Peak Ski Area road and 5.1 mi. to Jay Village. Montgomery Center is 6.7 mi. west.

Just north of the highway is **Atlas Valley Shelter**. This small structure, not intended for overnight use, was built in 1967 by a plywood company that owned the adjacent timberlands. Water is located at the spring across the highway, but there is no outhouse and wood fires are prohibited. Just north of Atlas Valley Shelter the LT reaches the **south end of Jay Loop (11.5 mi.)**, leading 0.2 mi. west to **Jay Camp**. The Catamount Trail shares the Jay Loop south.

Jay Camp, built in 1958, is a frame cabin with bunk space for 10. A tent platform is passed just before reaching the camp. Water is 50 ft. in front of the camp. Jay Loop continues north 0.2 mi. to join the Long Trail, giving hikers a southbound approach to the camp. **Hazen's Notch Camp to Jay Camp, 5.7 mi., 9.2 km, 4¼ h (SB 4¼ h).**

From the Jay Loop junction the LT trends northwesterly, meets the **north end of Jay Loop (11.7 mi.)** and ascends the southeast shoulder of Jay Peak. Bearing sharply left at the ridge saddle, the Trail climbs steadily, steeply at times, finally reaching a ski trail (12.9 mi.). The Long Trail crosses it and ascends in the open to the rocky summit of **Jay Peak** (el. 3,861') **(13.1 mi.)**. In bad weather the actual summit may be bypassed by turning left onto the ski trail and following it to the top station of the **Jay Peak Tramway**, which is located just below the summit.

From the summit there are good views in all directions. In the immediate foreground to the southwest are Big Jay (el. 3,800') and Little Jay, recently protected by the GMC's Long Trail Protection Program. To the south the Green Mountains are visible to Camel's Hump and, in clear

---

STAY ON THE FOOTPATH

Short cuts erode the land and make more work for the volunteers who take care of hiking trails for you.

---

weather, the White Mountains may be seen in the southeast and the Adirondacks in the southwest. To the north is the Green Mountain ridge to the border, and its extension into Canada known as the Sutton Mountains, culminating in Round Top (3,175'). To the northwest in Canada, Mt. Pinnacle stands alone, and to the northeast are Sugarloaf, Owl's Head, and Bear Mtn., over which the border passes. The international waters of Lake Memphremagog lie beyond Bear Mtn.

Dropping from the summit and past the tramway station the LT descends northwesterly along a ski trail, which then turns to the west and joins another ski trail at right angles (13.3 mi.). The Long Trail crosses this ski trail and the water pipes for snowmaking that parallel it. The LT then turns right and after entering the woods begins, in a northerly direction, a steep, circuitous descent to another ski trail. Crossing a corner of this trail it re-enters the woods (13.8 mi.). Descending unevenly near the top of the ridge the Trail soon reaches **Laura Woodward Shelter (14.6 mi.)**, named after a pioneer supporter of the Long Trail project.

Built in 1956, this open log shelter sleeps 8. Water is located at a spring beside the LT, about 200 ft. north of the shelter. **Jay Camp to Laura Woodward Shelter, 3.1 mi., 5.0 km, 2½ h (SB 2¼ h).**

Continuing in a northerly direction along the ridge, the Long Trail ascends **Doll Peak (15.5 mi.)**, named after Charles G. Doll who, with Phillips D. Carleton, both University of Vermont professors, cut the route from Jay Peak to Canada. After dropping from Doll Peak, the Trail, following the ridge, ascends to an **unnamed peak of the North Jay massif (16.0 mi.)**. It now begins a long and sometimes steep descent to the east before reaching a small stream (17.9 mi.). Bearing northerly again the LT follows the ridge over several low summits before reaching **Shooting Star Shelter (18.9 mi.)**.

This log structure, built in 1934 by the Long Trail Patrol, was so named because of a display of shooting stars

12

observed one night during its construction. It has sleeping space for 6. **Laura Woodward Shelter to Shooting Star Shelter, 4.3 mi., 6.9 km, 2¾ h (SB 3 h).** The primary water source is a well with a hand pump, located at the end of a short spur trail leading west off the Long Trail, 190 ft. south of the shelter. Pump water, like all water along the Long Trail System, should be treated. The quality and quantity of water cannot be guaranteed. In case of pump failure, water might be found 450 ft. downhill east from in front of the shelter. This source is unreliable.

From the shelter the Trail ascends **Burnt Mtn. (19.5 mi.)**, where a spur trail leads left to a lookout with a limited view from south to northwest including North Jay Peak, Lucas Brook Valley in the foreground, and Québec's Mt. Pinnacle beyond. Following the ridge and gradually descending, the LT reaches **North Jay Pass** and **Vt. 105** (Jay-Richford Highway) **(20.7 mi.)**. To the east it is 5 mi. to Jay and 8 mi. to North Troy. To the west it is 11 mi. to Richford.

North of the highway the Long Trail turns right, follows along the top of the road cut, passes under a power line, then, turning to a northerly direction, briefly parallels a logging road on the left. After ascending to the ridge the Trail turns east and after some easy hiking ascends moderately to the summit of **Carleton Mtn. (21.9 mi.)**, named after Phillips D. Carleton, who, with Charles G. Doll, cut the LT from Jay Peak to the border. A spur trail on the right leads to a lookout with a broad southerly view in which the Jay Mountains are prominent. Turning north, the Long Trail de-

---

THANK YOU

Major portions of the Long Trail in northern Vermont have been permanently protected by the GMC's Long Trail Protection Campaign with donations from hikers, foundations, and businesses as well as the State of Vermont. Thank you.

---

scends unevenly over several minor summits, finally reaching **Journey's End Trail** and, a few feet beyond, the **United States–Canadian Border** at **Line Post 592 (23.3 mi.)**, the **northern terminus** of the **Long Trail**.

The present line post was set in 1907 in accordance with the Webster-Ashburton Treaty, which in 1842 finally settled the U.S.-Canada boundary. The view from the line post is west along the border swath cut through the trees, and northwest and north into the valley of the Missisquoi River and the Sutton Mountains in Canada.

Side Trails

JOURNEY'S END TRAIL. This trail is the only approach trail to the northern terminus of the Long Trail. From North Troy, take the gravel North Troy–Jay Road west and then south 2.6 mi. to a junction with a narrow unpaved road on the west (right); or from Vt. 105, follow the North Troy–Jay Road 2.0 mi. north. There is a dairy barn east of the junction. Follow the unpaved road 1.3 mi. to its end, being sure to stay on the main road and passing a private-gated road on the left. The road is usually driveable by automobile. However, as it is sometimes used for logging, exercise caution. Springtime conditions may be poor. There is ample parking at the trailhead.

From the end of the road **(0.0 mi.)**, the **Journey's End Trail** follows an old country lane, gradually climbing to a small clearing and **Journey's End Camp (0.5 mi.)**. This frame cabin, built in 1933 by the Long Trail Patrol, has space for 8. Water is found at a brook 300 ft. north.

From the camp the Journey's End Trail bears to the right, crosses a sizable brook, then rejoins the old road again to reach an old farm settlement evidenced by stone foundations and rock piles. Turning left here, the trail ascends gradually and circuitously in a northwesterly direction, crosses several old woods roads, then reaches the border swath, which it parallels briefly before reaching the **Long Trail (1.3 mi.)**. **Shooting Star Shelter to Journey's End Camp 5.2 mi., 8.4 km, 3¼ h (SB 3½ h).**

12

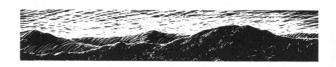

Appalachian Trail 1

Long Trail (Maine Junction) to Vt. 12

Take Note

The Appalachian Trail in Vermont leaves the Long Trail at Maine Junction, 1.0 mile north of U.S. 4 and 104.6 miles north of the Massachusetts state line, and bears easterly 43.9 miles to the Connecticut River at Norwich.

The Appalachian Trail from Maine Junction south to the Vermont-Massachusetts state line is covered in Divisions 1 through 6. The AT between Vt. 12 and the Connecticut River is covered in Appalachian Trail 2.

Camping and Fires

Much of the trail is on state land and a narrow strip of federal land surrounded by private property. Some of the AT remains on private property. Camping is allowed only at shelters. Wood fires, although discouraged, are permitted at the shelters in established fire rings. Follow leave-no-trace guidelines (pages 4 to 6) to minimize impact on the trail.

Access to Appalachian Trail

Vt. 100. The Appalachian Trail crosses this highway at the Gifford Woods State Park maintenance driveway 0.5 mi. north of the junction of Vt. 100 and U.S. 4. Parking is available at the boat landing on the east side of the highway.

River Road. Follow U.S. 4 east from its junction with Vt.

100 North. At 2.0 mi. turn left (north) onto the River Road. Continue on this road 1.5 mi. to the trail crossing. The trail crossing is also 2.4 mi. south of Vt. 100.

VT. 12 (BARNARD GULF ROAD). The AT crosses Vt. 12 4.2 mi. north of Woodstock and 12.2 mi. south of Bethel. Parking is available on the west side of the highway.

Appalachian Trail Description

From **Maine Junction** at **Willard Gap (0.0 mi.)**, the AT leaves the Long Trail and proceeds east, soon passing one end of the **Deer Leap Trail (0.1 mi.)**. The AT continues southeasterly, slabbing the side of Deer Leap Mtn. and passing the second end of the of the **Deer Leap Trail** just 200 ft. before reaching the northern end of the **Sherburne Pass Trail (0.9 mi.)**. The AT continues east, makes a short ascent over a low ridge, then descends to a spur on the right leading 50 ft. to **Ben's Balcony (1.2 mi.)**, a small clearing offering views toward Pico and Killington Peaks. Descending steadily, the AT reaches the upper camping area of **Gifford Woods State Park (1.9 mi.)**, passes through the camping and picnic areas and then reaches **Vt. 100 (2.1 mi.)** west of the park entrance and 0.5 mi. east of U.S. 4.

Gifford Woods State Park provides open shelters, tent sites, and picnic tables. Make reservations for the use of overnight facilities through the park office (Killington, VT 05751; 802-775-5354). Gifford Woods itself, located elsewhere within the park, is one of the few remaining stands of virgin hardwood forest in Vermont.

The AT turns right on Vt. 100 and follows it south a short distance to Kent Pond Fishing Access, 0.4 mi. north of U.S. 4. Here the trail turns left and then immediately right into an overgrown meadow. Crossing Kent Brook on a footbridge, the trail bears left along the brook and descends to the shore of **Kent Pond (2.5 mi.)**. Following the shore through the woods, it then passes through a field to the gravel Thundering Brook Road (3.0 mi.), a short distance north of Mountain Meadows Inn and 0.4 mi. north of U.S.

AT 1

4 and Vt. 100. Leaving the AT and following the road north, there are views of Pico Peak over Kent Pond from the earthen dam. The trail crosses the road and ascends to a height of land. It descends to the road again to follow it downhill to the crossing of the headwaters of the Ottauquechee River. After the crossing, the AT reaches the unpaved **River Road (4.4 mi.)**, 1.5 mi. north of U.S. 4 and Vt. 100.

After crossing the River Road, the trail ascends through mixed hardwood forest to an old logging road (4.8 mi.). After turning left and ascending on the road for a short distance, it bears right, leaving the road. The AT continues to climb, in part on old logging roads, to a vista (5.2 mi.) with good late fall and early spring views of the Ottauquechee River Valley and the Coolidge Range.

From the vista the trail continues on a logging road for a short distance, levels out, then begins to climb via switchbacks to the summit of an unnamed hill (5.7 mi.). From the summit the AT descends to a ridge, which it follows to a power line clearing (6.3 mi.). Continuing along the ridge, the trail crosses a woods road (6.6 mi.) and begins to ascend. After reaching an unnamed summit (6.9 mi.), the AT begins a steep descent before ascending to the north shoulder of Quimby Mtn. The trail descends to a shallow saddle, then climbs to a **height of land (7.7 mi.)**, the divide between the Ottauquechee River and Stony Brook.

Beyond the height of land the AT descends, steeply at times, to a spur on the right to **Stony Brook Shelter (8.7 mi.)**. Stony Brook Shelter, a frame lean-to with space for 6, was built in 1997. Water is from a brook just north of the spur. **Pico Camp to Stony Brook Shelter, 14.6 mi., 23.5**

IT'S YOUR DRINKING WATER

Safeguard water supplies. Use outhouses and wash your dishes and yourself away from the water source. The next hiker may be thirsty, too.

km, 8¼ h (SB 8¼ h). Climbing through conifers, the trail soon reaches a vista with a fine view of the Stony Brook drainage (9.0 mi.). Descending once again, the trail reaches another vista and continues to **Stony Brook (9.3 mi.).** Crossing the brook on a logging bridge, the trail turns left before Notown Clearing, which is used for logging operations. The AT crosses Mink Brook and ascends, via switchbacks at first, to a ridge. It then follows the ridge across several knolls to a **height of land (11.1 mi.).** Passing a small pond, the AT follows a ridge to a sag. Descending from the sag, the trail crosses an intermittent brook and several logging roads. It climbs over several small hills, winding just north of Bull Hill. There are occasional views to the west. The AT then descends via switchbacks to the gravel **Chateauguay Road (13.1 mi.).**

The trail crosses the road and, just beyond, Locust Creek. After climbing over a low hill, the trail crosses a brook (13.5 mi.). Shortly, the AT begins to switchback up a steep, evergreen-covered hillside. The grade moderates as the trail enters a mixed hardwood forest and crosses an intermittent brook (14.0 mi.). Continuing to ascend through a stand of paper birches, the AT passes a fine southwestern view before reaching **Lakota Lake Lookout (14.2 mi.).** Lakota Lake is below with the White Mountains in the distance.

From the lookout the trail follows the ridge with gradual elevation changes, crosses an old woods road, and reaches a spur trail on the left, which leads uphill 100 yds. to **The Lookout (15.9 mi.),** located on private property outside the AT corridor. Please respect this property.

From the spur trail the AT turns sharply right down an old woods road, which continues to the **Lookout Farm Road (16.7 mi.).** It crosses this road and soon reaches the King Cabin Road (16.8 mi.). Turning right, the trail follows the road for a distance, then turns left (17.0 m.), leaves the road, and gradually ascends the south slope of the Pinnacle. Presently, a fine southwestern view (17.5 mi.) of Killington and Pico Peaks is reached. The AT continues its ascent and soon reaches the height of land on Sawyer Hill (17.7 mi.). It

**AT
1**

then begins a gradual descent, crosses a woods road, and reaches a **spur trail (18.3 mi.)** on the left, which leads 0.2 mi. to **Wintturi Shelter**. Wintturi Shelter, a frame lean-to with room for 6, was reconstructed by Erik and Laurel Tobiason and friends in 1994. It is named in honor of Mauri Wintturi, a long active GMC member and trail maintainer. A spring is found 300 ft. north of the shelter. **Stony Brook Shelter to Wintturi Shelter, 9.8 mi., 15.7 km, 6 h (SB 6 h).**

From the Wintturi Shelter spur, the AT follows the contour of a wooded slope, then descends to an old road (19.1 mi.). Beyond the road the trail climbs to the crest of a low

WINTER HIKING?

- The LT and AT are marked with white blazes, which are difficult to see against a snowy background and frequently buried beneath the snow.

- Deep snow may obscure all signs of the trail. Topographical maps and a compass are helpful.

- Daylight is short in the winter. Darkness may come suddenly.

- Stay alert to the dangers of hypothermia and frostbite. Know the signs and how to treat them.

- Keep group size between four and ten people.

- Be prepared to keep warm and sheltered with nothing more than the equipment you carry.

- You may encounter winter weather at higher elevations during the fall and spring.

- Use skis or snowshoes. Post-holing makes the trail unpleasant and dangerous for the next person.

ridge (19.3 mi.), where a short spur leads right to a view of North Bridgewater. Descending, the trail soon crosses a little used woods road (19.9 mi.), where an old cellar hole and stone chimney on the left are all that remain of a past dwelling. The Appalachian Trail continues along the contour, then climbs to an open ridge (20.7 mi.), which provides excellent views of Mt. Ascutney. A second bald hilltop with panoramic views (20.9 mi.) is a short distance beyond.

Re-entering the woods, the AT makes an abrupt left turn and descends through an open area. Continuing through the woods with minor changes in elevation, it reaches the edge of a field where a wooden stile crosses an electric fence. The trail descends through two more fields with stiles, which provide excellent views of the valley and hills beyond. The trail crosses **Gulf Stream** on a footbridge and then reaches **Vt. 12** (Barnard Gulf Road) **(22.0 mi.)**.

AT 1

Side Trails

DEER LEAP TRAIL. This trail is part of a popular day hike to Deer Leap Overlook. The Deer Leap Trail begins on the AT 200 ft. west of the northern end of the Sherburne Pass Trail. The Deer Leap Trail forks west off the AT (0.0 mi.) and climbs through an attractive birch forest to the Overlook Spur (0.4 mi.). The spur is 0.2 mi. south to a dramatic rock outcropping with views of the Coolidge Range and the Adirondacks. The Deer Leap Trail continues north, drops precipitously to a brook (0.5 mi.), climbs to the height of land on Deer Leap Mtn. (0.7 mi.), and descends gradually to junction with the AT (1.3 mi.) 0.1 mi. east of Willard Gap and 0.8 mi. west of the Sherburne Pass Trail. Deer Leap Trail from the AT near the Sherburne Pass Trail to the AT near Willard Gap, 1.3 mi., 2.1 km, 1¼ h (Rev. 1¼ h).

SHERBURNE PASS TRAIL, NORTH HALF. This trail is part of a popular day hike to Deer Leap Overlook. See directions to the trailhead and a description for the southern half of this trail on page 95. From U.S 4 in Sherburne Pass (0.0 mi.) the trail enters the woods about 100 ft. east of the Inn at Long Trail and winds uphill to the AT (0.5 mi.).

APPALACHIAN TRAIL 2

Vt. 12 to the Connecticut River

Take Note

A relocation is planned between Totman Hill and the Pomfret-South Pomfret Road. Cloudland Shelter, outside the AT corridor, was replaced by Thistle Hill Shelter in 1995. Contact the Dartmouth Outing Club (DOC) for updates. See address information on page 226.

The AT south of Vt. 12 is covered in Divisions 1 through 6 and Appalachian Trail 1.

Camping and Fires

Much of the route is on a fairly narrow strip of federally owned AT corridor land surrounded by private property. Some of the trail remains on private property.

Camping is limited to the shelters and campsites described below. Small wood fires, although discouraged, are permitted at shelters and designated campsites. Follow leave-no-trace guidelines (pages 4 to 6) to reduce the impact on the trail.

Access to Appalachian Trail

Vt. 12 (Barnard Gulf Road). Refer to description on page 179 in Appalachian Trail 1.

Woodstock Stage Road. This road intersects the AT 0.9 mi. north of South Pomfret and 4.1 mi. north of Woodstock.

POMFRET–SOUTH POMFRET (COUNTY) ROAD. The AT crosses this road 1.3 mi. north of South Pomfret and 4.5 mi. north of Woodstock. There is parking available at a small pull-off on the west side of the road.

VT. 14. The AT joins this road at the bridge over White River in West Hartford, Vt., 6.9 mi. north of U.S. 4 and U.S. 5 in White River Junction.

U.S. 5. The AT crosses this highway in Norwich Village, 4.6 mi. north of Vt. 14 in White River Junction.

Appalachian Trail Description

From **Vt. 12** (Barnard Gulf Road) **(0.0 mi.)**, the Appalachian Trail crosses a small field and re-enters the woods. After ascending steadily, the trail reaches an upland field on **Dana Hill (1.2 mi.)**, which offers good views of the surrounding countryside. From Dana Hill the AT descends, easily at first and then more steeply, to the paved **Woodstock Stage Road (1.5 mi.)**. The trail crosses the road and a footbridge over Barnard Creek and gradually ascends through a field. Entering the woods, the AT climbs to a sag between Totman and Breakneck Hills, then descends bearing right at an obvious fork to cross a narrow road.

The AT ascends through a field past some foundations to a height of land, then takes a right-hand fork downhill. Utilizing woods roads, the Appalachian Trail descends to a field and meets the gravel **Bartlett Brook Road (3.0 mi.)**. Crossing the road and a small creek, the AT follows an old fencerow through woods and fields before descending, crossing Pomfret Brook and the paved **Pomfret-South Pomfret (County) Road (3.7 mi.)**. The Teago Store and South Pomfret post office are 1.3 mi. south on this road.

The trail crosses the road and climbs steeply through mixed woods to a field with fine views. At the edge of the field, it turns left and follows an old woods road. This is a remnant of the old "Kings Highway," which used to be a major thoroughfare through Pomfret (the trail crosses another section of this old road near Bunker Hill). Following the woods road, the trail passes an old four-way junction and climbs a small hill before descending to the east. The AT leaves the former highway at a spur trail (4.6 mi.), which goes uphill 50 ft. to an unreliable spring. It then ascends to the top of DuPuis Hill, a bald summit with panoramic views. The trail then descends gradually through the woods to the gravel **Cloudland Road (5.5 mi.)**.

The Appalachian Trail turns right onto the road for 200 ft., then left into a field north of a red house. It follows the southern side of the field, then crosses it to a gap in the stone wall. The trail turns right through this gap and enters the woods. It ascends through woods, passing under a power line. After crossing over the top of Thistle Hill (7.5 mi.), the trail reaches the **spur trail (7.8 mi.)** to **Thistle Hill Shelter** to the right. Thistle Hill Shelter, with space for 8, was built by the DOC in 1995. Ample water is available in nearby streams. **Wintturi Shelter to Thistle Hill Shelter, 11.7 mi., 18.8 km, 6¾ h (SB 6¾ h).**

From the spur trail, the AT descends to cross a small brook, then climbs to an open field atop Arms Hill, with fine views. The trail follows a woods road to a second field, with good views to the north and northeast. It continues to drop via switchbacks to the unpaved **Joe Ranger Road (9.3 mi.)**.

The AT crosses Joe Ranger Road by a small pond with a stone dam. It then climbs via switchbacks to the wooded summit of Bunker Hill. Descending Bunker Hill, the Trail crosses an old town road (10.0 mi.) by a cemetery and several hilltop pastures with fine views to the southeast. Crossing an old farm road before descending through a stand of pines and bearing left through a sag, the AT climbs to another hill-

CONTROL BACKCOUNTRY WASTE

Please use outhouses to control backcountry wastes. Follow instructions on the outhouse door. To reduce outhouse odor, however, urinate in the woods.

top pasture with views of the White River Valley. After leaving the field (11.6 mi.), it descends steadily through open hardwoods. The trail crosses a small swampy area and puncheon over a creek and turns left onto the paved Quechee–West Hartford Road. It follows this road to cross an iron bridge over the White River to **Vt. 14 (12.6 mi.)** in the village of **West Hartford**.

The Appalachian Trail turns left (north) on Vt. 14, passing a store and a post office, and follows it to **Tigertown Road (13.0 mi.)**. The AT turns right on Tigertown Rd., crosses a railroad track, and bears left at a fork. After passing under Interstate 89, the trail on the road reaches a junction with Podunk Road. It turns right onto **Podunk Road (13.2 mi.)** and then immediately left into the woods.

The AT climbs steeply through overgrown pasture and woods before descending back to Podunk Road (14.0 mi.). It crosses the road, then a brook, before ascending and crossing a woods road. The trail makes a sharp left turn across a brook and several old town roads, and then traverses the southern shoulder of Griggs Mtn. (16.1 mi.) to reach a **spur trail (16.6 mi.)** that leads 0.1 mi. right to **Happy Hill Shelter**. Happy Hill Shelter, with accommodations for 8, was built in 1918 by the DOC. A brook runs by the cabin

Thistle Hill Shelter to Happy Hill Shelter, 8.8 mi., 14.1 km, 5 h (SB 5 h).

From the shelter, the Appalachian Trail descends on an old road to a junction with the **William Tucker Trail (16.8 mi.)**. The AT then bears to the right and follows the south side of the ridge and crosses Newton Lane (18.2 mi.). The trail soon passes under a power line on the north flank of Mosley Hill (19.5 mi.). There is a view of the Connecticut River and Wilder Dam about 50 ft. south along the power line. From the clearing the AT descends, crosses a small stream, and follows the contour to **Elm Street (20.1 mi.)**. Bearing right on Elm Street and descending, the trail passes Hickory Ridge Road on the right, and follows the street to **U.S. 5 (20.9 mi.)** on the **Norwich Village Green**. A grocery store and the Norwich post office are a short distance to the left. From Norwich Village, the Appalachian Trail proceeds south on U.S. 5 and east on Vt. 10A under Interstate 91, enters New Hampshire, and crosses the **Connecticut River (21.9 mi.)** on the Ledyard Bridge.

Side Trail

WILLIAM TUCKER TRAIL. This trail provides an alternative route to the AT and the highlands around Griggs Mtn. from Norwich. From its junction with Dutton Hill and Meadow Brook Roads, 0.5 mi. west of the Norwich Village Green, Bragg Hill Road leads 1.3 mi. to a crossroads. The trailhead is another 0.5 mi. straight ahead beyond the road junction. There is a turn-around with limited parking. The trail follows an old woods road uphill for 0.8 mi. to the Appalachian Trail. **Road to AT, 0.8 mi., 1.3 km, ⅔ h (Rev. ½ h).**

SUMMARIES
AND MAPS

Massachusetts-Vermont State Line to Vt. 9

miles north-bound	NORTH	elevation at Long Trail (feet/meters)	miles south-bound
14.3	**Vt. 9** (Bennington-Brattleboro Highway)	1360/415	0.0
12.5	**Harmon Hill**	2325/709	1.8
10.6	**Old Bennington–Heartwellville Road**	2220/677	3.7
10.0	**Congdon Shelter**	2080/634	4.3
8.4	**Sucker Pond Outlet Brook,** crossing	2180/665	5.9
7.0	**Consultation Peak**	2810/857	7.3
5.8	**Roaring Branch,** bridge crossing at dam	2470/753	8.5
4.9	**North power line**	2890/881	9.4
3.1	**Mill Road** to Vt. 8 and 100, 4.2 mi. E	2290/698	11.2
2.8	**Seth Warner Shelter,** 300 yds. W via spur	2200/671	11.5
2.6	**Broad Brook Trail**	2130/649	11.7
0.0	**Massachusetts-Vermont state line**	2330/710	14.3

WILLIAMSTOWN APPROACH
VIA PINE COBBLE AND APPALACHIAN TRAILS

3.2	**Southern terminus of Long Trail**	2330/710	0.0
2.4	**Eph's Lookout**	2254/687	0.8
2.0	**Appalachian Trail**	2010/613	1.2
1.4	**Pine Cobble** (el. 1894/577 m), 0.1 mi. south via spur	1850/564	1.8
0.0	**Williamstown, Mass., Pine Cobble Road**	630/192	3.2

BLACKINTON APPROACH VIA APPALACHIAN TRAIL

3.8	**Southern terminus of Long Trail**	2330/710	0.0
3.0	**Eph's Lookout**	2254/687	0.8
2.6	**Pine Cobble Trail**	2010/613	1.2
1.4	**Pete's Spring, Sherman Brook Primitive Campsite,** 0.1 mi. W via spur	1300/396	2.4
0.0	**Blackinton, Mass., Mass. 2**	660/201	3.8

SOUTH
▼

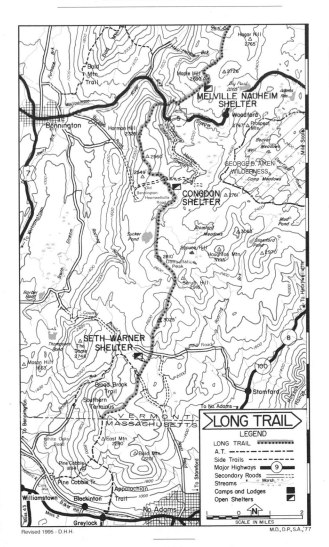

Vt. 9 to Arlington–West Wardsboro Road

miles north-bound	NORTH	elevation at Long Trail (feet/meters)	miles south-bound
22.6	**Arlington–West Wardsboro Road**	2230/680	0.0
21.7	**Black Brook**, bridge crossing	2220/677	0.9
20.6	**USFS Road 71**	2380/726	2.0
19.0	**Story Spring Shelter**	2810/857	3.6
18.1	**South Alder Brook**, crossing	2600/793	4.5
14.4	**Caughnawaga Shelter**	2800/854	8.2
14.2	**Kid Gore Shelter**, 60 yds. E via spur	2800/854	8.4
13.7	**Big Rock**	3250/991	8.9
10.4	**Glastenbury Mtn.**, fire tower	3748/1143	12.2
10.1	**Goddard Shelter** **West Ridge Trail** to **Bald Mtn. Trail**, 7.8 mi. S	3560/1085	12.5
7.6	**Glastenbury Lookout**	2920/890	15.0
5.8	**Little Pond Lookout**	3060/933	16.8
4.4	**Porcupine Lookout**	2815/858	18.2
3.2	**Hell Hollow Brook**, bridge crossing	2350/716	19.4
2.1	**Maple Hill**, power line	2630/802	20.5
1.6	**Melville Nauheim Shelter**, 250 ft. E via spur	2300/701	21.0
0.7	**Split Rock**	1900/579	21.9
0.0	**Vt. 9** (Bennington-Brattleboro Highway) **City Stream** **William D. MacArthur Memorial Bridge**	1360/415	22.6

SOUTH

2

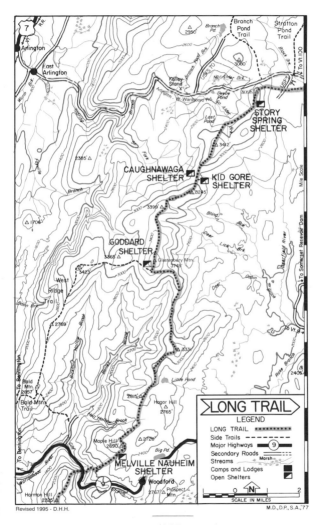

LONG TRAIL
LEGEND
LONG TRAIL ••••••••••
Side Trails - - - - - - -
Major Highways 9
Secondary Roads = = =
Streams
Camps and Lodges ■
Open Shelters ◩

0   1   2
SCALE IN MILES

Revised 1995 - D.H.H.

M.D.,D.P.,S.A.,'77

Arlington–West Wardsboro Road
to Mad Tom Notch

miles northbound	▲ NORTH	elevation at Long Trail (feet/meters)	miles southbound
22.7	**Mad Tom Notch,** USFS Road 21	2446/746	0.0
20.2	**Bromley Mtn.,** observation tower	3260/994	2.5
18.2	**Bromley Tenting Area**	2080/634	4.5
17.5	**Vt. 11 and 30** (Manchester-Peru Highway)	1800/549	5.2
15.1	**Spruce Peak,** 300 ft. W via spur	2040/622	7.6
14.7	**Spruce Peak Shelter,** 0.1 mi. W via spur	2200/671	8.0
12.6	**Prospect Rock,** 50 yds. W via spur Vt. 11 and 30, 2.0 mi. N via Rootville Road	2150/655	10.1
11.7	**Branch Pond Trail** to **William B. Douglas Shelter,** 0.5 mi. S	2280/695	11.0
8.9	**Winhall River,** bridge crossing	2175/663	13.8
7.1	**North Shore Trail** to **North Shore Tenting Area,** 0.5 mi. W	2555/779	15.6
7.0	**Stratton Pond** **Willis Ross Clearing** **Lye Brook Trail**	2555/779	15.7
6.9	**Stratton Pond Trail** to Arlington–West Wardsboro Road, 3.7 mi. S, **Stratton Pond Shelter,** 0.1 mi. S via spur	2620/799	15.8
3.8	**Stratton Mtn.,** south peak, fire tower **North Peak of Stratton Mtn.,** 0.7 mi. N via spur	3936/1200	18.9
0.0	**Arlington–West Wardsboro Road**	2230/680	22.7

SOUTH

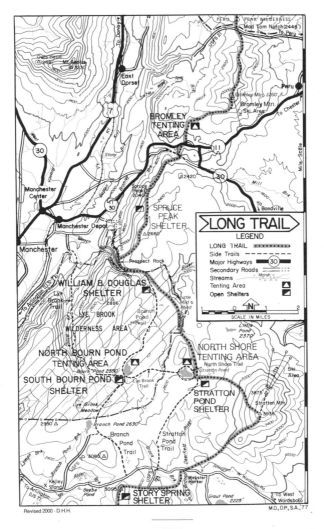

Revised 2000 - D.H.H.

M.D., D.P., S.A., '77

Mad Tom Notch to Vt. 140

miles north-bound	▲ NORTH	elevation at Long Trail (feet/meters)	miles south-bound
20.3	**Vt. 140** (Wallingford Gulf Road)	1300/396	0.0
20.2	**Sugar Hill Road**	1680/512	0.1
19.6	**Bully Brook**, crossing	1230/375	0.7
19.5	**Keewaydin Trail**	2300/701	0.8
18.9	**Greenwall Spur** to **Greenwall Shelter** (el. 2020/616 m), 0.4 mi. E	2300/701	1.4
18.6	**White Rocks Cliff Trail** to view, 0.2 mi. W	2400/732	1.7
17.8	**White Rocks Mtn.**, west slope	2560/780	2.5
15.6	**Homer Stone Brook**, bridge crossing	1900/579	4.7
14.7	**Little Rock Pond Shelter**, 100 ft. E via spur	1820/555	5.6
14.6	**Homer Stone Brook Trail**	1840/561	5.7
14.6	**Green Mtn. Trail** to USFS Road 10	1854/565	5.7
14.3	**Little Rock Pond Tenting Area**, 100 ft. E **Little Rock Pond Loop Trail** to Green Mtn. Trail, 0.4 mi. N	1854/565	6.0
14.0	**Lula Tye Shelter**, 100 ft. E via spur	1865/569	6.3
12.3	**USFS Road 10 at Big Black Branch**	1500/457	8.0
12.1	**USFS Road 10 at LT South**	1530/466	8.2
11.0	**Big Branch Shelter**	1470/448	9.3
10.9	**Big Branch**, suspension bridge crossing	1500/457	9.4
10.8	**Old Job Trail**, north end, to **Old Job Shelter**, 1.1 mi SE	1525/465	9.5
9.3	**Lost Pond Shelter**, 100 ft. W via spur	2150/655	11.0
7.3	**Baker Peak**	2850/869	13.0
7.2	**Baker Peak Trail** to public road, 2.9 mi. W	2760/841	13.1
5.4	**Lake Trail** to public road, 3.3 mi. W	2620/799	14.9
5.3	**Old Job Trail**, south end	2600/793	15.0
5.1	**Griffith Lake Tenting Area**	2600/793	15.2
4.6	**Peru Peak Shelter**	2550/777	15.7
3.3	**Peru Peak**	3429/1045	17.0
1.6	**Styles Peak**	3394/1035	18.7
0.0	**Mad Tom Notch**, USFS Road 21	2446/746	20.3

SOUTH
▼

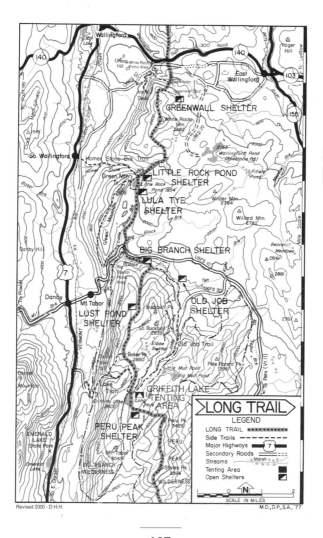

Revised 2000 - D.H.H.

M.D., D.P., S.A., '77

Vt. 140 to U.S. 4

miles north-bound	NORTH	elevation at Long Trail (feet/meters)	miles south-bound
23.7	**U.S. 4**	1880/573	0.0
21.9	**Brook**, crossing	2490/759	1.8
21.5	**Mendon Lookout**	2990/911	2.2
19.9	**Sherburne Pass Trail**, south end, to **Pico Camp**, 0.5 mi. N and U.S. 4 (Sherburne Pass) and Inn at Long Trail, 3 mi. N	3480/1060	3.8
17.5	**Bucklin Trail** to Brewers Corners, 3.3 mi. W	3770/1149	6.2
17.4	**Cooper Lodge** **Killington Spur** to Killington Peak (el. 4241/1293 m), 0.2 mi. E	3850/1174	6.3
15.7	**Shrewsbury Peak Trail** to Shrewsbury Peak (el. 3720/1135 m), 2.4 mi. SE and CCC Road, 4.2 mi. S	3500/1067	8.0
13.1	**Governor Clement Shelter**	1850/564	10.6
11.7	**Upper Road**, unpaved	1630/497	12.0
11.0	**Gould Brook**, crossing	1480/451	12.7
10.2	**Cold River (Lower) Road**, paved	1400/427	13.5
8.2	**Lottery Road**	1700/518	15.5
7.8	**Beacon Hill**	1740/530	15.9
7.3	**Clarendon Shelter**, 400 ft. S via spur	1350/412	16.4
6.3	**Vt. 103** (Rutland–Bellows Falls Highway)	860/262	17.4
6.2	**Clarendon Gorge** **Mill River**, suspension bridge crossing	800/244	17.5
5.5	**Airport Lookout**	1400/427	18.2
4.2	**Spring Lake Clearing**	1600/488	19.5
3.6	**Minerva Hinchey Shelter**, 200 ft. E via spur	1530/466	20.1
2.1	**Bear Mountain** height of land	2215/675	21.6
1.0	**Lookout Spur**, view of White Rocks 300 ft. W	1575/480	22.7
0.0	**Vt. 140** (Wallingford Gulf Road)	1300/396	23.7

SOUTH

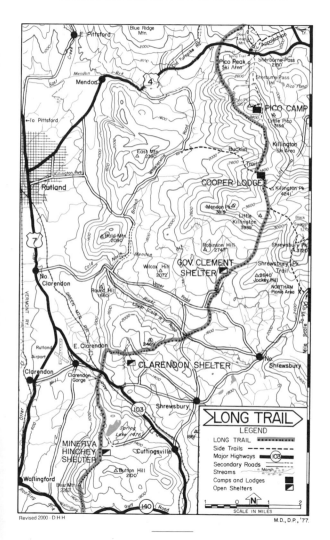

U.S. 4 to Vt. 73 (Brandon Gap)

miles northbound	▲ NORTH	elevation at Long Trail (feet/meters)	miles southbound
19.9	**Vt. 73, Brandon Gap**	2183/665	0.0
19.0	**Sunrise Shelter**	2564/782	0.9
17.6	**Chittenden Brook Trail** to USFS Road, 3.7 mi. E	2951/899	2.3
16.2	**Farr Peak**, east spur, (summit el. 3522/1074 m)	3150/960	3.7
15.7	**Bloodroot Gap**	3110/957	4.2
14.0	**Bloodroot Mtn.**, east ridge, (summit el. 3485/1063 m)	2900/893	5.9
13.2	**Wetmore Gap**	2600/792	6.7
12.7	**New Boston Trail** to **David Logan Shelter** (el. 2620/799 m), 0.2 mi. S and Road, 1.2 mi. S	2760/841	7.2
10.8	**Telephone Gap**	2300/701	9.1
8.9	**Green Road**, abandoned	2500/762	11.0
5.0	**Rolston Rest Shelter**	2240/683	14.9
3.3	**Elbow Road**	1951/595	16.6
1.4	**Tucker-Johnson Shelter**	2250/686	18.5
1.0	**Maine Junction, Willard Gap,** **Appalachian Trail** to Vt. 100, 2.1 mi. E, and Hanover, NH, 44 mi. E, and Katahdin, Baxter Peak, ME, 396 mi. E **Deer Leap Trail,** south end	2250/686	18.9
0.0	**U.S. 4**	1880/573	19.9

SOUTH

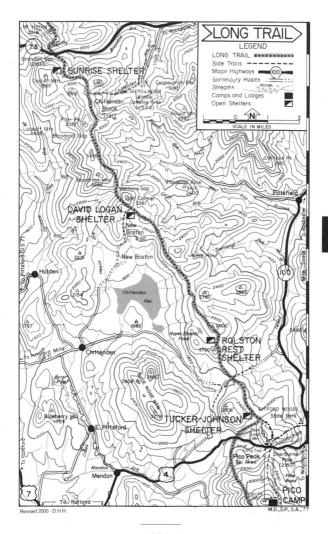

Revised 2000 - D.H.H.

M.D.,D.P., S.A.,'77

Vt. 73 (Brandon Gap) to Cooley Glen Shelter

miles north-bound	▲ NORTH	elevation at Long Trail (feet/meters)	miles south-bound
22.5	**Cooley Glen Shelter** **Cooley Glen Trail** to road, 3.2 mi. W	3130/954	0.0
22.0	**Mt. Cleveland**	3482/1061	0.5
18.9	**Mt. Roosevelt** and **Killington View**	3528/1075	3.6
18.5	**Clark Brook Trail** to road, 3.0 mi. E	3390/1033	4.0
17.7	**Mt. Wilson**	3745/1141	4.8
16.8	**Emily Proctor Shelter** **Emily Proctor Trail** to road, 3.5 mi. N	3460/1055	5.7
16.2	**Bread Loaf Mtn.**, lookout, 0.1 mi. W	3835/1169	6.3
15.0	**Skylight Pond Trail** to **Skyline Lodge**, 0.1 mi. E and USFS Road 59, 2.5 mi. W	3420/1042	7.5
14.9	**Battell Mtn.**	3482/1061	7.6
13.9	**Mt. Boyce**	3323/1013	8.6
13.0	**Boyce Shelter**	3020/920	9.5
12.4	**Burnt Hill Trail** to road, 2.2. mi. W	2950/899	10.1
10.3	**Silent Cliff Trail** to cave and cliff, 0.4 mi. E	2480/756	12.2
9.9	**Middlebury Gap, Vt. 125**	2144/653	12.6
9.5	**Lake Pleiad** (el. 2128/649 m), 0.1 mi. W	2150/655	13.0
8.9	**Middlebury Snow Bowl**, chair lift	3180/969	13.6
7.2	**Worth Mtn.**, summit	3234/986	15.3
5.4	**Sucker Brook Trail** to **Sucker Brook** **Shelter** (el. 2420/738 m), 0.1 mi. W and USFS Road 67, 1.0 mi. W	2440/744	17.1
4.5	**Romance Gap**	2685/818	18.0
4.1	**Romance Mtn.**, east summit	3125/953	18.4
3.3	**Gillespie Peak**	3366/1026	19.2
1.8	**Cape Lookoff Mtn.**	3320/1012	20.7
1.3	**Mt. Horrid**, summit	3216/980	21.2
0.7	**Great Cliff of Mt. Horrid**, 0.1 mi. E	2800/853	21.8
0.0	**Vt. 73, Brandon Gap**	2183/665	22.5

SOUTH
▼

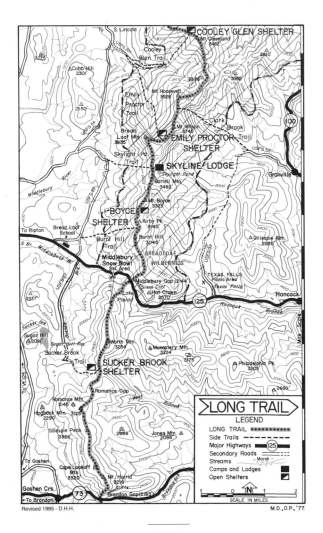

Cooley Glen Shelter to Birch Glen Camp

miles northbound	NORTH	elevation at Long Trail (feet/meters)	miles southbound
18.9	**Beane Trail** to **Birch Glen Camp,** 100 ft. W and Carse Road, 1.5 mi. W	2020/616	0.0
17.6	**Molly Stark's Balcony,** lookout	2900/884	1.3
17.3	**Molly Stark Mtn.,** summit	2960/903	1.6
16.7	**Baby Stark Mtn.,** east slope, (summit el. 2830/863 m)	2807/856	2.2
16.3	**Appalachian Gap, Vt. 17**	2365/721	2.6
14.5	**Theron Dean Shelter** **Dean Panorama and Cave,** via spur	3320/1012	4.4
13.8	**Stark's Nest**	3644/1111	5.1
13.2	**General Stark Mtn.,** highest summit	3662/1116	5.7
12.9	**Barton Trail** to **Glen Ellen Lodge** (el. 3250/991 m), 0.3 mi. E	3430/1045	6.0
12.8	**Jerusalem Trail** to road, 2.4 mi. W	3430/1045	6.1
11.4	**North boundary of the Green Mountain National Forest**	3800/1158	7.5
11.0	**Mt. Ellen,** chair lift, highest summit of Lincoln Mtn.	4083/1244	7.9
10.6	**Cutts Peak**	4022/1226	8.3
9.5	**Holt Hollow**	3710/1131	9.4
9.4	**Castlerock Chair Lift**	3750/1143	9.5
8.7	**Nancy Hanks Peak**	3812/1162	10.2
8.1	**Lincoln Peak**	3975/1212	10.8
7.3	**Mt. Abraham**	4006/1221	11.6
6.5	**Battell Shelter**	3250/991	12.4
6.4	**Battell Trail** to road, 2.0 mi. W	3250/991	12.5
4.7	**Lincoln Gap, Lincoln-Warren Highway** to Warren and Vt. 100, 4.7 mi. E	2410/735	14.2
0.8	**Mt. Grant**	3623/1104	18.1
0.0	**Cooley Glen Shelter**	3130/954	18.9

SOUTH

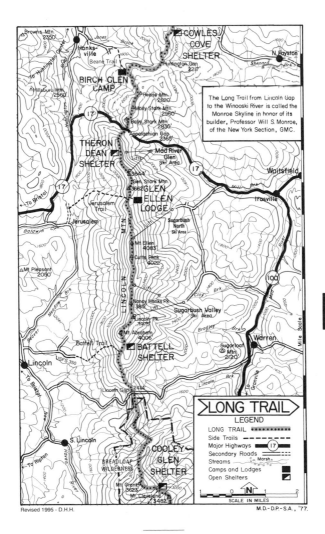

The Long Trail from Lincoln Gap to the Winooski River is called the Monroe Skyline in honor of its builder, Professor Will S. Monroe, of the New York Section, GMC.

LONG TRAIL

LEGEND

LONG TRAIL	••••••••••
Side Trails	– – – – –
Major Highways	17
Secondary Roads	
Streams	Marsh
Camps and Lodges	■
Open Shelters	◪

SCALE IN MILES

Revised 1995 - D.H.H.

M.D.-D.P.-S.A., '77.

8

Birch Glen Camp to Bolton Mountain

miles north-bound	▲ NORTH	elevation at Long Trail (feet/meters)	miles south-bound
30.3	**Bolton Mtn.**	3725/1135	0.0
27.6	**Harrington's View**, 150 ft. via spur	2585/788	2.7
26.6	**Buchanan Shelter**, 0.3 mi. via spur	2310/704	3.7
24.3	**Bolton Notch Road** to U.S. 2, 2.7 mi. S	1120/341	6.0
21.0	**Duck Brook Shelter**	670/204	9.3
19.3	**Jonesville, U.S. 2**, Winooski River Bridge	326/99	11.0
16.1	**River Road**	400/122	14.2
15.5	**Gleason Brook**	580/177	14.8
14.2	**Spruce Knob**	1720/524	16.1
11.0	**Alpine Trail** (5), northern end	2800/853	19.3
10.6	**Gorham Lodge**	3400/1036	19.7
10.2	**Camel's Hump Hut Clearing** **Burrows Trail** (6) to road, 2.1 mi. W **Monroe Trail** (7) to road, 3.1 mi. E	3800/1158	20.1
9.9	**Camel's Hump**, summit	4083/1244	20.4
9.7	**Alpine Trail** (5), south end	3800/1158	20.6
8.2	**Wind Gap, Dean Trail** (4) to **Hump Brook Tenting Area**, 0.8 mi. NE and Couching Lion Farm, 2.3 mi. NE	2800/853	22.1
8.0	**Forest City Trail** (3) to road, 2.2 mi. W	2660/811	22.3
8.0	**Montclair Glen Lodge**	2670/814	22.3
7.8	**Allis Trail** (2), south end, to LT, 0.3 mi. N	2890/881	22.5
7.0	**Mt. Ethan Allen**, north peak, lookout	3680/1122	23.3
5.9	**Mt. Ira Allen**, east slope, (el. 3506/1069 m)	3380/1030	24.4
4.4	**Burnt Rock Mtn.**	3168/966	25.9
3.8	**Hedgehog Brook Trail** (1) to road, 2.0 mi. E	2800/853	26.5
2.9	**Cowles Cove Shelter**	2520/768	27.4
1.5	**Huntington Gap**	2217/676	28.8
0.0	**Beane Trail** to **Birch Glen Camp**, 100 ft. and Carse Road, 1.5 mi. W	2020/616	30.3

SOUTH
▼

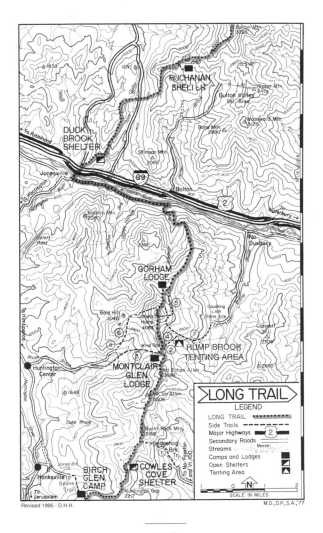

Bolton Mountain to Vt. 15

Part 1, Bolton Mountain to Chin

miles north-bound	▲ NORTH	elevation at Long Trail (feet/meters)	miles south-bound
10.1	**Chin**, Mt. Mansfield's highest peak	4395/1339	16.2
9.9	**Sunset Ridge Trail** (24) to road, 3.1 mi. W **Profanity Trail** (25), south end	4260/1298	16.4
9.7	**Cliff Trail** (16), north end	4020/1225	16.6
9.6	**Lower Lip**	4030/1228	16.7
9.4	**Upper Lip**	3964/1208	16.9
8.9	**Halfway House Trail** (21)	3880/1183	17.4
8.8	**TV Road, Amherst Trail** (15), south end	3860/1177	17.5
8.7	**Visitor Center, Toll Road, Triangle Trail** (12) to **Nose** (el. 4062/1238 m), 0.2 mi.	3849/1173	17.6
8.6	**TV Road**, at LT North	3860/1177	17.7
8.4	**TV Road**, at LT South **Forehead Bypass** (8), north end	3900/1189	17.9
8.1	**Forehead**, Mt. Mansfield's southernmost peak **Wampahoofus Trail** (10)	3940/1201	18.2
7.4	**Forehead Bypass** (8), south end **Needle's Eye**	3080/939	18.9
7.3	**Butler Lodge Trail** (4) to **Butler Lodge**, 0.1 mi. W and road, 1.9 mi. W	3040/927	19.0
7.2	**Wallace Cutoff** (5) to **Butler Lodge**, 0.1 mi. W	2900/884	19.1
6.0	**Twin Brooks Tenting Area**, 100 ft. W	2300/701	20.3
4.6	**Nebraska Notch Trail** (3) to road, 1.5 mi. W	1780/548	21.7
4.3	**Clara Bow Trail** (2), north end	1860/567	22.0
3.9	**Lake Mansfield Trail** (1) to **Taylor Lodge** and **Clara Bow Trail** (2), 0.1 mi. E and road, 1.6 mi. E	1850/564	22.4
2.8	**Mt. Clark**, east slope, (summit el. 2979/908 m)	2800/853	23.5
1.4	**Mt. Mayo**	3160/963	24.9
0.5	**Puffer Shelter**	3200/975	25.8
0.0	**Bolton Mtn.**	3725/1135	26.3

SOUTH
▼

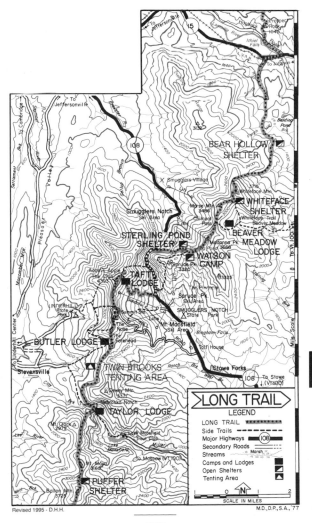

15

To Jeffersonville

Lamoille River

Prospect
Rock
1040

Ithiel
Falls

To Johnson

108

To Cambridge

To Jeffersonville

Belding
Pond
Brk

3132

BEAR HOLLOW
SHELTER

Smugglers Village

Whiteface Mtn.
3715

Smugglers Notch
Ski Area

Morse Mtn.
3446

Chin

Pass

WHITEFACE
SHELTER

Whiteface Trail
Beaver Meadow

STERLING POND
SHELTER

Madonna Pk.
3668

BEAVER
MEADOW
LODGE

WATSON
CAMP

Spruce Pk.
3320

Adams Apple
The Chin
4393

TAFT
LODGE

3125

Spruce Pk.
Ski Area

SMUGGLERS NOTCH
State
Park

UNDERHILL
State
Park

Summit Sta.

Line

The Nose

Mt. Mansfield
Ski Area

Bingham Falls

BUTLER LODGE

The Forehead

Toll House

To Underhill Center

Stevensville

Ranch
Brk

Stowe Forks

To Stowe
(Vt. 100)

108

TWIN BROOKS
TENTING AREA

10

Frey Mtn.
3377

Nebraska Notch

TAYLOR LODGE

LONG TRAIL

LEGEND

Mt. Clark
2973

Lake Mansfield
Trout Club

LONG TRAIL ....

Side Trails ━ ━ ━ ━

Major Highways ━━━ 108

Secondary Roads ‒ ‒ ‒ ‒

Streams   Marsh

Camps and Lodges

Open Shelters

Tenting Area

Mt. Major
3360

To Moscow (VT 100)

Brown

LONG
TRAIL

PUFFER
SHELTER

Bolton Mtn.
3725

0   1   2

N

SCALE IN MILES

Bolton Mountain to Vt. 15

Part 2, Chin to Vt. 15

miles north-bound	▲ NORTH	elevation at Long Trail (feet/meters)	miles south-bound
26.3	**Vt. 15** at LT North, **Lamoille River Bridge**	500/152	0.0
25.7	**Vt. 15** at LT South, **Lamoille Valley R.R.**	500/152	0.6
22.4	**Bear Hollow Shelter**	1380/421	3.9
19.3	**Whiteface Mtn.**	3715/1132	7.0
18.8	**Whiteface Shelter, Whiteface Trail** (33) to Beaver Meadow Lodge, 1.0 mi. S	3000/914	7.5
18.0	**Morse Mtn.**, east slope, (el. 3486/1063 m)	3380/1030	8.3
17.7	**Hagerman Overlook**	3100/945	8.6
17.3	**Chilcoot Pass, Chilcoot Trail** (32) to Beaver Meadow Lodge, 0.8 mi. E	2950/899	9.0
16.5	**Madonna Peak**, chair lift	3668/1118	9.8
15.3	**Elephant's Head Trail** (30), north end, to Watson Camp and Spruce Peak Sterling Pond Shelter	3030/924	11.0
15.1	**Sterling Pond Outlet**	3000/914	11.2
13.9	**Vt. 108** at LT North	2120/646	12.4
13.8	**Smugglers' Notch**, height of land	2162/659	12.5
13.3	**Big Spring, Hell Brook Trail** (29)	1803/550	13.0
12.6	**Smugglers' Notch Picnic Area** **Elephant's Head Trail** (30), south end	1600/488	13.7
12.4	**Vt. 108** at LT South	1600/488	13.9
10.7	**Taft Lodge, Hell Brook Cutoff** (28) to **Hell Brook Trail** (29) **Profanity Trail** (25), lower end	3650/1113	15.6
10.4	**Eagle Pass, Hell Brook Trail** (29), south end **Adam's Apple Trail** (27) to **Adam's Apple** (el. 4060/1237 m), 0.1 mi.	3990/1216	15.9
10.3	**Story Trail** (26) to Sunset Ridge Trail (24)	4050/1234	16.0
10.1	**Chin**, Mt. Mansfield's highest peak	4395/1339	16.2

SOUTH
▼

PROTECT MT. MANSFIELD'S ALPINE PLANTS. DO THE ROCK WALK!

- Walk on marked trails.
- Walk only on the rocks, not the plants.
- Leash dogs and keep them off the plants.
- Camping is not permitted in this alpine zone.

Vt. 15 (Lamoille River Bridge) to Tillotson Camp

miles north-bound	▲ NORTH	elevation at Long Trail (feet/meters)	miles south-bound
26.7	**Tillotson Camp**	2560/780	0.0
	Frank Post Trail to road, 2.0 mi. E		
23.9	**Belvidere Saddle**	3200/975	2.8
	Forester's Trail to **Belvidere Mtn.**		
	(el. 3360/1024 m), 0.2 mi. SE and		
	Frank Post Trail, 2.1 mi. E		
21.3	**Vt. 118** at Eden Crossing	1280/390	5.4
19.6	**Ritterbush Lookout**	1300/396	7.1
19.3	**Babcock Trail** to Vt. 118, 1.4 mi. N	1100/335	7.4
18.7	**Devil's Gulch**, south end	1260/384	8.0
18.3	**Spruce Ledge Camp**, 830 ft. E via spur	1540/469	8.4
17.4	**Bowen Mtn.**, north summit	2200/671	9.3
15.9	**Bowen Mtn.**, south summit	2290/698	10.8
14.7	**Basin Brook**	1890/576	12.0
12.9	**Butternut Mtn.**	2715/828	13.8
11.7	**Corliss Camp**	1900/579	15.0
	Davis Neighborhood Trail to road, 1.5 mi. S		
9.0	**Laraway Mtn.**, summit	2790/850	17.7
8.7	**Laraway Lookout**	2620/799	18.0
6.9	**Codding Hollow Road** to Vt. 109, 2.5 mi. W	1230/375	19.8
	and public road at Davis Neighborhood,		
	1.9 mi. E		
4.5	**Plot Road** (Johnson-Waterville Upper Road)	1254/382	22.2
3.6	**Roundtop Shelter**	1650/503	23.1
2.0	**Ed Derby Road** at LT South	960/293	24.7
1.7	**Prospect Rock**	1040/317	25.0
0.9	**Ithiel Falls Camp Meeting Ground**	510/155	25.8
0.0	**Vt. 15** at LT North	500/152	26.7
	Lamoille River Bridge		

SOUTH
▼

PLEASE RESPECT PRIVATE LAND

Use of the Long Trail in much of this area is provided through the cooperation and generosity of private landowners. Please be sure to:

- Camp only at GMC shelters and lodges. Camping between shelters is illegal without the written permission of the property owner.
- Build fires only in the one fireplace provided. No new fireplaces or fire rings should be built. Use only dead wood. Better yet, use a backpacking stove and spare the woods.
- As elsewhere on the Long Trail, carry all litter out.
- Clean the shelter and site before leaving. Treat the building and surroundings as if they were your own.
- Avoid parking in driveways or using people's lawns. Stay on the trail.

Thank you! Your cooperation will help assure the continued existence of the Long Trail and side trails on private lands.

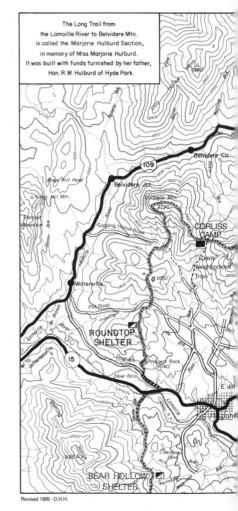

The Long Trail from
the Lamoille River to Belvidere Mtn.
is called the Marjorie Hulburd Section,
in memory of Miss Marjorie Hulburd.
It was built with funds furnished by her father,
Hon. R.W. Hulburd of Hyde Park.

Revised 1999 - D.H.H.

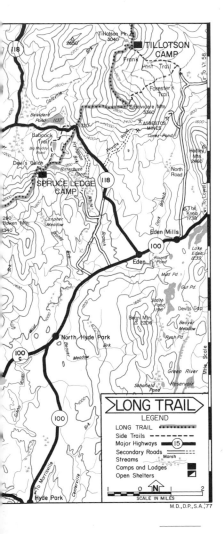

LONG TRAIL

LEGEND

LONG TRAIL ••••••••••
Side Trails ‑ ‑ ‑ ‑ ‑ ‑ ‑ ‑
Major Highways 15
Secondary Roads ====
Streams   Marsh
Camps and Lodges ■
Open Shelters ◣

0   N   2
SCALE IN MILES

M.D.,D.P.,S.A.,'77

Tillotson Camp to the Canadian Border

miles north-bound	▲ NORTH	elevation at Trail (feet/meters)	miles south-bound
	JOURNEY'S END TRAIL		
1.3	**Northern terminus of the Long Trail**	2100/640	0.0
0.5	**Journey's End Camp**	1550/472	0.8
0.0	**Journey's End Trail trailhead**	1020/311	1.3
	LONG TRAIL		
23.3	**U.S.-Canadian Border, Line Post 592 Northern terminus of the Long Trail**	2100/640	0.0
21.9	**Carleton Mtn.**, lookout	2670/814	1.4
20.7	**North Jay Pass, Vt. 105**	2150/655	2.6
19.5	**Burnt Mtn.**, lookout via spur	2570/783	3.8
18.9	**Shooting Star Shelter**	2260/689	4.4
16.0	**Unnamed peak of North Jay massif** (North Jay summit el. 3400/1036)	3320/1012	7.3
15.5	**Doll Peak**	3380/1030	7.8
14.6	**Laura Woodward Shelter**	2800/853	8.7
13.1	**Jay Peak Tramway**	3861/1177	10.2
11.7	**Jay Loop**, north end, to **Jay Camp**, 0.2 mi. S	2600/792	11.6
11.5	**Jay Loop**, south end, to **Jay Camp**, 0.2 mi. W	2200/671	11.8
11.4	**Jay Pass, Vt. 242, Atlas Valley Shelter**	2180/664	11.9
10.6	**Gilpin Mtn.**, south summit, lookout	2920/890	12.7
9.6	**Domey's Dome**	2880/878	13.7
8.6	**Chet's Lookout**	2900/884	14.7
8.4	**Buchanan Mtn.**	2940/896	14.9
7.5	**Bruce Peak**	2900/884	15.8
6.1	**Hazen's Notch Camp**, 0.1 mi. W via spur	2040/622	17.2
4.6	**Hazen's Notch, Vt. 58**	1780/543	18.7
2.7	**Haystack Mtn.** (el. 3223/982 m), summit 0.2 mi. W via spur	3180/969	20.6
0.6	**Tillotson Peak**, east slope (el. 3040/927 m)	2980/908	22.7
0.0	**Tillotson Camp** **Frank Post Trail** to road, 2.0 mi. E	2560/780	23.3

SOUTH
▼

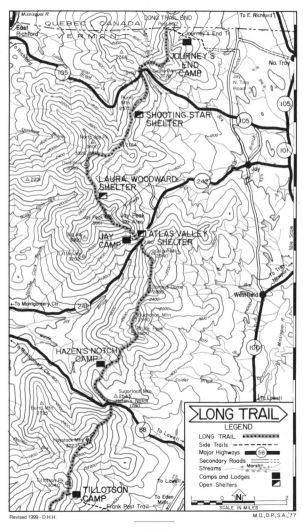

Appalachian Trail 1
Long Trail (Maine Junction)
to Vt. 12

miles north-bound	▲ NORTH	elevation at Trail (feet/meters)	miles south-bound
22.0	**Vt. 12** (Barnard Gulf Road) **Gulf Stream**, bridge crossing	882/269	0.0
18.3	**Wintturi Shelter**, 0.2 mi. N via spur	1900/579	3.7
16.7	**Lookout Farm Road**	2200/671	5.3
15.9	**The Lookout**, 100 yds. N	2320/707	6.1
14.2	**Lakota Lake Lookout**	2640/805	7.8
13.1	**Chateauguay Road**	2000/610	8.9
11.1	**Height of land** between Stony Brook and Chateauguay Road	2260/689	10.9
9.3	**Stony Brook**	1600/488	12.7
8.7	**Stony Brook Shelter**, 0.1 mi. via spur	1360/415	13.3
7.7	**Height of land** between Ottauquechee River and Stony Brook	2550/777	14.3
4.4	**River Road**	1214/370	17.6
2.5	**Kent Pond**	1540/469	19.5
2.1	**Vt. 100**	1580/482	19.9
1.9	**Gifford Woods State Park**	1660/506	20.1
1.2	**Ben's Balcony**	2220/677	20.8
0.9	**Sherburne Pass Trail**, north end, to U.S. 4 (Sherburne Pass) and Inn at Long Trail, 0.5 mi. S **Deer Leap Trail**, north end	2440/744	21.1
0.1	**Deer Leap Trail**, south end	2280/695	21.9
0.0	**Maine Junction, Willard Gap Long Trail to Canada**, 165.9 mi. N	2250/686	22.0

SOUTH
▼

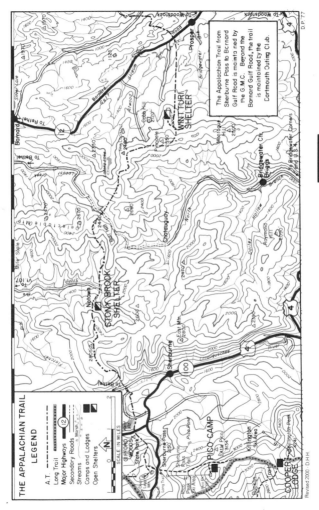

The Appalachian Trail from Sherburne Pass to Barnard Gulf Road is maintained by the G.M.C. Beyond the Barnard Gulf Road, the trail is maintained by the Dartmouth Outing Club.

THE APPALACHIAN TRAIL LEGEND

A T – · – · –
Long Trail ――――――
Major Highways ■■■■■■■■
Secondary Roads 12
Streams – – – – –
Camps and Lodges ■
Open Shelters ■

SCALE IN MILES

Revised 2000, D.H.H.

AT 1

Appalachian Trail 2
Vt. 12 to the Connecticut River

miles northbound	▲ NORTH	elevation at Trail (feet/meters)	miles southbound
21.9	**Connecticut River**, Vt. 10A, Ledyard Bridge	380/116	0.0
20.9	**Norwich Village Green**, U.S. 5	537/164	1.0
20.1	**Elm Street**, at AT South	750/229	1.8
16.8	**William Tucker Trail** to road, 0.8 mi. E	1320/402	5.1
16.6	**Happy Hill Shelter**, S via spur	1420/433	5.3
13.2	**Podunk Road**	860/262	8.7
13.0	**Tigertown Road**	390/119	8.9
12.6	**West Hartford, Vt. 14**, White River crossing	390/119	9.3
9.3	**Joe Ranger Road**	1280/390	12.6
7.8	**Thistle Hill Shelter**, S via spur	1480/451	14.1
5.5	**Cloudland Road**	1370/418	16.4
3.7	**Pomfret–South Pomfret (County) Road**	980/299	18.2
3.0	**Bartlett Brook Road**	980/299	18.9
1.5	**Woodstock Stage Road**	820/250	20.4
1.2	**Dana Hill**	1530/466	20.7
0.0	**Vt. 12** (Barnard Gulf Road)	882/269	21.9

SOUTH
▼

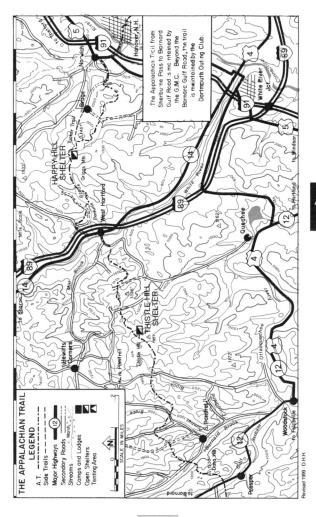

The Appalachian Trail from Sherburne Pass to Barnard Gulf Road is maintained by the G.M.C. Beyond the Barnard Gulf Road, the trail is maintained by the Dartmouth Outing Club.

THE APPALACHIAN TRAIL
LEGEND

A.T. — — —
Side Trails - - - - -
Major Highways
Secondary Roads
Streams
Marsh
Camps and Lodges
Open Shelters
Tenting Area

SCALE (IN MILES)

N

Revised 1999 - D.H.H.

AT
2

Public Campgrounds
Near the Long Trail

Many Vermont state parks and U.S. Forest Service campgrounds make excellent bases for day hiking on the Long Trail. Campgrounds closest to the Trail are listed below. The location of the campground and the closest LT system trailhead are noted. Reservations are highly recommended at state campgrounds. Rates are between $10 and $16. At U.S. Forest Service campgrounds, a small fee is charged (generally $5) and the sites are first come, first served, except where noted. For more information, call the numbers listed below.

Divisions 1 and 2

Woodford State Park, Woodford
- (802) 447-7169 or Jan. to May (802) 483-2001
- From Bennington: 10 mi. east on Vt. 9

Red Mill, Woodford (U.S. Forest Service)
- (802) 362-2307
- From Bennington: 10 mi. east on Vt. 9, then 1 mi. north on USFS Rd. 274

Closest trailhead: LT crossing on Vt. 9

Divisions 2 and 3

Grout Pond, Stratton (U.S. Forest Service)
- (802) 362-2307
- From Stratton: 2.5 mi. west on Arlington–West Wardsboro Rd., then south on USFS Rd. 262

Closest trailheads: LT and side trails to Stratton Mtn., and Stratton and Bourn Ponds

Divisions 3 and 4

Emerald Lake State Park, North Dorset
- (802) 362-1655 or Jan. to May (802) 483-2001
- On U.S. 7 in North Dorset

Closest trailheads: LT on USFS Rd. 10, and Lake Trail and Baker Peak Trail

Hapgood Pond, Peru (U.S. Forest Service)
- (802) 362-2307
- From Vt. 11 in Peru: 2.0 mi. north on Hapgood Pond Rd.
- Reservations accepted

Closest trailhead: LT on Vt. 11 and 30 South

Division 5

Coolidge State Park, Plymouth
- (802) 672-3612 or Jan. to May (802) 886-2434
- From junction of Vt. 100 and Vt. 100A in Plymouth Union: 3.0 mi. north on Vt. 100A

Closest trailhead: Shrewsbury Peak Trail

Divisions 5 and 6

Gifford Woods State Park, Killington
- (802) 775-5354 or Jan. to May (802) 886-2434
- From junction of U.S. 4 and Vt. 100: 0.5 mi. north on Vt. 100

Closest trailheads: AT leaves from park; LT on U.S. 4 in Sherburne Pass

Divisions 6 and 7

Branbury State Park, Brandon
- (802) 247-5925 or Jan. to May (802) 483-2001
- From junction of Vt. 73 and Vt. 53: 6.0 mi. north on Vt. 53

Moosalamoo, Ripton (U.S. Forest Service)
- (802) 388-4362
- From junction of Vt. 73 and Vt. 53 in Forest Dale: 1.6 mi. east on Vt. 73, then left on USFS Rd. 32 for 5.3 mi., and left again on USFS Rd. 24

Closest trailheads: LT at Brandon and Middlebury Gaps

Chittenden Brook, Chittenden (U.S. Forest Service)
- (802) 767-4261 or (802) 767-4777
- From the junction of Vt. 100 and Vt. 73: 5.2 mi. west on Vt. 73, then 2.5 mi. south on USFS Rd. 45

Closest trailheads: LT is 3.7 mi. west via Chittenden Brook Trail; LT in Brandon Gap nearby

Divisions 8, 9, and 10

Little River State Park, Waterbury
- (802) 244-7103 or Jan. to May (802) 479-4280
- From the northern junction of U.S. 2 and Vt. 100 in Waterbury: 1.5 mi. west on U.S. 2 to Little River Rd., then right (north) for 3.5 mi.

Closest trailheads: Hiking on the LT and side trails to Mt. Ellen, Camel's Hump, and Mt. Mansfield nearby

Division 10

Underhill State Park, Underhill
- (802) 899-3022 or Jan. to May (802) 879-5674
- From Underhill Center: 1.0 mi. north on Pleasant Valley Rd., then east 2.7 mi. on the Mountain Rd. (Town Highway 2)

Closest trailheads: Explore Mt. Mansfield via many trails from the park.

Divisions 9, 10, and 11

Smugglers' Notch State Park, Stowe
- (802) 253-4014 or Jan. to May (802) 479-4280
- From Stowe: 8 mi. north on Vt. 108

Vermont State Ski Dorm
- (802) 253-4010
- From Stowe: 7 mi. north on Vt. 108

Closest trailheads: LT and side trails to Mt. Mansfield and Sterling Pond nearby

Divisions 10 and 11

Elmore State Park, Lake Elmore
- (802) 888-2982 or Jan. to May (802) 479-4280
- From Morrisville: south 5 mi. on Vt. 12

Closest trailheads: Trails to Mt. Mansfield and northern areas of Division 10 nearby

Post Offices and Stores

The communities listed below are those nearest the Long Trail and its side trails. Each has at least one grocery or general store. Those in boldface are larger communities offering more goods, services, and accommodations. Communities without a postal zip code following the name do not have a post office. Address hiker's mail sent to post offices: "General Delivery—Hold for Long Trail hiker—Arriving [date]."

Division 1
North Adams, MA 01247; Greylock, MA; Williamstown Station, MA; **Williamstown, MA 01267**; Stamford, VT; **Bennington 05201**

Division 2
East Arlington 05252; **Arlington 05250**; West Wardsboro 05360

Division 3
Peru 05152; Manchester Center 05255; **Manchester 05254**

Division 4
Danby 05739; South Wallingford; East Wallingford 05742; Wallingford 05773

Division 5
Cuttingsville 05738; North Clarendon 05759; Sherburne (Killington 05751); **Rutland 05701**

Division 6
Chittenden 05737; Rochester 05767; Forest Dale 05745; **Brandon 05733**

Division 7
Hancock 05748; Ripton 05766; East Middlebury 05740; **Middlebury 05753**; Granville 05747

Division 8
Warren 05674; Lincoln; **Bristol 05443**; Waitsfield 05673

Division 9
Huntington 05462; Jonesville 05466; Richmond 05477; **Waterbury 05676**

Division 10
Moscow 05662; Underhill Center 05490; **Stowe 05672**; Morristown Corners; **Morrisville 0561**

Division 11
Johnson 05656; Waterville 05492; Belvidere Center 05442; Eden 05652

Division 12
Lowell 05847; Montgomery Center 05471; Westfield 05874; Jay; **North Troy 05859**; **Richford 05476**

Useful Addresses

Green Mountain Club
4711 Waterbury-Stowe Rd., Waterbury Center, VT 05677
(802) 244-7037   www.greenmountainclub.org

Appalachian Trail Conference
New England Regional Office
P.O. Box 312, Lyme, NH 03768-0312
(603) 795-4935

Appalachian Trail Conference
799 Washington St., P.O. Box 807, Harpers Ferry, WV 25425
(304) 535-6331   www.atconf.org

Catamount Trail Association
1 Main St., Suite 308, Burlington, VT 05401-5291
(802) 864-5794   www.catamounttrail.together.com

Dartmouth Outing Club
Outdoor Programs Office
119 Robinson Hall, Hanover, NH 03755
(603) 646-2834   www.dartmouth.edu/student/doc

Department of Forests, Parks and Recreation
Barre Regional Office
324 N. Main St., Barre, VT 05641-4109
(802) 476-0170

Department of Forests, Parks and Recreation
Essex Junction Regional Office
111 West St., Essex Junction, VT 05452
(802) 879-6565

Department of Forests, Parks and Recreation
Pittsford Regional Office
317 Sanitorium Rd., West Wing, Pittsford, VT 05763-9358
(802) 483-2314

Department of Forests, Parks, and Recreation
Vermont Agency of Natural Resources
103 S. Main St., Waterbury, VT 05671-0601
(802) 241-3655   www.state.vt.us/anr/fpr

Green Mountain National Forest
Forest Supervisor's Office
Route 7, 231 N. Main St., Rutland, VT 05701
(802) 747-6700   www.fs.fed.us/r9/gmfl

U.S. Forest Service
Manchester Ranger District
2538 Depot St., Manchester Center, VT 05255
(802) 362-2307

U.S. Forest Service
Middlebury Ranger District
1007 Route 7 South, Middlebury, VT 05753
(802) 388-4362

U.S. Forest Service
Rochester Ranger District
99 Ranger Rd., Rochester, VT 05767
(802) 767-4261

Vermont State Police Headquarters
Waterbury State Complex
103 S. Main St., Waterbury, VT 05676
(802) 244-8727

Vermont Department of Travel and Tourism
6 Baldwin St., Drawer 33
Montpelier, VT 05633
(800) VERMONT   (802) 828-3237
www.travel-vermont.com

GMC Publications

The Green Mountain Club welcomes inquiries about hiking and backpacking in Vermont. For more information, or to order GMC publications, write or call:

The Green Mountain Club, Inc.
4711 Waterbury-Stowe Road
Waterbury Center, Vermont 05677
Phone: (802) 244-7037
E-mail: gmc@greenmountainclub.org
www.greenmountainclub.org

Guidebooks

Day Hiker's Guide to Vermont (3rd edition, 1987, new edition in 2000). Companion volume to *Long Trail Guide*; describes most of the hiking trails in Vermont outside of the Long Trail System. Comprehensive coverage of more than two hundred trails throughout the state, thirty-six topographical maps, hiking tips and suggestions.

The Long Trail End-to-Ender's Guide (New edition annually). Handy supplement to *Long Trail Guide* for long-distance hikers. Up-to-date information on trail conditions, overnight accommodations, equipment sales and repairs, mail drops, and transportation.

Trail Maps

Mt. Mansfield (2000). Color, foldout topographical map of the Mt. Mansfield area; weather resistant, with trail mileages, overnight facilities, trailheads, and regulations.

Mt. Mansfield Booklet

Tundra Trail, A Self-Guiding Walk: Life, Man and the Ecosystem on Top of Mt. Mansfield, Vermont. Twelve-page booklet with illustrations describes a natural history hike along the Long Trail on the ridge of Mt. Mansfield.

GMC History

Green Mountain Adventure, Vermont's Long Trail (1st edition, 1989). An illustrated history of the Green Mountain Club by Jane and Will Curtis and Frank Lieberman. Ninety-six pages of rare black-and-white photographs and anecdotes of the Club's first seventy-five years.

Pamphlets

A Group Hiking Guide for Vermont's Long Trail and Appalachian Trail. Information about group permits, Leave No Trace™, group size, and more. Free with self-addressed stamped envelope (SASE).

The Long Trail: A Footpath in the Wilderness. Information and suggestions on hiking the Long Trail. Free with SASE.

Winter Trail Use in the Green Mountains. Basic information about using the Long Trail System in winter. Free with SASE.

Periodicals

The Long Trail News. GMC's quarterly membership newsletter provides trail and shelter updates, hiking, statewide trail information, Club history, and a Club activities calendar.

The Patroller. Trails and shelters newsletter; mailed to active trail maintainers.

Additional Reading

The Green Mountain Club suggests the following books as you make your way through the natural world. They may make your trip safer and more enjoyable and help you identify the plants and animals you may encounter as you hike in the Northeast. All books are available from the Green Mountain Club headquarters.

Natural History and Field Guides

- *AMC Field Guide to Mountain Flowers of New England*, Appalachian Mountain Club Books, 1964.
- *Field Guide to the Birds of North America*, National Geographic Society, 2nd edition, 1994.
- *The Nature of Vermont,* Charles W. Johnson, University Press of New England, 1980.
- *Newcomb's Wildflower Guide*, Lawrence Newcomb, Little, Brown & Co., 1989.
- The *Peterson Field Guides Series,* Houghton Mifflin Co., or *Stokes Nature Guides,* Little Brown & Co., include guides to flora, fauna, and ecology.
- *Tracking and the Art of Seeing: How to Read Animal Tracks and Sign*, Paul Rezendes, Camden House, 1992.

Hiking "How to" Books

- *Backpacking: One Step at a Time*, Harvey Manning, Vintage Books, 1986.
- *The Complete Walker III*, Colin Fletcher, Alfred A. Knopf, 1984.
- *Mountaineering First Aid, A Guide to Accident Response and First Aid Care*, The Mountaineers, 1990.
- *The NOLS Cookery: Experience the Art of Outdoor Cooking,* National Outdoor Leadership School, 1991.

Winter Outings

- *AMC Guide to Winter Camping: Winter Travel and Adventure in the Cold-Weather Months,* Stephen Gorman, AMC Books, 1991.

- *Winterwise, A Backpacker's Guide*, John M. Dunn, Adirondack Mountain Club Books, 1988.

Ethics and History of Outdoor Recreation
- *Backwoods Ethics, Environmental Issues for Hikers and Campers*, 2nd edition, Laura and Guy Waterman, Countryman Press, 1993.
- *Forest and Crag, A History of Hiking, Trail Blazing, and Adventure in the Northeast Mountains*, Laura and Guy Waterman, AMC Books, 1989.
- *Green Mountain Adventure, Vermont's Long Trail*, Jane and Will Curtis and Frank Lieberman, Green Mountain Club, 1989.
- *Wilderness Ethics, Preserving the Spirit of Wildness*, Laura and Guy Waterman, Countryman Press, 1993.

Green Mountain Trail Guides and Maps
- *Appalachian Trail Guide to New Hampshire-Vermont*, 8th edition, Appalachian Trail Conference, 1995.
- *Best Hikes with Children in Vermont, New Hampshire, and Maine*, Cynthia C. Lewis and Thomas J. Lewis, The Mountaineers, 1991.
- *Day Hiker's Guide to Vermont*, GMC Publications, 1987.
- *Fifty Hikes in Vermont*, 4th edition, Green Mountain Club, Backcountry Publications, Countryman Press, 1990.
- *Guide to the Taconic Crest Trail*, Taconic Hiking Club, 1992.
- *Hiker's Guide to the Mountains of Vermont*, Jared Gange, Huntington Graphics, 1994.
- *The Long Trail End-to-Ender's Guide*, GMC Publications.
- *Mt. Ascutney Guide*, 5th edition, Ascutney Trails Association, 1992.
- *Trail Map: Mt. Mansfield*, GMC Publications, 1995.

Index

abbreviations xiii
Abraham, Mt. 113
Adam's Apple 145
Adam's Apple Trail 144–145, 159
Airport Lookout 89; hike, 86
Allis Trail 122, 123, 129
alpine areas 10, 44–46
Alpine Trail 123, 126, 130–131
Amherst Trail 143, 155–156
Appalachian Gap 112, 116
Appalachian Trail 1, 33; approach to Long Trail, 49–51
Appalachian Trail Conference 30, 33
Arlington–West Wardsboro Rd. 57, 62, 65, 66
Arms Hill 186
Atlas Valley Shelter 174

Babcock Trail 167, 169
Babcock Trail Extension 167, 168–169
Baby Stark Mtn. 116
Baker Peak 77; hike, 74
Baker Peak Trail 77, 83
Bald Mtn. 62–63
Bald Mtn. Trail 59, 62–63
Bamforth Ridge hike, 119
Barnard Gulf Road. See Vt. 12
Barton Trail 114
Battell Mtn. 105
Battell Shelter 113
Battell Trail 112–113, 116–117
Beacon Hill 89; hike, 86
Beane Trail 116, 117, 121
Bear Hollow Shelter 149; hike, 135
Beaver Meadow Lodge 147; hike, 135

Beaver Meadow Trail 147, 160–161
Belvidere Mtn. 167–168; hike, 163
Big Branch Shelter 78
Big Branch Wilderness 10, 74, 77, 78; hike, 75
Big Muddy Pond 169; hike, 162
Birch Glen Camp 116, 121; hike, 110
Black Swamp Trail 94
blazes, trail, 2
Bloodroot Mtn. 99
Bolton Mtn. 128, 139
Bolton Notch Road 120, 127
Bourn Pond 70, 71, 72
Bowen Mtn. 167
Boyce, Mt. 105
Boyce Shelter 105
Branch Pond 72
Branch Pond Trail 68, 72
Brandon Gap 97, 100, 103
Bread Loaf Mtn. 106
Breadloaf Wilderness 10, 102, 105, 110, 112
Broad Brook Trail 53, 55
Bromley Mtn. 69–70; hike, 64
Bromley Tenting Area 69
Bruce Peak 173
Buchanan, Bruce 26, 173
Buchanan Mtn. 173
Buchanan, Roy O. 25, 26, 27, 32, 127, 173
Buchanan Shelter 127–128
Bucklin Trail 92, 94–95
Burnt Hill 105
Burnt Hill Trail 105, 108
Burnt Mtn. 176
Burnt Rock Mtn. 122
Burrows Trail 125, 131

Butler Lodge 141; hike, 135
Butler Lodge Trail 141, 142, 151
Butternut Mtn. 166
Button Hill 88

Camel's Hump 118, 120–121, 123, 125
campgrounds, public, 222–224
camping 7–8; winter, 18–19
Cantilever Rock Trail 158
Canyon North Extension 144, 157
Canyon North Trail 143, 156–157
Canyon Trail 143
Cape Lookoff Mtn. 104
caretakers 3–4, 28, 32
Carleton Mtn. 176; hike, 170
Carleton, Phillips D. 26, 176
Catamount Trail 19–20
Caughnawaga Shelter 61
Chateauguay Road 181
Chilcoot Trail 147, 161
Chin, Mt. Mansfield's, 144
Chittenden Brook Trail 99, 101; hike, 96
Clara Bow Trail 139, 141, 151
Clarendon Gorge 89
Clarendon Shelter 89
Clark Brook Trail 107, 109
Clark, Mt. 139
Cleveland, Mt. 107
Cliff Trail 144, 156
Cloudland Road 186
Codding Hollow Road 164, 165
Cold River (Lower) Road 88, 90
Congdon Shelter 54
Consultation Peak 54
Cooley Glen Shelter 107, 112
Cooley Glen Trail 107, 109
Cooper Lodge 92
Corliss Camp 166
Cowles Cove Shelter 121

Cutts Peak 114
Dana Hill 185
David Logan Shelter 99
Davis Neighborhood Trail 166, 168
Dean Trail 123, 130
Deer Leap Trail 179, 183
Devil's Gulch 167; hike, 162
Dewey, Mt. 141
distances, hiking, 13
Doll, Charles G. 26, 175, 176
Doll Peak 175
Domey's Dome 173
Duck Brook Shelter 126–127; hike, 118
DuPuis Hill 186

East Mtn. 50
Ed Derby Road 165
Elephant's Head Trail 145, 146, 160; hike, 135
Ellen, Mt. 114; hike, 111
Emily Proctor Shelter 106
Emily Proctor Trail 106, 108–109
end-to-end, Long Trail, 25, 27
equipment 11–13
Ethan Allen, Mt. 122; hike, 119

Farr Peak 99
fire, restrictions, 7–8
Forehead, Mt. Mansfield's, 142
Forehead Bypass 142, 152
Forest City–Burrows Connector 133
Forest City Trail 123, 129–130
Forester's Trail 167–168, 169
Frank Post Trail 168, 169, 172
Frost Trail 152
Gameroff Hiker Center 24
gear. See equipment
General Stark Mtn. 115

geology, of Green Mtns., 37–38
Gillespie Peak 104
Gilpin Mtn. 173
Glastenbury Mtn. 59; hike, 56
Glen Ellen Lodge 114
Goddard Shelter 59
Gorham Lodge 125
Governor Clement Shelter
    90–91
Grant, Mt. 112
Green Mtn. 84; hike, 74
Green Mountains: geology of,
    37–38; history of the land,
    36–42; native peoples,
    39–40; natural history,
    36–46; plants and animals,
    42–46
Green Mountain Club:
    Gameroff Hiker Center, 24;
    headquarters, 24, 28; history,
    25–29; land protection,
    34–35; membership, 23;
    publications, 228–229;
    recognition by Vt. Gen.
    Assembly, 29; sections, 23,
    31–32; volunteers, 31–32
Green Mountain National
    Forest 49, 56, 65, 75, 96,
    103, 111; camping, fires, per-
    mits, 7–9; management of
    trail in, 30; northern bound-
    ary of, 114; shelter fees, 4
Green Mountain Parkway 28
Green Mountain Trail 79, 84
Greenwall Shelter 81
Griffith Lake 77
Griffith Lake Tenting Area 77
group use 8–9; permits 9

Halfway House Trail 143, 157
Happy Hill Shelter 187
Harmon Hill 54; hike, 48
Haselton Trail 143, 155

Haystack Mtn. 172; hike, 171
Hazen's Notch 171, 172
Hazen's Notch Camp 170,
    172–173
Hedgehog Brook Trail 122,
    129
Hell Brook Cutoff 145, 159
Hell Brook Trail 145, 159–160
Hogback Road 163
Homer Stone Brook Trail 79,
    84–85
Horrid, Mt. 104; Great Cliff of,
    104; hike, 102
Hump Brook Tenting Area 123,
    130
hunting 16
hypothermia 14–15

Ira Allen, Mt. 122

Jay Camp 174
Jay Loop 174
Jay Pass 171, 173
Jay Peak 174–175; hike,
    170–171
Jerusalem Trail 114, 117
Joe Ranger Road 186
Journey's End Camp 177
Journey's End Trail 177

Keewaydin Trail 81, 85
Kelley Stand Road. See
    Arlington–West Wardsboro
    Road
Kent Pond 179
Kid Gore Shelter 61
Killington Peak 91; hike, 87
Killington Spur 91, 94
Kirby Peak 105

Lake Mansfield 150
Lake Mansfield Trail 139,
    150–151
Lake of the Clouds 144, 145

Lake Pleiad 105; hike, 102

Lake Trail 77, 83

Lakeview Trail 142, 143, 155

Laraway Lookout 166; hike, 162, 163

Laraway Mtn. 166; hike, 163

Laura Cowles Trail 158

Laura Woodward Shelter 175

leave-no-trace 4–6

lightning 15–16

Lincoln Gap 111–112

Lincoln Mtn. 113

Lincoln Peak 113

Lincoln-Warren Highway. *See* Lincoln Gap

Little Killington 91

Little Pond Mtn. 58

Little Rock Pond 79; hike, 74

Little Rock Pond Loop Trail 79, 83

Little Rock Pond Shelter 81

Little Rock Pond Tenting Area 79

Lockwood Pond 168

Long Trail: end-to-end of, 25, 27; guidelines for, 2–21; history of, 25–29; length of, 1; management of, 30–33; northern approach to, 176–177; protection of, 34–35; southern approach to, 49–51; transportation to, 20–21

Long Trail News 23, 27, 229

Long Trail Patrol 27, 32

Lookout Farm Road 181

Lost Pond Shelter 78

Lottery Road 89

Lula Tye Shelter 79

Lye Brook Trail 67, 71–72

Lye Brook Wilderness 10, 64, 68, 70, 71; hike, 65

MacKaye, Benton 33, 66

Madonna Peak 147

Mad Tom Notch 66, 70, 75, 76

Maine Junction 97, 179

Mansfield, Mt., 134, 137–139, 142–145; Toll Road, 143, traverse of, 135; Visitor Center/Summit Station, 142–143

Maple Hill 58

Maple Ridge Trail 142, 152–153

Mass. 2. 50

Mayo, Mt. 139

Melville Nauheim Shelter 58

membership, in GMC, 23

Middlebury Gap 103, 105

Mill Road 49, 53

Minerva Hinchey Shelter 88

Molly Stark's Balcony 116; hike, 110

Molly Stark Mtn. 116

Monroe Trail 125, 131-132

Montclair Glen Lodge 122–123

Morse Mtn. 147

mud season 9–10

Nancy Hanks Peak 113

National Park Service 30

native peoples, in Green Mtns., 39–40

natural history 36–46

Nebraska Notch 139; hike, 135

Nebraska Notch Trail 141, 151

New Boston Trail 99, 100–101

North Bourn Pond Tenting Area 72

North Jay Pass 171, 176

North Shore Tenting Area 68, 72

North Shore Trail 68, 71–72

Old Bennington–Heartwellville Rd. 54

Old Job Shelter 78, 82
Old Job Trail 77, 78, 82–83
overnight sites 3–4

parking 21
peregrine falcons 11
permits, group 9
Peru Peak 76
Peru Peak Shelter 76
Peru Peak Wilderness 10, 74, 76
Pico Camp 92–93
Pico Link 92, 95
Pico Peak 92; hike, 86–87
Pine Cobble 51; hike, 48
Pine Cobble Trail 48, 50, 51
Pinnacle 181
plants and animals, in Green
  Mtns., 42–46
Plot Road 164, 165
Podunk Road 187
Pomfret–South Pomfret
  (County) Road 185
Porcupine Lookout 58; hike, 56
post offices near Long Trail 225
Profanity Trail 144, 145, 159
Prospect Rock (Div. 3) 68
Prospect Rock (Div. 11)
  164–165; hike, 162
public campgrounds 222–224
publications, GMC, 228–229
Puffer Shelter 139

Quimby Mtn. 180

rabies 17–18
Ritterbush Pond 167; hike, 162
River Road (Div. 9) 119–120,
  126
River Road (AT 1) 179, 180
Roaring Branch 53; hike, 48
Rock Garden Trail 142, 152
Rolston Rest Shelter 98
Romance Mtn. 104
Roosevelt, Mt. 107; hike, 102

Rootville Road 68
Roundtop Shelter 165

safety 11–13
Sawyer Hill 183
sections. *See* Green Mountain
  Club
Seth Warner Shelter 53
shelters 3–4
Sherburne Pass Trail 92, 95,
  179, 183
Sherman Brook Primitive
  Campsite 50
Shooting Star Shelter 175–176
Shrewsbury Peak 93; hike, 86
Shrewsbury Peak Shelter 94
Shrewsbury Peak Trail 91, 93
Silent Cliff Trail 105, 108
skiing. *See* winter trail use
Skylight Pond 105–106
Skylight Pond Trail 105, 108
Skyline Lodge 105–106
Smugglers' Notch 136–137,
  145–146
snowshoeing. *See* winter trail use
South Bourn Pond Shelter 71,
  72
South Link 153, 155
Split Rock 58; hike, 56
spring and fall hiking 9–10
Spruce Ledge Camp 167
Spruce Peak 69; hike, 64
Spruce Peak Shelter 69
Stark's Nest 115
state lands: camping and fires,
  7–8; permits, 9
Sterling Pond 146
Sterling Pond Shelter 146
Stony Brook Shelter 181
stores near Long Trail 225
Story Spring Shelter 61
Story Trail 159
Stratton Mtn. 66–67; hike, 64

Stratton Pond 67–68
Stratton Pond Shelter 67, 68
Stratton Pond Trail 67, 70
Styles Peak 76; hike, 74
Subway 144, 157
Sucker Brook Shelter 104
Sucker Brook Trail 104, 107–108
Sugar Hill Road 81
Summit Station, Mt. Mansfield, 142
Sunrise Shelter 99
Sunset Ridge Trail 144, 158

Taft Lodge 145
Taylor, James P. 25, 26, 66
Taylor Lodge 139, 141
Theron Dean Shelter 115
Thistle Hill 186
Thistle Hill Shelter, 186
Thundering Brook Road 179
Tigertown Road 187
Tillotson Camp 168, 172
Tillotson Peak 172
trail marking 2
Triangle Trail 155
trip planning 11–13
Tucker-Johnson Shelter 97
TV Road 142, 143
Twin Brooks Tenting Area 141

U.S. Forest Service 30
USFS Road 10. 75–76, 78
USFS Road 21. See Mad Tom Notch
USFS Road 71. 62
U.S. 2. 120, 126
U.S. 4. 88, 95, 97, 178, 183
U.S. 5. 185, 187
Upper Road 90

vandalism, avoiding, 21
Vermont Department of Forests, Parks, and Recreation 30

Vt. 9. 49, 55, 57
Vt. 11 and 30. 65–66, 69
Vt. 12. 179, 183, 184, 185
Vt. 14. 185, 187
Vt. 15. 137, 150, 163–164
Vt. 17. See Appalachian Gap
Vt. 58. See Hazen's Notch
Vt. 73. See Brandon Gap
Vt. 100. 178–179
Vt. 103. 87, 89
Vt. 105. See North Jay Pass
Vt. 108. See Smugglers' Notch
Vt. 118. 164, 167
Vt. 125. See Middlebury Gap
Vt. 140. 76, 81, 87, 88
Vt. 242. See Jay Pass

Wallace Cutoff 141, 152
Wampahoofus Trail 142, 153
water concerns 6–7
Watson Camp 146–147
weather, in Green Mtns., 14
West Ridge Trail 59, 62
Whiteface Mtn. 149
Whiteface Shelter 147, 149
Whiteface Trail 149, 161
White Rocks Cliff Trail 81, 85
White Rocks Mtn. 81
White Rocks National Recreation Area 74, 76, 81
wilderness areas, cautions, 10
Willard Gap 97, 179
William B. Douglas Shelter 68, 73
William Tucker Trail 187, 188
Wilson, Mt. 107
winter trail use 18–20; hypothermia, 14–15; sanitation, 19. See Catamount Trail
Wintturi Shelter 183
Woodstock Stage Road 184, 185
Worth Mtn. 104

Green Mountain Club

Providing and Protecting Vermont's Hiking Trails Since 1910

Your membership or gift supports the Long Trail; contact the GMC at 4711 Waterbury-Stowe Road, Waterbury Center, Vermont 05677; (802) 244-7037; www.greenmountainclub. org. Thank you!